# THE EARLY YEARS OF LIFE

# THE EARLY YEARS OF LIFE

Psychoanalytical Development Theory According to Freud, Klein, and Bion

*Gertraud Diem-Wille*

**KARNAC**

First published in 2011 by
Karnac Books Ltd
118 Finchley Road
London NW3 5HT

Originally published in Germany as *Die frühen Lebensjahre—Psychoanalytische Entwicklungstheorie nach Freud, Klein und Bion* © 2007 W. Kohlhammer GmbH Stuttgart.

Translated from the German by Norman Merems (Chs. 1–3), Camilla Nielsen (Chs. 4–6) and Benjamin Mcquade

British Library Cataloguing in Publication Data

A C.I.P. for this book is available from the British Library

ISBN-13: 978-1-85575-710-3

Typeset by Vikatan Publishing Solutions (P) Ltd., Chennai, India

Printed in Great Britain

www.karnacbooks.com

*One who possesses virtue in abundance*
*Is comparable to a new born babe:*
*Poisonous insects will not sting it;*
*Ferocious animals will not pounce on it;*
*Predatory birds will not swoop down on it.*
*Its bones are weak and its sinews supple*
*Yet its hold is firm.*
*It does not know of the union of male and female*
*Yet its male member will stir:*
*This is because its virility is at its height.*
*It howls all day yet does not become hoarse:*
*This is because its harmony is at its height.*

*To know harmony is called the constant;*
*To know the constant is called discernment.*
*To try to add to one's vitality is called ill-omened;*
*For the mind to egg on the breath is called violent.*

*A creature in its prime doing harm to the old*
*Is known as going against the way.*
*That which goes against the way*
*Will come to an early end.*

*Chapter 55*

From: Tzu, L. (1963) *Tao Te Ching*, trans. D.C. Lau,
Harmondsworth, Middlesex: Penguin Books Ltd. p. 116.

# CONTENTS

vii

# PREFACE

This book provides a powerfully argued and beautifully constructed account of the early development of the child in the family context from a psychoanalytic perspective. It draws particularly on the theoretical trajectory from Freud to Klein and Bion. It is written in a clear, accessible, and jargon-free style and it is evident that the author wishes to reach and interest a wide audience of parents and others involved in the upbringing of children in the broadest sense. The growth of the child's mind is the story she most wants to tell. The wealth of detailed examples drawn from the systematic observation of babies and young children, from everyday observation of children's behaviour in family and social contexts, and from a range of clinical interventions, draws the reader into a vivid understanding of the author's conceptual framework and provides many memorable vignettes of children's lives.

The method of presentation, in which the descriptive material is followed by an interpretation of its psychological and developmental significance, offers the opportunity to immerse oneself in an account of the detailed play and interactions of a child with parents, or therapist, or other children, and to then draw back and consider the complex processes one has been privileged to observe.

The breadth of the scholarship, depth of the clinical thinking, and skill that is in evidence will also make the book of real interest and relevance to readers already familiar with the psychoanalytic terrain. To an impressive degree the author brings together fundamental theories of psychoanalysis, insights from infant observation, knowledge of empirical research in child development, aspects of modern neuroscience, and a very substantial experience of clinical work in parent–infant psychotherapy and child analysis. This latter is particularly welcome since the importance of child analysis for the contemporary understanding of child developmental issues is sometimes not adequately appreciated. The examples drawn from sustained analytic work with children demonstrate both the nature of the children's suffering and the way in which analysis, through close attention to their unconscious anxieties, can relieve this and open up their capacity for emotional and cognitive development and for enjoyment of their lives.

I will mention briefly some points which particularly struck me. The first is the way that the pedagogical significance of the psychoanalysis of children, so strong in the early years of the growth of psychoanalysis as a discipline and perhaps especially linked to German traditions of psychoanalytic thinking and practice, is present as a theme in the author's approach. Her aims include a strong desire for parents and others to be able to benefit in the taxing tasks of child rearing from the specific understanding that psychoanalysis can offer: undertaking of infantile anxieties; understanding the way in which the birth of babies evokes unprocessed infantile emotion in adults; and recognizing the need for solid psycho-social support for parents during pregnancy and the early years of children's lives to ensure that the necessary layers of containment are in place. There is a generosity of spirit in this conviction in the liberating impact of awareness of unconscious aspects of experience and an ambition to communicate both realism and hopefulness in which the book succeeds admirably.

The second remarkable feature is the thoughtful interpretation of the place of fathers in modern children's lives—rarely does one read such natural accounts of mothers, fathers, and babies together as in some of the examples used here.

The third is the distinctive mix of German and British psychoanalytic traditions on which the author draws and which should stimulate wider awareness of the potential inherent in such exchanges of ideas.

Lastly, is the overall sense of balance which characterizes the voice of the author. She is as attentive to all that enables human growth and happiness as she is to what stands in its way. Her positive account of what psychoanalysis can contribute to people's lives is a splendid antidote to any tendency to an excessive focus on the pathological, and I think her devotion to infant observation probably partly explains an overall perspective so respectful of human potentialities.

Contemporary preoccupation with the early years of children's lives makes this a timely as well as potentially long-lasting contribution to the field, and it is to be most warmly welcomed.

*Margaret Rustin*
*London, July 2009*

Understanding the nature of a baby with all its potentialities, being totally unaltruistic, and simultaneously soft and strong, leads us to the heart of psychoanalysis as Freud discovered it. In the fifty-fifth chapter from *Tao Te Ching* by Lao Tzu, the baby is considered as a metaphor of the Tao: it embodies the eternal beginning, the ever-springing source. The baby is seen in many ways as ideal, being full of the true and perfect energy, having soft bones and weak muscles but a firm grip and a sexual energy (Le Guiun, 1998). In psychoanalysis we do not only take the baby as a metaphor but seek to understand in detail the growth of the child's mind, developing only when another mind is available for it. When already working as an analyst in Vienna, I was introduced in London to Esther Bick's method of a psychoanalytic way of observing the development of a personality in its natural environment in the family, when the seminar group works carefully with the empiric observational material in order to make hypotheses about the inner world of the baby. The psychoanalytic theories of Sigmund Freud, Melanie Klein, and Wilfried Bion can be understood in a fresh way in the discussion of the observations and can be connected with my analytic experience of having worked as an analyst with grown-ups. In this book I try to bring together three approaches which I was so grateful to integrate into my analytic training and my analytic work: the *Infant Observation Method* to understand the unfolding of the inner world in the inter-action of the infant with its parents; the *parent–infant therapy* when early problems with the baby are addressed; and the *analytic work with children*. These different sources for understanding a baby in the early years, the baby in a child, and the baby in an adult, are based on the psychoanalytic theory of Freud, Klein, and Bion. Students who engage in training in psychoanalysis or psychotherapy often find it very difficult to integrate the metapsychology of psychoana-lytic terms with their observation of infants and their parents and the clinical material of patients.

I wish to thank the analysts Betty Joseph and Anne Alvarez, with whom I could discuss the material of the child analytic cases, and Elisabeth Bott Spillius and Michael Feldman, with whom I discussed my analytic work with grown-ups. With Dilys Daws I saw families and infants with early developmental or sleeping problems and am grateful to her for sharing her experience with me. Particular thanks are due to Margaret Rustin, who encouraged my research work of the *Follow-up Study of Infant Observation*, as well as to Isca Salzberger Wittenberg, who came to Vienna to support our Infant Observation Group in Vienna.

The translation shows the interest in the blending of psychoanalytic work with children and adults with the Infant Observation Method of Esther Bick. The balance of examples from observed babies in "normal families" and children in an analysis is based on the conviction that the awareness of unconscious emotional patterns between parents and child can have a helpful liberating impact on people who work with children and parents.

My special thanks go to the FWF Der Wissenschaftsfonds (Funds for Scientific Research) who made possible the translation of the book into English, ensuring its availability to English readers and enabling it to have resonance in the English scientific community.

*Gertraud Diem-Wille*
*Vienna*
*July 2009*

# ACKNOWLEDGEMENTS

The thought of writing an introduction to psychoanalytic development psychology according to the teachings of Freud, Klein, and Bion arose during my teaching activities in training seminars for psychoanalysts in the Vienna Psychoanalytic Association. In the discussion following the seminar "Psychoanalytic Development Theory", it became clear to me what made Melanie Klein's concepts difficult to understand and comprehend if the participants had no previous familiarity with the idea of "instinct theory". When I was directing the university course "Psychoanalytic Observational Studies", both the students and I became aware that neither in German nor English was there a general and clear representation of normal development in the first three years of life. Thanks to my teachers Isca Salzberger-Wittenberg, Anne Alvarez, and Margaret Rustin, I became familiar with the rich clinical experiences of Infant Observation according to Esther Bick, documentation that had been collected over more than fifty years, especially in the Tavistock Clinic in London. Through Lisa Miller and Dilys Daws I learned about clinical work in parent–infant therapy under the model of "Under Five Counselling Service", and I choose to make frequent reference to this in this book. I am very grateful for the aid and encouragement

I received. I was able to draw on the prolific clinical experience of analysts in London, especially that of Betty Joseph, Michael Feldman, Robin Anderson, Elisabeth Bott Spillius, and Irma Brenman-Pick, experiences which supported my analytical work with children and adults. I welcome this opportunity to express my appreciation for their generous support and clinical accompaniment.

I have learned a great deal both from my patients of all ages and from my colleagues. I am thankful to the Kohlhammer Publishers, represented by Dr. Klaus-Peter Burkarth and Prof. Günther Bittner, for the stimulus to plan an in-depth study of developmental psychological themes following the widespread interest in my book *Das Kleinkind und seine Eltern: Perspektiven psychoanalytischer baby-beobachtung* (*The Young Child and its Parents: Psychoanalytic perspectives on infant observation*) (2003, 2009). I recognize connections more clearly due to intensive discussions at the Interuniversity Faculty for Interdisciplinary Research and Advanced Training at the Alpen-Adria University Klagenfurt, with the professors Wilfried Datler, Helga Reiter, Kornelia Steinhardt, Irmtraud Sengschmied, and Barbara Lehner. Participants in university courses, through their questions and interest, have helped me to recognize which basic assumptions and thought patterns had to be made explicit in order to become comprehensible. I am grateful to Konrad Krainer, dean of my institute, for his generous support and encouragement of my work and for facilitating my work's core theme of psychoanalytic pedagogy.

To my best friend and first reader Christiane Siegl I am grateful for her refreshingly friendly criticism and suggestions while reading the manuscript. With his critical questions, Peter Marginter helped me to communicate descriptions more clearly. His fine feeling for language, concern for clarity when expressing ideas, and numerous suggestions for formulation, have contributed importantly to the text. Sylvia Zwettler-Otte, a competent analyst and loyal friend, has supported me with her encouragement and appreciative words, and edited the manuscript with a sharp eye. My editor Frau Alina Piasny has gone through the manuscript with great care and knowledge and has compiled a subject and a person index.

My children Katharina and Johanna and my son-in-law Ramsy have helped me with their comments and support. The observation of, and experiences with, my lively and curious grandchildren

Samira and Karim have supplied me with rich material for examples. Both my grandchildren were not only theoretically interested in the evolution of the book, but also worked with me, sitting in my lap during corrections at the computer. I have to thank Werner Koenne, the man at my side, for his partly humorous and partly serious questions and suggestions from the viewpoint of a natural scientist and sceptical logician. His natural support and acceptance made it easier for me to carry out this time-consuming activity.

Special thanks to the parents Hanna and Ramsy Hadaya, Agnes Turner, and Lucki Dostal for permission to reproduce their family photos.

*Gertraud Diem-Wille*
*Vienna*
*Summer 2007*

# The relevance of the first years for personality development

"The past is not dead,
it isn't even gone."

—William Faulkner

At first, Freud's (1905) insight that the early years are of paramount importance in personality development encountered strong opposition and lack of understanding. His view of the child as a sexual being that from birth on struggled with the emotions of love and hate, Eros and the death instinct, clashed with the widely held sentimental understanding of a child's innocence. The Bible verse, "Let the little children come to me and do not hinder them, for to such belongs the kingdom of heaven" (Matthew 19: 14, The Bible, English Standard Version, 2001) was wrongly understood as a confirmation of the inexperience, naiveté, and innocence of children. Children's cruel sides, their jealousy and envy or exhibitionistic behaviour, were barely noted or only smiled at, since such behaviour in a child had a strange effect, and adults averted their shock with laughter. The assumption was that children did not yet understand anything about painful feelings. We can compare the psychoanalytical

xix

understanding of the early years as a foundation of personality development with the taking root of a young tree. The early aspects of development form the roots, without which a living tree cannot exist. A deep, affectionate relationship to the parents/caregivers permits the development of deep and strong-building roots, which also provides firmness and security during stormy phases of life. Insufficient mothering and adverse environmental conditions allow only a superficial building of roots, which then perhaps offer insufficient stability in developmental crises. The high child mortality in orphanages[1], where only the child's physical well-being is attended to, indicates that a minimum of life-sustaining functions, such as emotional allocation and positive surroundings, must be present for the child to survive psychologically. Early maldevelopments such as autism or hospitalism can be traced back to early experiences of deprivation (Alvarez, 2001; Spitz, 1945).

The assessment of childhood in each historical period determines the typical dealings with children. In the twentieth and twenty-first centuries Freud's assumption prevailed, namely that early childhood experiences also persisted in the later phases of a normal development. According to Williams (2003), this is also true for a pathological development. It is only in the last decade that the study of the early years has aroused scientific interest. The observation of early childhood behaviour and interaction in the family with its significance for psychological development requires special training, as made possible by the psychoanalytical observation of infants by Esther Bick (1964), for example. The image of a tree taking root to describe the quality of the relationships between parents and child, points out its central significance for personal stability; however, this image neglects the other aspect—how pervasively the parents or caregiver, through their personality and behaviour vis-à-vis the child, influence its view of the world and perception of other people. Similar to a cloth's pattern, early experiences are absorbed and remain alive in the unconscious as "experience in feeling" (Klein).

It was only in the twentieth century, the "Century of the Child", that the child was taken seriously as a person. Ellen Key (cited in Hermann, 1992: 43) called for an "upbringing from the child's

---

[1]René Spitz (1945) mentions that up to 80% of infants sent to orphanages do not survive their first year.

viewpoint", and Maria Montessori (1982: 15) spoke about the particular activities of the child and its desire to learn. But let us consider what sort of adult behaviour was permitted when one takes into account the prejudices regarding the child's inexperience. Since it was assumed that little children could not distinguish between their own mother and father and another adult, the child's care was left to strangers. The parents' withdrawal was abrupt and without any preparation. As long as the child could not speak, it was assumed that it could not understand anything. Therefore, everything was negotiated in the child's presence. Children were treated as objects and, as Rousseau (1762) vehemently criticized in *Emile*, were wrapped in baby pillows to keep them quiet and hung on a hook on the wall.

No problem was seen in giving away the child to a wet nurse as one did not assume that the child had an emotional relationship to its mother. In fact, however, the opposite was true. Badinter (1980) describes how in eighteenth-century France, children spent their first years with a nanny, with a high child mortality rate. In 1857, Flaubert very casually mentioned (in his novel *Madame Bovary*, shockingly realistic for that time) how Emma only visited her child at the nanny's twice a week. It is therefore not surprising that Emma Bovary, the main character, could not establish an emotional relationship with her daughter, and continued to feel that her life was empty and monotonous.

Sending children of age six to eight years away from home in order to learn court customs was the rule in royal and aristocratic circles. (Mary Stuart was sent to the French court at the age of seven, and at seventeen married the crown prince.) It was also the rule in rural settings, where children had to work as servants or maids. A difficult childhood was usual in most parts of the world up into the twentieth century.

In his very comprehensive study, *"Hört ihr die Kinder weinen"* ("Hear the Children Crying") (1977), Lloyd deMause wrote a psychogenetic story of childhood which examines (with the aid of biographical reports) the different attitudes of parents to children in different centuries in Europe and the USA. Contrary to a belief in child innocence, the study shows that up into the nineteenth century the usual rearing practices of beating, ordering, and ridiculing were meant to combat the evil in the child: savageness and the archaic were to be tamed with drills, force, and severe punishment. The "enlightened" pedagogue Schreber, whose psychotic son[2] acquired fame with his autobiography *Denkwürdigkeiten eines Nervenkranken* (*Memoirs of My Nervous Illness*) (Schreber, 1903), favoured a surfeit of outdoor physical activity for children, but also developed "pedagogic machines and apparatus" in order to prevent masturbation and thumb-sucking, or to force an upright posture while writing (Schreber, 1879; 1891).

Even today children are ridiculed, beaten, left alone without forewarning, or separated from their parents in hospital for weeks. Nowadays we know that this inflicts damage on the child, that a long separation from the parents is traumatic. Especially during an illness, or before and after surgery, children need the particular support of their parents in order to be able to deal with these frightening experiences.

This book will attempt to make the insights of psychoanalysis useful for answering pedagogical questions, and show how the experiences we have as babies and as young children determine our basic attitude towards the world. As babies we first learn to feel. How we start to organize our feelings influences our later behaviour and our capacity to think. This attempt at clarification breaks new ground, as psychoanalysis does not represent a single closed system of theories. Within the various schools of psychoanalysis, varying assumptions exist about the start of the development of the ego, and consequently different theories about the workings of the human psyche, which are often the cause of fierce controversies. In the following observations we refer principally to Freud's conception and its further development by Melanie Klein, Wilfried Bion, and the London post-Kleinians Betty Joseph, Michael Feldman, John Steiner, and Hanna Segal. The focus of our attention (using the technical term "object relation theory")[3] is

---

[2] In his paper "Psycho-Analytic Notes on an Autobiographical Account of a Case of Paranoia" (1911), Freud was concerned with the roots of paranoia. Schatzman (1973: 36) pursues the question of how delusions, which Daniel Paul Schreiber reports, could be connected to his father's "rearing apparatus".

[3] The term "object relation" was used by Freud (1915: 127) as a description of the intrapsychic dimension of individual experiences (or internalized "object relation"); it denotes the representation of the self, the other. Melanie Klein (1955: 138) was the first to formulate a theory of object relation which placed the relationship of the child to its caregivers at the centre of emotional development.

the description of intrapsychic processes, and how they develop out of the relationship to relevant persons ("objects").

The central significance of the emotions, which Freud pointed out at the start of the twentieth century, has been increasingly seized on by different sciences, such as neurology, psychology, psychoanalysis, and biochemistry. Interest centres on the question of how our emotions determine our thinking, and why human beings only become human when they learn to relate emotionally to other humans. The biological explanation of our social behaviour assumes a "social brain" and the biological system of regulating our feelings (Gerhardt, 2004: 37; Schore, 2003: 45). In neurology and biology today one is in agreement that "our rationality, which science from its inception praises so highly, is built on emotions and cannot exist without it" (Gerhardt, 2004: 5). Damasio (1995: 128; emphasis in original) emphasizes that the rational part of the brain cannot function independently, but only simultaneously with the fundamental regulatory and emotional part of the brain: "Nature appears not simply to have built the apparatus of rationality onto the apparatus of biological regulation, but also *from* it and *with* it." The upper part of the cortex cannot operate independently of the primitive emotional component. The scientific confirmation of the fundamental significance of early experiences in the womb and in the first three years of life supports the arguments and clinical results of psychoanalysis and psychoanalytical social work which have pointed out the connection between early deprivations and later criminality, violence, and drug addiction.

Recognizing the significance of emotions is of central interest especially for pedagogues, that is, not only the emotions of the children to be brought up but above all the feelings of the pedagogues themselves. For a long time in pedagogy there existed the firm conviction that the pedagogue should put aside his or her own feelings as much as possible in order to be able to treat the student "objectively" and "fairly". Some teachers could not acknowledge that their sympathy with or rejection of the students influenced the children's behaviour. Psychoanalytical pedagogy seeks to help teachers not to brush aside their feelings but rather to recognize them and to learn to reflect on them. They can then use emotions as a source of understanding, not only comprehending their own motives but also as an additional dimension of information about the student. Training is required to correctly evaluate both the teacher's own feelings and those of the student, and to observe the behaviour and details of the student's relationship to the teacher and to other schoolmates. As we have learned all our lives to hide our feelings from ourselves and from others—especially the deeply affectionate or aggressive ones— we are, as Bergmann shows in his film *Scenes of a Marriage* (1973), "emotional illiterates", who can only (re)discover access to our own emotions and those of others through a painful learning process.

The psychoanalytical treatment technique in the Kleinian tradition emphasizes above all the interpretation of transference and countertransference. Instead of orientating him or herself to the contents of what is told by the patient, the analyst concentrates more on the minute description of the interaction between patient and analyst. Betty Joseph (1993) puts the focus on the reconstruction of the patient's story in the here and now, which is illustrated in the recorded case descriptions of children's analyses.

In a university course dealing with psychoanalytical observation this new approach was discussed. A participant said: "A great deal happened in the last two years (in the course), outside and also within; it was often walking a tightrope. It was painful to see my own reflection in observation and in group discussions. It was an intense phase of personality development—sometimes very difficult—but I wouldn't have missed a minute." A kindergarten teacher, who often had had to conduct observation tasks during her training, was astonished at the new dimension to be learned through psychoanalytical observation. Above all, she found the precise, descriptive note-taking instructive, as she experienced how difficult it was to forego premature evaluations.

This book shows the development of the child in the first three years—in the important dimensions of thinking, of emotional development, and psychosexual development—not only in theory, but through examples of observation of babies and small children.

# CHAPTER ONE

# The nature versus nurture controversy

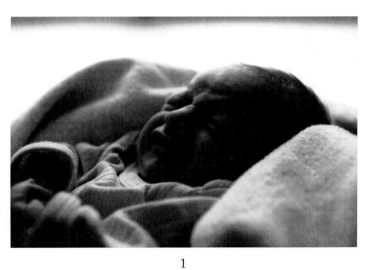

One of the fundamental questions about child development concerns the significance of biologically inherited genetic features and the influence of the environment. The different answers are based on varying assumptions about the nature of human beings, the research perspective, and varying interpretations of empirical data. Today, there is widespread agreement that the child's development follows equally a universal pattern, exhibits individual differences, and is influenced by environmental conditions. How much importance is attached to each of these three influences is dependent on the theoretical orientation of the psychologist and the questions he or she asks.

At the beginning of the twentieth century, viewpoints were extremely opposing. Advocates of the racial theory emphasized biological heredity, implying an indisputable racial correlation. This was supposed to prove the superiority of the "Aryan race" as "superhuman", above all other "inferior races" and the "subhuman". Under National Socialism, this spurious "scientific" argument was used to legalize the extermination of "inferior lives"—all deformed and abnormal people and the Jews. The systematic and bureaucratically organized murder of more than six million Jews, gypsies, homosexuals, and war prisoners in the concentration camps of the "master race" in Germany and Austria between 1933 and 1945 has proven forcefully that, under National Socialism, "racial superiority" served as a pretext for a dehumanized, systematic criminality.

But it was not only in the social sciences in Central and Eastern Europe that the nature of personality and intelligence was accepted as being of leading importance. In the United States, even today every marriage applicant has to fill in a health form with questions about psychic illnesses in the family and inherited maldevelopments. Due to the conviction that intelligence was primarily genetic, up to the Second World War it was the practice of the social services in the USA not to release infants for adoption, but to place them in orphanages for six months in order to find out if they possessed normal intelligence. As emotional relationships and intellectual stimulation in the orphanages were minimal and frequently resulted in delayed development, the children were often assessed as being mentally retarded and sent to corresponding institutions (Mussen et al., 1990: 16). What led to a re-thinking of the social agencies was René Spitz's (1945: 53) groundbreaking investigation into American orphanages and his discovery of the "hospitalism syndrome",[1] consequent of the infant's emotional and intellectual neglect in institutions that were hygienic and correctly run but which did not provide constant offers of relationships. A slow apprehension of the psychoanalytic mindset and Piaget's (2001) cognitive theories led to the realization that development represented the result of an interaction of maturity-contingent changes and individual experience.

Freud (1905: 179) assumed that children were active creatures who passed through a series of psychosexual development phases, in which they were confronted with certain inner conflicts, desires and fantasies; the manner in which they overcame these was critical for whether they became mature adults capable of work and love, or whether they remained fixated at an earlier stage of development. This thesis—that the early development and early relationship to the parents is highly significant—was revolutionary for its time, had widespread influence, and is generally recognized today. In the standard work on American developmental psychology, it is only in the third printing that Berk goes into the complex "bidirectional connection between biology and environment" and speaks of a "decoupling of the correlation between genetics and environment in psychological illnesses and antisocial behaviour" (Berk, 2004: XXXVI).

Freud (1905) spoke of constitutional factors that play a role in the development of the personality, in addition to experience. Exponents of psychoanalysis today emphasize individual disposition and family influences. The baby's personality, its temperament, its inborn tendency towards robustness or sensitivity, towards impatience, envy, and tolerance of frustration, all these are factors in the development of psychic illnesses equally important as burdensome family relationships, traumatic experiences, or deprivation. Psychoanalysis and psychoanalytic pedagogics have effectively shown to what degree infantile behaviour is influenced by emotional encouragement or conflicts. After a therapy in which the inhibiting factors

---

[1] "The term "hospitalism" designates a vitiated condition of the body due to long confinement in hospital, or a morbid condition of the atmosphere of a hospital. The term has been increasingly pre-empted to specify the evil effect of institutional care of infants, placed in institutions from an early age, particularly of the psychiatric point of view" (Spitz, 1945: 53).

of fear, aggression, or repressed conflicts can be discussed, children who were classified as "stupid" are able to fully utilize their intelligence and social competence. However, before a therapy or child analysis can be recommended, a thorough investigation of the possible somatic and genetic origins of the disorder must be undertaken. Encouragement of the child's intellectual and social capabilities can only take place within the scope of its given aptitudes; at present there is no way to measure this scope, there is only the psychotherapeutic-diagnostic experience, which shows whether a child demonstrates emotional inhibitions in its development.

In view of advances in biology and psychology, today both assumptions—a predispositional as well as an environmental determinism—are seen as equally naive. Research assumes that a combination of inherited potential and individual experience has made a person what they are and determined how they experience the world. Let us now turn first to the inherited dispositions and then to the environmentally contingent influences.

## 1.1   Inherited dispositions

The term "genetically contingent" is colloquially equated with a necessary transmission of a genetic factor from the parents to all of their children. This naive assumption will now be compared with several perspectives of biological research into heredity, in order to show that heredity is not a one-dimensional passing on of the parents' genetic makeup to their children, but rather constitutes a highly complex phenomenon. After this, we will deal with both the beneficial and damaging aspects of inherited dispositions.

Each of us consists of billions of cells. Within each cell there is a nucleus (a control centre) which contains rod-like structures called chromosomes, which preserve and transmit  genetic information. The human genetic equipment lies in the chromosomes, which originate in equal parts from the biological parents. Human cell nuclei contain forty-six chromosomes (diploid chromosome complement) in the form of twenty-three correlating pairs (an exception being the gender chromosome pair XY in men). Each half of the chromosome pair corresponds with the other in size, shape, structure, and genetic function. One half originates from the mother and one from the father. Every body cell has forty-six chromosomes, apart from the egg and semen cells. These have only one-half of the chromosome complement (twenty-three chromosomes). In fertilization, when the semen cell penetrates the wall of the egg cell, twenty-three chromosomes are released, just as the egg cell itself releases twenty-three chromosomes; the nuclei of both merge together, and a double chromosome complement exists again, that is, each individual starts life with forty-six chromosomes. Chromosomes consist of chemical modules which are banded together in a giant molecule, deoxyribonucleic acid—or DNA for short. In 1945, Oswald Averyn at the Rockefeller Institute investigated the previously unknown matrix. It took nearly 20 years, until 1962, for Nobel Prize winners James Watson and Francis Crick to discover the substance and structure of DNA, the basis of genetic material. They developed a DNA model that consisted of two molecule chains winding around a single imaginary axis, and built the so-called double helix (similar to a flexible ladder that winds around its own axis like a spiral staircase) (Fraser and Nora, 1986; Moore, 1982). Each rung consists of a specific pair of chemical modules, nucleotide base pairs, connected between the columns by a hydrogen bridge. The specific sequence of chemical elements forms a sequence of nucleotide bases forms—a so-called nucleotide. The varying sequences construct the specific genetic code of an individual, which is significant in protein synthesis and specifies the individual's genetic programme. A gene is a segment of the DNA. Genes, which carry the genetic makeup, can be of varying lengths—from about one hundred to several thousand ladder rungs. One human cell contains about one million genes; on average, thirty thousand genes lie along the human chromosome. The entire biological inheritance is contained in these twenty-three pairs of chromosomes.

Each body cell has twenty-two pairs of homologous chromosomes at its disposal. The twenty-third pair consists of gender chromosomes, which are different in men and women. Normally, women have two X chromosomes (XX) and men one X and one Y chromosome (XY); the other twenty-two chromosome pairs are equal in both men and women. In cell division (mitosis) the genetic information is conserved and transmitted unchanged to the divided cells. A unique characteristic of DNA is that it can double itself (identical replication) during this process. A surprising result of DNA research was that the genetic makeup of human beings was largely similar to simple organisms such as bacteria and fungi, and was 98 to 99% identical to DNA in chimpanzees and monkeys. Genetic variation between one human and another is 0.9%. How did human beings, with only twice the number of genes of a worm or a fly, manage to develop into such complex creatures? The answer lies in the proteins of protein biosynthesis, a process performed in our genes. They break up and rejoin again in an unbelievable multiplicity—about ten to twenty million types—on the ribosomes, which also lie in the cytoplasm. The genetic information creates the biological data storage and by means of transcription this information is brought from the cell nuclei to the location of protein synthesis. The communication system between cell nucleus and cytoplasm, which fine-tunes gene activity, is substantially more complex in humans than in one-celled creatures. As factors from the environment influence gene formation within the cell, even biological circumstances are equally the result of genetic and non-genetic forces (Davis, Howell, and Gardner, 2001; Berk, 2005: 61).

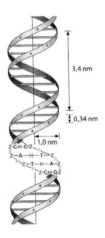

The ladder like structure of DNA.

In cell division, the double (diploid) chromosome complement with twenty-three pairs is preserved. In the genesis of egg and semen cells (gender cells, gametes) the chromosome complement has to be halved (haploid complement). This occurs in the process of reduction-division (miosis). The "crossing over" in the first phase of this process is the most significant event. The homologous chromosomes—one maternal and one paternal—lie parallel to each other; each has already been divided lengthwise (duplicated) and they have a common "contact point". Genetic material is exchanged in this "tetrade". Further along in this process the divided chromosome halves draw apart from each other, resulting in the formation of four daughter cells, each containing half of a chromosome complement, although it is left to chance which chromosome half lands in which cell. In the case of a male there are two semen cells with X chromosomes and two with Y chromosomes; females have only the X gender chromosomes. In the process of fertilization, when the egg and semen cells merge, the resulting cell (zygote) again has forty-six chromosomes (double chromosome complement) at its command. In the cell division process (mitosis) the chromosomes pair off and exchange segments, so that the gene of one chromosome can be replaced by the gene of another. Then chance determines which part of each pair joins another and lands in the same gender cells (gametes). "If one leaves aside the possibility of crossings-over, the total number of different combinations of semen and egg cells of one pair of parents is about 64 billion" (Mussen *et al.*, 1990: 52). So it is understandable how different siblings from the same parents can be, as each child inherits only half the genes from each parent and those in varying combinations. The number of different inheritances is larger than the entire world population. With the exception of identical twins, we can assume that each human being is genetically unique. The probability that the offspring of two parents (if they are not twins) are genetically the same is about one to seven hundred trillion (Gould and Keeton, 1997).

Physical characteristics are largely inherited: eye colour, skin complexion, hair quality and colour. What colour eyes a child actually inherits is not only dependent on the father's and mother's eye colour, but on how many genes (for example, for dark eyes) the father or mother has. It is important to point out that all physical characteristics are culturally evaluated. The ideal of beauty in each society has to do with ethnic association. Thus, in European cultural circles white skin colour is considered of positive importance, while dark skin is seen as foreign. The light-skinned ideal of beauty is often held in high esteem even among dark-skinned people. In mythology, the white skin colour is sometimes described as a deficiency. In the Balinese myth of creation brown skin colour is ascribed to "children of the sun". In this myth, God created human beings by day; they had brown skin and were called children of the sun. Those humans which God created only later, by pale moonlight, had a lighter skin colour and were called "children of the moon". The characterization of dark skin as good and strong is an obvious one, clearly related to creation in sunlight; whites are lacking something, they only have the weak light of the moon. The same is valid for the length of the nose. In China, Europeans are called "long noses", a description which evokes sympathy and curiosity, as they do not correspond to the beauty ideal of a dainty nose. Therefore, it is important for personality development how exactly the environment reacts to physical characteristics, if there are socially discriminating or rewarding reactions. In Hans Christian Andersen's fairy tale "The Ugly Duckling", the theme is the cruelty of social exclusion based on different appearances. Only when the duckling becomes a swan and finds his parents and siblings is he accepted—a sombre world view, since the duckling/child cannot escape their destiny (Bettelheim, 1977: 101).

In child upbringing, it is therefore important to acquaint children with children's books about different ethnic myths and fairy tales, in order to treat cultural variety as something natural. For example, in the African myth "The Turtle's Dream", included in the series "Folk Tales of the World", children learn not only the Bantu story of the wonder tree, which bears all the world's fruit and is discovered not by powerful animals but by the slow and more attentive turtle, but also the African grandmother Koko in her hut with brightly coloured dresses, who knows the secret name "Omumbo-rombonga" (Throughton, 1994: 12).

## Parents' support in view of inherited abilities or deficiencies

We bequeath our children good and bad physical qualities, talents such as musicality or absolute pitch, and greater or smaller impediments to seeing, hearing, and so forth. How children and parents deal with these physically inherited features depends on the quality of their relationship. Here are two short examples.

A nine-year-old girl was sent to the eye doctor because she screwed up her eyes while watching television. The doctor detected moderate short-sightedness and prescribed eyeglasses. The girl was appalled and did not want to wear glasses. She was afraid of being laughed at by the other students in her school. As both her mother and father were severely short-sighted, the mother remarked that the girl's "impediment" was not surprising; the child had clearly inherited short-sightedness from them. Instead of being placated, the girl came to her mother, hit her on the leg, cried heavily, and complained that her mother had done this to her, that she had given her this defective sight during her pregnancy. The mother felt guilty and discussed the situation with her husband and the girl's grand-mother and aunt—all spectacle wearers.

Instead of laughing at her or wanting to talk her out of her fears, all the family members helped the girl to deal with this new situation. Her father accompanied her to the opticians and she chose six frames in order to decide on one of them at home. While she tried them on, her father told her grandmother that his daughter had a real spectacle face, that eyeglasses suited her well. The grand-mother had all the frames shown to her. The girl's brother, two years younger, also wanted to try on the frames, especially the cool Harry Potter glasses. Looking at himself modelling them in the mirror he laughed with joy and decided that he also wanted glasses. He finally calmed down when his father explained that later on he would also get glasses if he saw poorly and needed them. His sister tried on the different frames with noticeably increasing pleasure. Later, her grandmother told her about when she had tried to hide her short-sightedness, had moved to the front row in class, and nevertheless still had to copy everything from her neighbour. In the afternoon, her aunt rang up, spoke with the girl about the new glasses, and told her about when she had noticed her own short-sightedness. In the evening, the girl mentioned casually that she looked forward to seeing everything clearly with the new glasses.

At first the girl had protested and blamed her parents for her defective vision. With the help of the entire family she succeeded in accepting reality—an important emotional achievement towards bearing frustrations and dealing with restrictions or handicaps.

A second example: a music teacher, who had been a concert gui-tarist, noticed her daughter's musicality very early on. At the age of three the daughter could sing many international children's songs alone and without mistakes. As she observed her mother playing the guitar, she expressed a desire to play too. Her mother bought her a good instrument, taught her the basics of playing, and was delighted at how readily and gladly the little girl made music. Two years later, when the girl expressed a wish to play the violin just as the mother's violinist duet partner did, the mother took this wish seriously. She hired a young violin teacher to teach the girl how to play. At the age of six, alone in her room, she played the violin with concentration for up to an hour, practiced various songs, and also played together with her mother.

How did the mother succeed in perceiving and supporting her daughter's talent so early? She herself, as the youngest daughter in a musical family, had learnt the guitar in elementary school on the director's initiative. Later, she had been taught by a young, dedicated music teacher, studied at the music university, and at sixteen had won an important international music competition. Without bitterness, she had forsaken a promising career as a concert guitarist in order to realize her desire for children. She was emotionally predisposed to be delighted that her daughter had inherited her musicality, and—by purchasing a good instrument and hiring a music teacher—to show her how seriously she took her wish. Even in the absence of excessive parental ambition, there are many successful examples of encouraging children, who then maintain an enjoyment and delight in music.

In the first example, the family responds to the girl and helps her to accept her visual impairment; in the second, the special musical talent is recognized and encouraged. We see the close interconnection between inherited disposition and the significance of environmental reaction. In the first case, making fun of the girl as "four-eyed" could threaten her self-esteem. In the second case, the mother could have either dismissed the girl's request because she was still too small, or bought her a plastic guitar to play with. Encouraging talent is only possible within the framework of inherited abilities, but even a moderate talent can be encouraged—if the child takes pleasure in it.

### 1.1.1   Chromosome anomalies

Especially significant is the question of the inheritance of qualities and abilities in genetic maldevelopment and the treatment of children with anomalies. There are more than one hundred and fifty known genetic maldevelopments which lead to developmental disturbances; most of them appear only very seldom (Scarr and Kidd, 1983).

Down's syndrome (earlier mongolism) is the most prevalent chromosome anomaly; it appears in one out of eight hundred live births. In 95% of the cases, the cause of the anomaly is an additional chromosome in the twenty-first chromosome pair. The risk of Down's syndrome increases dramatically with the mother's age. With a twenty-year-old woman the probability of a maldevelopment is 1: 1,900 births; with a thirty-five year-old woman this increases to 1: 300, and with a forty-five year-old woman 1: 30 (Halliday *et al.*, 1995).

Children with Down's syndrome have an IQ of from 25 to 40, occasionally up to 70. They have memory and speech problems, a limited vocabulary, and a slow motoric development. Visual and cardiac defects frequently appear. Children with Down's syndrome are generally cheerful, have a marked talent for mimicry, and love music. Their physical characteristics are a small, thickset frame, a flattened face, a protruding tongue, almond-shaped eyes, and an unusual fold over the ball of the hand. When these children grow up in stimulating surroundings, where their special needs are met and they feel loved and accepted, their social, emotional, and motoric abilities can improve more markedly than their intellectual capacities (Hines and Bennette, 1996).

*1.1.2   Autism*

Child autism, a serious disorder which influences children in their mental and emotional development, proceeds from a genetic and an environmental influence. Autism ranges from docile, highly functional children with Asperger's syndrome to children with severe handicaps. In therapy and in dealing with autistic children, parents and teachers can learn to find the "non-autistic child behind the autism" (Alvarez and Reid, 1999: xiii). Children with autism fail to establish emotional relationships with people, instead treating human beings no differently than they would pieces of furniture. Autistic children do not communicate in normal ways with people, and do not play, instead performing unusual, repetitious rituals and movements whose meanings are secretive (Kanner, 1943). They appear to live in their own world, to which no one can gain admittance. Sometimes they have strong partial capacities, for example, remarkable mathematical skill. Often these behaviour patterns are accompanied by developmental delays in all other areas. Children with autism seem to have no interest in the world and do not assume that anyone could be interested in them.

There are scientific controversies over the possible causes of autism and what constitutes the central disorder. Some authors, such as Leslie (1987) and Firth (1989), favour a cognitive explanation, namely that children with autism are born without the capability of forming an adequate "theory of mind". Others, such as Hobson (1993) and Trevarthen *et al.*, (1996) consider autism as a disorder of intersubjectivity, as a deficiency in recognizing another person. Alvarez and Reid (1999: 2; emphasis in original) characterize autism as "impairment of the normal *sense of emotionally-based security about, and desire for, interpersonal relationships*".

It is important to understand that autism develops in early childhood. To make clear the behaviour of a child with autism, I will cite a description of the first therapy hour with the family of patient Sally, as Sue Reid (1999) describes it. For the past two years, at the Tavistock Clinic in London, Reid and Alvarez have been conducting a Workshop for autism, in order to do research into and develop special therapeutic work for families with an autistic family member.

## Sally, a child with autistic symptoms

Seven-year-old Sally comes into the therapy room with her parents, her older sisters, her older brother, her baby sister, the au pair, and the therapist. As the siblings chatter animatedly, Sally shows no interest and says nothing. She is an exquisitely pretty child, with large eyes and long eyelashes, but her eyes focus on nothing and nobody.

In the consulting room she stares in front of herself, sits without movement and without interest, and suddenly stands up and goes to the door. When her father follows her, she places his hand on the door handle. He tries to pick her up in order to put her on his lap, but she struggles vehemently and her body is rigid. He gives up. The therapist assesses Sally as fragile and vulnerable, but with a solid muscular body.

She moves around as if neither furniture nor people were there, steps on the therapist's feet, bumps into the table and pushes it ahead of her as she proceeds, all without noticing anything.

Neither frustration nor irritation can be detected. She shows no pain upon this obviously painful contact with the table. All attempts to reach her, to call her name, are not even registered by her; it is as though she were deaf. She seems to be trapped in her own world. Occasionally she smiles to herself, and sometimes she speaks to herself in a high-pitched, strained voice or in a whispering sing-song. When a family member tries to seat her in his lap, she refuses. If she is hindered in her wandering about the room, she protests and starts to scream.

Her parents relate that Sally has no language, only strange noises all her own; she doesn't play or look at anyone. The therapist had little confidence of being able to help Sally. There was only a single glimmer of hope—Sally had reacted to the therapist's colourful watch. She had stood still briefly and looked at the watch. Then she had also looked sideways at the therapist—a momentary contact which she quickly broke off (Reid, 1999: 13f).

This first description conveys the intensity of Sally's disorder, which dictated her rigid control of her world at any cost and made her appear inaccessible to any form of contact. Is it possible to penetrate this nearly complete shielding of the private world of autistic children and to enable them to establish contact with the general world of human relationships, including love and hate, joy and pain?

Although the prognostic chances in general are estimated as very small, psychoanalysts and psychotherapists have attempted to develop a therapy for children with autism. It should be noted once again that there are various degrees of autism, from the mild form of Asperger's syndrome—in which children participate in several dimensions of life and withdraw in certain emotional areas—to severe autistic disorders. In the preface to their book *Autism and Personality* (1999), Anne Alvarez and Susan Reid emphasize how important it is to see the non-autistic child behind the autism, and also to help the parents find this child. The psychic pain of autistic children is often underestimated, since they seem outwardly impassive. If successful contact is made with the child, this is always associated with mental pain; it is comparable to the physical pain felt by Chinese women when the bandages on their feet are removed. Some parents of children with autism discontinue therapy because they cannot endure their child's pain or the aggressive behaviour associated with it.

In the best-seller *The Curious Incident of the Dog in the Night-Time*, the story of a highly intelligent boy with Asperger's syndrome is described in the form of a detective story. It is indirectly apparent not only how the difficult child is a burden on the parental relationship, but also how the parents protect the child from the pain of their divorce by telling him that his mother has died (Haddon, 2003).

I would now like to describe an important therapy session with the aforementioned Sally in which, for the first time, successful emotional contact with her was made and her parents were helped to understand how Sally expressed her wishes. This session took place after longer work with the whole family. Reid has developed a fourteen-phase psychotherapeutic evaluation of problems with autistic children, in which parents are to a large extent included. The particular session described here took place in the ninth phase, where the needs of the child, the parents, and the siblings were all explored (Reid, 1999: 27–31).

At this meeting of the family with the therapist (to which they arrived late), Sally immediately went to the doll's house in the consulting room. The therapist interrupted the talk with the parents and told Sally that she would bring the doll's house to the small table in the middle of the room. Sally showed minor irritation with this interference. While the parents discussed what had been happening since the last session, the therapist saw that Sally had taken two small plastic people from the house and placed them beside each other; opposite them she had placed a small figure which she had brought with her. (It was the head of a plastic ornament which her parents explained had been broken long ago but which Sally had kept saved. The part of the ornament which remained was a round shape with a rather simple doll-child's face on the front with prominent eyes.) The therapist's interpretation consisted of a description of the situation: "Sally is showing us something about what is happening with two people speaking to one person who was very busy with her eyes." Sally showed no noticeable response to this and quietly continued to talk to herself in her own private language.

Her parents continued to describe recent events: Sally had begun to like looking at herself in the mirror. The therapist remarked that it could be a good thing that Sally was showing an interest in herself. The parents commented that Sally approaches the mirror in their bedroom, looks at herself, and then moves away from the mirror. Her mother was worried that this behaviour could easily become stuck and repetitive. The therapist then suggested that the mother could play with Sally near the mirror: she could hide, then step together in front of the mirror, let Sally stand there alone, and describe what happens. She could play hide and seek with Sally as she would with a small child, a rather ordinary peek-a-boo game. The therapist spent some time discussing with the parents how they could play with Sally in a way that would feel right to her. The parents explained how difficult it was to avoid being pushed away by Sally, and yet also to not go to the other extreme, namely not pushing themselves into Sally's world. The therapist encouraged the parents to form emotional contact with Sally lightly and playfully, and to remember that Sally had to catch up with several things she had missed as a baby, for example, playing hide and seek, which usually starts between the sixth and eighth month.

When her mother spoke about Sally's being put to bed, the therapist noticed that Sally took a doll's bed out of the doll's house, quickly put a small doll into it, and put the bed back into the house. Her parents hadn't noticed Sally's actions, and continued describing how Sally now slept in the au pair's room, because she always woke the baby up in the night. Since Sally was not allowed to go out of the au pair girl's room and was told she must stay in the room with her. At this Sally had screamed: "Let me out, let me out!" over and over. Her parents were overjoyed that Sally had spoken and were amazed at this new development.

At the next therapy session, the therapist suggested that she would play with Sally and the parents should look on. The therapist took several dolls out of a toy box and said, "Here are some more people for your house." At the same time she held out the box to Sally and was careful not to look at her directly—knowing that that would probably be understood by Sally as an intrusion into her private world. Sally peered into the box hesitantly, reached into it slowly, and emptied all of the dolls onto the table, during which she did not look once at the therapist.

Sally inspected the dolls. The therapist said, "Sally, look to see if one of the dolls looks like Sally." Thereupon Sally selected from the group a small doll and a mother figure, placed them side by side on the table, and began to chat with them in her high voice. As Sally looked from one figure to the other and then at her hand, the therapist hypothesized that she was carefully observing the skin colour of the dolls and was thinking about the difference between their skin colour and that of the dark-skinned au pair girl. She then rummaged among the dolls and picked up a mother doll who was holding a tiny cloth baby in her arms. In the way in which Sally considered both dolls—the mother and the baby, the therapist recognized an inner participation. She said, "Sally is showing us that she knows what she needed—to feel safely held, and then perhaps she could begin to grow."

Sally opened the arms of the mother doll and closed them around the baby. Then she lay the baby doll down and took up a small, pink, rubber baby doll. As her mother had previously told the therapist that Sally often undressed in order to feel objects directly against her skin, the therapist suggested that the small pink doll represents Sally without clothes, who wanted to feel her skin. Then Sally took the pink baby doll and tried to give it to the mother doll to hold, which was not really successful. The therapist said that Sally was the pink doll and was trying to show that she wants to be held, to feel safe, without finding a way of achieving this.

Sally moved the pink baby doll in different directions, which the therapist associated with Sally's desire to find a way to be near to her mother. When she was successful, the therapist commented, "Now she feels held." But again and again, the mother doll let the doll baby somehow slip out of her arms. The therapist said, "Sally knows what she wants and what she needs, but she often can't find it. She is showing how she often feels not held and not thought of by anyone." Sally placed the baby doll in the arms of the mother doll as if it immediately wanted to breast-feed. The therapist postulated that Sally had presumably already seen babies held by their mothers in this way, and she herself also wished to be held like this in order to feel safe. "And if she feels understood by me [the therapist], she feels herself held just as safe and sound as the pink doll." To the therapist's astonishment, Sally then took the baby doll and made it kiss the mother doll. The therapist connected this with what had just happened between them: when Sally felt understood, she also felt loving emotions, and wanted to kiss her mother and be near her. Sally's mother, who had observed everything carefully, began to cry, stroked Sally's hair, and kissed her gently on the head. Sally then played with other, more powerful stuffed animals, such as lions.

At the end of the session Sally didn't want to leave, although the therapist told her that she would be coming back again in the following weeks. Sally had the mother doll and the baby doll embrace firmly and didn't want to return them; the therapist said that Sally was showing how important both of them were for her and that she was frightened to let them go because she feared she would never get them back. As the parents became impatient, the therapist suggested giving Sally a few more minutes in order to talk about her anxieties and fears; she emphasized how important it was for everyone to think about Sally. Sally began to cry bitterly and was not capable of placing the doll in the therapist's hand, so the therapist carefully took it out of her hand. Her father picked Sally up, and she cried and called, "Bye, bye!" It was a painful separation for all, but it was encouraging for the parents to see Sally demonstrate a very human reaction in her unwillingness to be separated from the loving mother doll. The therapist encouraged Sally's parents to talk with her about her painful feelings, instead of merely distracting or comforting her when they arose. This would make Sally feel emotionally held by her parents, the wish she had expressed in her playing.

In the last session, before she was transferred to a more frequent child analysis, Sally showed her wish to create contact. To the surprise of the therapist and her parents, she said, "Gonna be happy," and lifted her arms up in a delicate, beautiful movement, like a plant turning towards the light.

This improbable shift of autistic children towards human communication does not occur frequently; descriptions of psychotherapeutic work with autistic children show how difficult it is to make contact with them. However, it is often possible—to varying degrees (Alvarez, 1992). An essential factor is the way in which parents, educators, and therapists face disorders that are due to genetic causes. Two harmful attitudes are: 1) labelling the child as "autistic", mongoloid, stupid, or aggressive, and 2) the opinion that one cannot do anything because everything has been genetically determined. Labelling conveys to the parents that they have been robbed of "their special child", receiving in its place simply a stereotype. This fear of experts' labelling intensifies parents' feelings of hopelessness and often causes them to become apathetic.

Usually, the child brought to therapy is seen by one therapist, and another talks to the parents.

In therapeutic work with autistic children, distance is taken from the usual diagnostic procedures. In the case of parents of children where autism is suspected, great value is placed on inviting the child together with its parents and siblings for a session. Reid and Alvarez, in their work at the Tavistock Clinic in London, use a multi-phase procedure as their basis.

Psychotherapeutic procedure in work with autistic children

**Phase 1:** Referral: First, no reports about the child are read, in order to remain open and to avoid adopting the judgements of other experts. The child can then more easily be seen through the family's eyes.

**Phase 2:** Observation: Observation of the child and the emotions that are triggered off in the therapist (countertransference). Unstructured observation: to achieve a fair grasp of complex cases.

**Phase 3:** Sharing observation and learning the child's history: Discuss the observation of the child with the parents and find out about the child's history.

**Phase 4:** Contact with other professions: Establish contact with other experts, in order to prepare a help network.

**Phase 5:** Containment of possible family trauma: Offer a containment of the family trauma; investigate what it means for each family member to live with a child with autistic symptoms.

**Phase 6:** Consultation: Advise the family and set up a connection between the child's behaviour and the parents' reactions, in order to make possible a new strategy for improving the family's quality of life.

**Phase 7:** Diary: Encourage the parents to keep a weekly diary of their observations of the child's behaviour, and to note down their positive and negative changes.

**Phase 8:** Family history: On the basis of the developing trust, the stories of the individual family members can be collected, in order to reveal sound development tendencies in the siblings, or to make contact with earlier traumatic experiences in the parents' lives. Meetings with the individual family members should be conducted in order to find out their needs.

**Phase 9:** Assessment of child: Assessment of the effect of the therapeutic work on the child concerned and the child's family.

**Phase 10:** Review of impact of assessment process on child and family: Offer a feedback meeting with the parents to sound out different perspectives, and to give the parents more strength ("empowerment") to consider a therapy plan.

**Phase 11:** Feedback: Build up a network of communication with other experts. Meeting of the parents with other experts should be organized, and plans developed for treatment at home, at school, and in the therapy.

**Phase 12:** Network communication: Develop a treatment for the family, and evaluate who needs help, with consideration given to the resources of the Tavistock Clinic. (Other care facilities can also be used.)

**Further treatment—Phases 13 and 14:** A single meeting per trimester is suggested in order to critically discuss the therapy plan and to reflect on the child's response to the therapy (Reid, 1999: 21ff).

This digression on the treatment of an autistic child should help to make clear how temporary all diagnoses and test results are. Again and again, it is impressive how children react to therapy when they feel themselves understood for the first time in their lives. Even if there is only moderate success, therapy is an important support in helping the parents and the whole family to better organize living with an autistic child. Some families hardly trust themselves to socialize or leave the house with the child because they fear the reactions of friends and acquaintances. The quality of life for the entire family is the focus of therapeutic assistance.

Regarding the initial question of genetic versus environmental influences, today it is generally assumed that genetically contingent factors are insufficient for an actual illness. In other words, even if a genetic disposition for a specific illness or for an artistic talent exists, triggering factors in the environment are needed for this encumbering or enriching facility to be developed. This means that whether a person with an inherited disposition for depression, schizophrenia, or obesity actually becomes ill, or a person with a special talent for music or mathematics actually develops it, depends on how encouraging or impeding are the family relations to which they are exposed.

### 1.1.3   Intelligence

Numerous studies with monozygotic (identical) and dizygotic (non-identical) twins and with adopted children have been carried out concerning intelligence. The complexity of the questions and the design of the studies cannot be explained in depth here. It is nevertheless clear that even identical twins have different experiences. They grow up in the same family, but can develop very different relationships with their parents; for example, the child born five minutes earlier can see himself as older and can more actively explore the world, and show greater curiosity, than the child born five minutes later. Piontelli (2002) has carefully documented these behavioural differences of twins both during pregnancy, using ultrasound scans, and as they continue after birth.

A study was made of the genetic influence on intelligence by comparing the IQs (intelligence quotients) of children who were adopted when very young with the IQs of both their biological and their adoptive parents (Horn, 1983). At first it seemed that the results of the study supported an inheritance theory. The IQ of the adopted children correlated more strongly with that of their biological mother (0.24) than with that of their adoptive mother (0.15). However, in subsequent, more precise, analyses of individual cases, it was shown that the average IQ of a subgroup of adopted children was closer to that of the adoptive mother than it was to that of the biological one, especially when the IQ of the latter was below the average (Huston, 1984). This means that encouraging adopted children in a supportive environment was actually successful. A French research team (Schiff *et al.*, 1978, 1982) got similar results when they studied lower class children who had been adopted by university graduates from the upper income brackets. Their IQ was 14 points higher than that of the children of unskilled workers. The same result was achieved in a USA study of black and multi-racial children who had been adopted as infants by white middle-class families (Scarr and Weinberg, 1976). In summary, one can say that inherited as well as environmental factors play an important role in the enhancement of, or influence on, the intellectual capacity of children.

Case studies from child analyses demonstrate how a child who is considered "dull" can use its supposed deficiency to disguise its inner conflicts. In her treatment of "Erna", Melanie Klein (1924) discovered how the child's interest in the world reawakened after her repressed, aggressive fantasies of invading her mother's body were interpreted, thereby diminishing her fears. The knowledge urge is closely tied to the empowerment fantasy of penetrating the mother's body and stealing everything that she fantasizes is there—babies and the father's penis. The resulting guilt feelings and fear of punishment lead to a restriction of thinking, playing, or showing aggressions. If these unconscious inner conflicts can be cleared up, curiosity and play will be possible again.

## 1.2    Environmental influences

By environmental influences we understand, above all, the actual relationship of the parents to the child, their manner of upbringing, as well as the child's living conditions, its care, and social affiliation.

Growing up in a united family is considered the most important factor for a supportive environment. Children who live with foster parents have to learn to change caregivers at an early age, and seldom have the opportunity to establish a stable emotional relationship with one person. Therefore, even in foster care, the attempt is made to create small family groups or socio-pedagogic family-like care units for children and youths.

Within the family, socio-economic factors play as important a role as the quality of the parents' relationship to each other, the living conditions, and the personality of the parents.

Parents in a strained marriage tend to be less open to their children's needs, to be critical, to express annoyance, and to punish (Cox, Paley, and Harter, 2001). Additional social support systems can be very helpful. Thus, the direct support of the grandparents in caring for the children or indirect financial and emotional support of the child's parents can foster the child's development. Often, the relationship to a warm-hearted grandmother or an affectionate grandfather can be a lifeline for a child whose parents are emotionally unavailable or preoccupied with their own physical or psychic problems.

An important factor in the child's development is the family's socio-economic status, determined by the parents' level of education, the reputation and prestige of their occupations, and the income level. However, no correlation can be made between a mature identity, the ability to love and to work, and the level of social affiliation, that is, at all social levels there are persons with more mature personalities or with psychic problems. Dependence seems greater on whether the child's mother and father themselves (as babies and then children) could develop a loving and constant relationship to a caregiver. As we will be dealing with these questions in detail in the following chapters, I would like to present some short case studies to show what effect being born into a specific family and environment has. The family differences consist not only in their ethnic affiliations and socio-economic conditions, but also in emotional patterns which often have effects generations later.

Being born into a specific family constitutes an essential influential factor. Therefore, here are two biographical examples of women who made use of intensive family social work, as contrasted with a study of successful managers. In multi-problem families (Goldbrunner, 1989; Rauchfleich, 1996), characteristics and behaviour patterns are perpetuated nearly identically from generation to generation. Psychoanalysis can help us understand why these patterns repeat themselves and how it is possible to break out of the vicious cycles.

### 1.2.1   Example: problem families with family-social intensive care

Gerlinde, mother of ten children and at present receiving family-intensive care, hardly mentioned her family of origin during a two-hour interview; she only said that her father had died early, that she had a poor relationship to her mother, and that they didn't see each other. Asked what she remembered from her childhood, she said, "My own childhood ... partly it was great and partly ... concerning my mother, it was a horror. I never want to be like her ... My mother said: "Bitch, fetch me a coffee. Bitch, do this ..." These are things that really hit hard. And at some point—my second child was on the way—my mother said, "I would rather have had ten puppies than a daughter." Well, I will certainly not hurt my children in this way" (Liebletsberger, 2005).

At first, Gerlinde tries to maintain the picture of her "great" childhood, but she cannot finish her sentence as painful memories arise. Indeed, she begins to relate how terribly it hurt her not to have received any affectionate attention from her mother. However, she continues to struggle to see a connection between the behaviour towards her and her behaviour towards her children. This unprocessed traumatic experience is repressed, and her relationship to her alcohol-dependent father is idealized.

Gerlinde tried to escape from her callous mother and alcohol-dependent father by becoming pregnant at the age of seventeen and marrying the child's father. At the time of the socio-pedagogic assistance of the family-intensive care, she had ten children from six different fathers, and had been married and divorced three times. She had had no job training and lived on social welfare, child support, and alimony. Her seventeen-year-old son had fathered a child with her best woman friend and after a violent argument with his mother had moved out.

On the conscious level, Gerlinde wanted to be a completely different mother than her mother had been. The unconscious wish to repeat emotional patterns in a relationship similar to those she wanted to avoid on a conscious level was called "repetition compulsion" by Freud (1920: 63). Even if the experiences with her alcoholic father had been painful, they were nevertheless familiar to her. Unconsciously, Gerlinde initiated actions in order to create similar, known situations, as she chose men who drank and physically abused her. She always became pregnant before she could stabilize a relationship with a new partner, only to be completely overburdened by caring for ten children without financial security. She fights for her children and tries to treat them with respect, even if not always successfully. Due to stress and her unsure financial situation, she prompts her children to repeat her situation; for example, her oldest son fathering a child at the age of sixteen and thereby establishing a family in an insecure financial situation. But Gerlinde is able to accept and make use of socio-pedagogic help.

This compulsive repetition of painful experiences, dangerous life situations, or humiliating treatment, which creates suffering, unhappiness, and despair, belongs to the most baffling psychic mechanisms. This unconscious, strong urge to recreate earlier, familiar, yet painful, emotional patterns, as apparently asexual phenomena, contradicts the basic striving for satisfaction and desire and should be seen as an expression of masochistic and sadistic aspirations. This strong inclination to become involved in situations again and again in which one suffers and which, on a conscious level, one wants to avoid, can only be understood as the deep embedding of unconscious motives. In his later years Freud linked the repetition compulsion with the death instinct.

In another case of family-intensive care, the answer to the first question about Irina's contact with her family of origin already shows how rootless and lost the mother is. In a sad voice, she says she has no contact with her family—her mother has already died, and she wants no contact with her father and siblings.

> Well, when I was little my father already ... he lives in Vienna ... and I grew up at my great-grandmother's because my mother was ... an alcoholic and other siblings grew up in a Children's Home, and my great-grandmother took me in at the age of one and raised me.
>
> (Liebletsberger, 2005: 51)

The long pauses between sentences, the many interruptions, and the incomplete sentences show how difficult it is for Irina to speak about her experiences as a child. The interviewer also suffers so much that he cannot continue his questions. He has the impression of delving into an open wound, and feels the pain that Irina cannot. She relates these scraps of memory in a monotone and without emotional involvement. She came to her great-grandmother's house at the age of only one, that is, it was not only her alcoholic mother who was not in a position to take care of her as a baby, but her grandmother also was missing. Her father had abandoned the family early on. Irina's first year of life was particularly marked by piecemeal relationships, abandonment, limited stability, and emotional wounds. At the time of the family-intensive care she had no contact with either her siblings or her mother; she had broken off all contact and was not supported by either her family or her husband's.

It is therefore not surprising when we learn that Irina was not in a position to understand the situation of her own young children. They were taken away from her because she had left them at home alone and unattended while she worked as a waitress. She could not comprehend that one cannot leave one- and two-year-old children alone with their four-year-old brother. Because she herself had never experienced someone taking care of her, she also could not take care of her children. Her early experiences of lack and deprivation and the hardships due to being separated from her mother left deep traces in her personality. She and her husband were incapable of putting their finances in order; their debts and interest costs became larger and larger. The house was a construction site which for years could not be completed. Her incapability of reflecting on her and her children's well-being also led to her unawareness of an increasingly dire financial situation—she simply threw away the notices of over-due bills. Only the removal of the children by the Youth Welfare Office presented her with a crisis, and gave her an opportunity to accept help. The experience of her problems being taken seriously and of being regularly supported by two social workers made it pos-sible for her to put her life in sufficient order that she got her chil-dren back again.

In both cases, long-lasting support by the family-intensive social work agency was necessary to help both families organize their financial situations and to assume responsibility for their children (Liebletsberger, 2005: 159 ff, 204 ff).

## Escape from the vicious circle of deprivation

Is it at all possible to break out of this vicious circle? Neglected children become mothers and fathers who then neglect their own children, and children who are beaten become adults who beat and mistreat their own children, often seeing this as correct upbringing which toughens the children. We know that the tendency to forget, to repress, or to trivialize these painful and humiliating experiences is the surest way of perpetuating this pattern. Even when people such as Gerlinde resolve to treat their children entirely differently, this pattern asserts itself behind their back, so to speak. They them-selves have experienced these brutal, abusive adults as strong and themselves as powerless. This intensive love–hate relationship was unconsciously connected with excitement, even though permeated with suffering. Unconsciously, they equate themselves with the aggressor, become just as strong and merciless as their mother or father, and let their children feel how it is to be helplessly handed over to an arbitrary fate. Anna Freud (1969: 85) called this intrapsy-chic pattern "identification with the aggressor". Of course, there are infinitely many variations of this constellation, which should always be understood as special and singular, case by case.

Only if one maintains emotional contact with these painful experiences of surrender, impotence, rage, and helplessness, and, ideally, has someone with whom to share these experiences—a friend, an aunt, a teacher, a priest, a psychotherapist—can the victim possibly develop an ability not to pass on these experiences to their own children and to not do them the same wrongs that they have suffered. Such openness in listening to the problems and pains of children makes high demands on educators, who cannot avoid the attendant pain and feelings of helplessness. Isca Salzberger-Wittenberg writes:

> ... one is making oneself available to the client's or student's excessive emotional pain, and holding or carrying it for them for a period of time. The possibility of the strain becoming too great, resulting in having to give up one's job, having a breakdown, or protecting oneself against pain by becoming more superficial, dogmatic and rigid, is one that needs to be taken seriously.

> (Salzberger-Wittenberg, 1999: 166)

She continues: "Knowing that we are not omnipotent, we sometimes wish to refer cases to other professional help" (Salzberger-Wittenberg, 1999: 167). The escape from this problem consists of acting as if one did not notice the problems of a beaten, maltreated, or neglected child. By looking away and letting things be, one supports a situation which sows the seeds for further burdensome cruelties in coming generations.

In psychoanalysis and social work, case studies are of patients and clients in treatment, so that mostly adverse behaviour patterns in the family are spotlighted. It is just as important to mention that affectionate support of children and help in overcoming difficult life and professional situations fall on just as fertile soil as mistreatment and neglect do. Parents who act as examples for their children help to pass on qualities such as courage, resilience, ambition, persistence, selflessness, and loving devotion to future generations. Their children have experienced being taken seriously and being loved, and they have seen examples of persistence in the face of difficult conditions, the overcoming of crises, and holding one's ground through hard work. Just as in problem families, family experiences—in this case, positive ones—offer a basis on which children can develop behaviour similar to the example set by their parents.

## 1.2.2   Example: professionally successful families

From a study of "Career Men and Career Women" (*"Karrierefrauen und Karrieremänner"*) (Diem-Wille, 1996) in management and academia, I would like to present the biography of a man and a woman who, in spite of difficult social conditions, showed their children positive strategies for mastering and coping with life, along with a loving acceptance of children. A top manager, whom I'll call Hermann, describes his family situation as follows:

> I was the only son ... was provided for, mothered, and kept as far away as possible from all bad images of life. I was a quiet, good child, read a lot. ... I have had no contact with my father all my life, as a German he was expelled from the country in 1945. ... My mother worked lots and lots, she lived totally for her profession ... grandmother ran the household.

(Diem-Wille, 1996: 42)

As an only child, he was brought up by his mother and grandmother after a separation of his parents caused by politics. Against his mother's will, he attended university and made a swift career in a computer company. He has been married for twenty years, and has one grown daughter and another young one. His warmhearted grandmother had cared for and mothered him, while his working mother took on more the role of father. His mother had a wholesale textile business in the countryside and sometimes had to go on trips as "country chandler", a very strenuous and atypical activity for women, which she performed very successfully. His grandmother also had to earn a living for herself and her illegitimate daughter. She rented rooms to students and made lunch at home for business people (Diem-Wille, 1996: 51). Hermann proudly told of the resourcefulness of both women, who were able to establish an existence without outside help. For both women, bringing up and encouraging the child were important purposes in life. Although he considered himself a "coddled only child", his achievements in school were always excellent. He was also able to realize his wish to make himself independent—again contrary to his mother's will.

Twenty-one years ago Hermann began as a consultant in a computer company, shortly thereafter became an assistant to the head of systems advisory, and then built up his own department. After only three years, due to his strong professional dedication, he was offered a management position in the planning area, which he subsequently headed. The department expanded to include marketing and staff tasks. Twelve years later Hermann received a leading position abroad, and was assigned very challenging projects. He described these two years abroad as his most interesting time, as he principally had to make new decisions about expanding the business relationships with Third World countries. After two years he was recalled to Austria to a position on the executive board and shortly thereafter, in a company re-organization, was appointed divisional director. A year later he was the general director's representative. He touches on his work effort and the stresses when he mentions "how quickly I had to change," and "always learning something new and just before one begins to reap rewards, one is doing something new again" (Diem-Wille, 1996: 42).

Now for the family background of a top woman manager, whom I shall call Erika. Outwardly, she had difficult social relationships similar to Irina's, who had had recourse to family-intensive social work, but the way in which her family overcame poverty and social decline, and the attitude she conveyed to her daughter, differ greatly from Irina's family.

In Erika's case, we find the mother's unspoken "message" was "to do it differently than I do". Without academic training, for which no money was available, Erika was able to pursue a fast-rising professional career in an international concern. Erika's mother was an illegitimate daughter who grew up at her maternal grandmother's. There was never enough money. Erika's great-grandmother ran a grocery, "a tiny general store in Lichtental", a work-intensive and physically strenuous occupation for a single woman:

> A tiny general store in Lichtental in wartime. Well, that's something that exceeds, I think, any reproaches. To walk to the Naschmarkt at three in the morning, pick up the wares and then back again with the cart and then selling and standing in the store, with hardly any holidays.
>
> (Erika)

The oppressive closeness and her mother's battle for survival were indicated by Erika in her narrative. She made slips of the tongue and said "exceeds any reproaches" instead of "exceeds our imagination"—presumably she had reproached her grandfather, who had abandoned her mother during the war. Asked what her mother's parents had been, she immediately speaks about her great-grandmother:

> Her mother—well her mother was an illegitimate child and was, I believe, very young—her mother was very young, very young. I don't know the woman, I've never seen her, and that was rather an unwanted child, and therefore she also took in grandmother, and the father is unknown. Rather dubious relationships.
>
> (Erika)

Erika comes from a family in which there were two generations of illegitimate children (girls). The great-grandmother had been abandoned along with her illegitimate child. The grandmother repeated this pattern. It demands great courage to bring illegitimate children into the world, as can be seen from two generations of reproaches, disappointments, and condemnation of the women of unreliable fathers. Erika's mother wanted to do it differently than her mother and grandmother had: marry a man from higher social circles and not have children. Erika was not planned; she was "an accident". Erika's mother didn't ever want to be hungry and wanted to lead a comfortable life. Her husband, Erika's father, admittedly did not fulfil his wife's ambitious plans; he led a "comfy life". Her mother was happy about Erika's professional successes and was proud of her. "I think I've attained what she actually wanted ... at least as far as getting ahead."

Erika speaks clearly about the connection between her life and her mother's in relation to professional success. This involves a parent's delegation of (unrealizable) wishes to their child, who is supposed to fulfil them vicariously for the parent. This model provides many examples of a burdensome "assignment" for the child, if the child is under pressure to lead their parent's life, not their own (Stierlin, 1980: 215). Those human objects of delegation have to master unconscious assignments from the family's areas of tension; through their problems, they induce one or both parents to take care of them or sacrifice for them, thereby giving meaning to their lives. Those delegated to receive the "assignment" unconsciously: they are representatives, acting out the parents' repressed instability, violence, or self-indulgence. Although on a conscious level the parents suffer from the child's behaviour, in family therapy it is clear that they secretly encourage and approve of this behaviour. One can say: "By means of deceptive and frequently self-destructive behaviour, such delegates make possible the psychological survival of one or both parents" (Stierlin, 1989: 217). In Erika's case a positive assignment could also be conveyed: to improve the family's status simultaneously for herself and, by proxy, for her mother and grandmother. Instead of the dynamics of revenge and spite, a redemption spanning generations can be experienced (as in Erika's case) if the grandchild opposes the injustice done to the last two generations with recognition and financial success, in which Erika allows her parents to participate by supporting them financially.

## Patterns of upbringing as an influential factor

The parents' upbringing constitutes an essential influence on child development. If we compare the upbringing of parents from problem families (Goldbrunner, 1989) with that of parents of successful children (Diem-Wille, 1996), a clear tendency is visible: problem families are characterized by frequent breaking off of contact, separation of the parents, and abrupt alternation between closeness and uncaring distance. The parents are separated or, if they remain together, live in love–hate, characterized by phases of bickering and reconciliation. In the bickering phase, the child is wooed by both sides with promises and attestations of love; in the reconciliation phase he is ignored. The children do not feel constant devotion, and attempt to force attention by means of negative behaviour. Child management fluctuates between laxity and strictness. There are no clear guidelines for punishment. The children's behaviour is criticized in a nagging way, and they are threatened with massive withdrawal of affection. Independent actions of the children are dismissed and criticized. The child is shaken out of their affect in an uncontrolled fashion. Rules which the child is required to obey are either not observed by the parents for their part, or observed only inconsistently. The spatial and economic cramped relationships are manifest in disorderly living quarters and housekeeping as well as in the parents' clothing. The parents are incapable of dealing with everyday tasks such as managing money and housekeeping, they cannot reflect on themselves, and they hold other people and situations responsible for their misfortune. The children become familiar with the world from a discouraging side, and are defensive and mistrustful. Daily failures can be borne only by fantasizing unrealistic wishes, ideas, and intentions as possibilities.

The parents of "career women and career men" were predominantly stable, thorough in their pursuits, and formulated rules of behaviour whose observance they held to be important. In the group studied, a success-oriented undertone prevailed. The subjects were self-confident, assertive, and had a high tolerance of frustration. On the whole, they felt accepted and wanted by at least one parent. Their joy in discovery and their curiosity had been supported, their ideas and conceptions were taken seriously, and their independence was encouraged. The parents played with them a great deal, gave them books, and also discussed the books with them. They considered their children capable of achievement, encouraged their independence, and enjoyed their successes with them. Even when the parents' expectations were potentially over-demanding, the subjects studied were able to produce results thanks to their talents. The parents set an example of regularity and order in their dress and housekeeping and expected the same of their children. An important factor was the parents' retaining their joy, determination, and resilience in spite of great difficulties. The parents' work ethic was described as austere: work stood at the centre of life. Those interviewed respected their parents—even when they had conflicting relationships with them—not because of their superiority, but because of their ability to master their own lives.

## Comparison between professionally successful families and problem families

The comparison between professionally successful families and problem families should not be misunderstood as a judgment. The goal of child-rearing is not to produce "career people". The examples are presented in order to describe the different influences in upbringing. The goal of an "adequate upbringing", according to Winnicott (1983), is to enable individuals to be capable of work and relationships, corresponding to the ideal picture of a "balanced identity", a balanced life between professional and private, between work and pleasure.

The case studies might leave the impression that certain family patterns represent a similar beneficial or unfavourable condition for all children. Actually, clinical work has shown that children in the same family have different chances of development. On the one hand, this is dependent on the child's disposition of robustness or vulnerability, patience or impatience, but, on the other, is dependent also on the differing relationships of the parents to each child, depending upon gender, similarity to the parent, the position in the sibling line, and the family's specific positive or traumatic circumstances. In *A Mingled Yarn: Chronicle of a Troubled Family* (1992) Beulah Parker, a renowned American psychoanalyst, describes her own family and tries to understand which factors determined that her brother became schizophrenic and later took his own life, while her sister became neurotic. Behind the façade of a white, successful, Anglo-Saxon family, it is shown *how* the disruption of feeling and thinking capacities is affected by a communicational dysfunction in the family, resulting in silences and the sending of contradictory messages. She shows how "environmental influences are extraordinarily significant … and that the genetic inheritance can be seen at most as a predispositional factor" (Parker, 1972: 11).

It is the story of a socially privileged family in the USA, whose paternal and maternal line goes back to the Pilgrims who landed in America in 1635. The family members were Protestants who had access to money and high social  positions. The father was a good-looking, highly gifted, and very successful businessman in the grand style, who was very devoted to his children as long as he lived with them in the same household. The mother was charming, well-educated, and concerned about the children. All three children possessed above-average intelligence, talent, and health, had an attractive home, and enjoyed a superior education in private schools. What was the reason that one son became schizophrenic? All family members had great difficulty in directly communicating what they felt. In many scenes, we can see how the parents sent contradictory messages to their children and expected them to keep to rules which they themselves did not follow. Religious pathos was used to emphasize the equality of human beings, and the children were encouraged to have contact with common Italian children, who were then talked about deprecatingly. What was said aloud contradicted indirectly communicated wishes—an "inner tug-of-war" took place.

Business ventures usually received a coating of human idealism and romantic glorification.

The father became entangled in business clashes in the Midwest, which kept him away from the family for ten years. His situation remained unclear for the children; ten years had passed as though he would return at any moment. He came for brief visits and disappeared again. The third, unwanted daughter soon manifested serious eating disorders, which only stopped after hiring an experienced nursemaid—an indication of the difficult relationship between mother and baby. The detailed descriptions give excellent insights into the diversity of experiences in the same family from the perspective of the three siblings.

Parker discusses how to recognize and understand the special type of communicational dysfunction in families with a schizophrenic member in relationship to an analyst in her famous book *My Language Is Me* (*Meine Sprache bin ich*) (1974) in the form of dialogues with an adolescent youth.

The question of the significance of inherited and environmental influences in the emergence of psychic disorders such as schizophrenia, or in aptitudes such as development of intelligence, or in misconduct such as delinquency or vandalism, is still the subject of controversial discussion. There is agreement that both factors play a role.

# CHAPTER TWO

# The emergence of the body-ego—individuation through the experience of separation and closeness

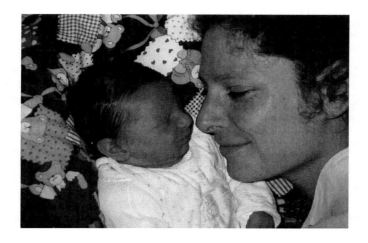

## 2.1    Being held by the parents

The baby, the product of a couple's sexual union, remains dependent on affection and care after birth. One can describe the baby as a "physiological premature birth" or as a "secondary home-nester"(Portmann, 1951: 45), because it is incapable of survival without the help of the parents or other caregivers.[1] In order to form a stable body-ego (that is, the ability to feel alive and a connection to one's own body), the capability of self-love, and to comprehend being a separate person than the parents, it needs the continuing experience of the relationship to adults who care for the baby's physical and spiritual well-being. The different dimensions of the incipient body-ego, the ability to feel and to think, the development of psychosexuality and creativity (which are expressed in play), all these are closely connected and together form a whole. One could compare this complex interaction with the score of a symphony. There are different superimposed melodies and a voice for each instrument, and from the polyphonic blending of these an entire musical works arises. In the following chapters, if emphasis is placed on a specific aspect, this should not be understood as an artificial separation, but serves to describe an individual phenomenon more clearly—the interplay of inherited and environmental influences should also be considered. The focus of attention is always on the development of the child's inner reality.

How does the newborn child become a reflective person who can engage in love relationships and shape its own life? Or into a person who assumes a fringe position in society due to criminality, drug addiction, violence, or psychological disorders such as eating problems, depression, or schizophrenia? How can we understand

---

[1] Human development has a special position among the vertebrates, writes Portmann. The specific upright posture and the typical way of communicating is reached a year after birth. "If this human condition paralleled that of a genuine mammal, human pregnancy would have to be a year longer than it actually is: it would have to be 21 months long. Therefore, the newborn is a type of "physiological", i.e., normalized premature birth, or a "secondary nest-squatter," the sole case in this category among mammals" (Portmann, 1951: 45). "This "ex-uterus springtime" is of fundamental significance: here the processes of maturation, which are also encouraged in the mother's body, are combined with the inflowing experiences of countless sources of stimulation; in dealing with these, maturation progresses, as does the attainment of upright posture and the means of movement and language" (Gehlen, 1971: 45).

which conditions lead to the formation of the diverse characters and uniqueness of individuals? By this we do not mean that the first three years of life once and for all determine a person's character, but that they shape basic patterns of experiencing the world; particularly in puberty there is a "secondary psychosexual development phase" which leads to changes—and, in addition, the entire experiences of life serve to modify our identity.

Today we know that the basic pattern of the personality is formed in the first years of life, especially in the first months, and is dependent on the quality of the relationship to the first caregivers—usually the mother and father. Physical and psychological development, as well as psychological and intellectual development, are closely connected. The focus of various sciences on the first years of life has consistently shown how central the first years are for the structuring and training of the brain, for the inner pattern of experiencing the world, and for the self-image. Body, mind, sexuality, and creativity are closely connected. In remarking that "There is no such thing as an infant, only an infant with its mother", Winnicott (1956: 303) clearly formulated the vitally important relation of the baby to its mother (caregiver).

Before I go into a detailed description of the different qualities of the maternal relationship with the baby and the resulting beneficial or complicating factors, I would like to point out a possible misunderstanding: The fundamental significance of maternal/parental care and love is often understood as though the entire "blame" for problems in development lies with the mother or parents, and only in the first years of life, so that teachers and educators often tend not to feel themselves responsible or accountable. A converse reaction would be helpful—that is, to understand how important it is to help the young parents-to-be deal with the upcoming task during the pregnancy. Of prime importance is not the physical care but the emotional preparation for parenthood. As I have thoroughly detailed in my paper, "Pregnancy as a Restructuring of the Inner World of Parents-to-be" ("*Psychoanalytische Aspekte der Schwangerschaft als Umgestaltung der inneren Welt der werdenden Eltern*") (Diem-Wille, 2004), due to the new parental tasks, deep-seated emotions and unfinished inner (often unconscious) problems with the prospective parents' own parents become newly activated.

If these newly activated feelings and conflicts with their own parents can be made conscious and reflected on, the prospective parents will gain inner space for dealing with the newly existing baby, and make room for it in their own inner world. Another common misunderstanding is to demand of a "perfect mother" that she always understands her baby, always cares for it lovingly, and selflessly puts aside her own needs. Psychoanalysis can make an important contribution here by revising this unrealistic assumption. There is no such thing as an "always good mother", only a "good-enough mother", who conveys predominantly positive experiences to the baby. Human emotions are seldom one-dimensional like love or anger, and appear in mixtures, that is, they are ambivalent: where there is love there is also hate and anger; generosity is accompanied by envy and resentment; patience and impatience alternate. All human beings—including mothers and fathers, teachers and educators—have their good and bad qualities, strengths and weaknesses, special talents and vulnerable areas, and they retain these when they have a baby or have to take care of a child. Each one of us was born into a particular family and had to learn to live with these people under specific socio-economic conditions and in a cultural-religious framework. Our children too will profit from the positive assets of our personalities, and therefore will also have to deal with our weaknesses, problems, and crises, with restrictions and obstructions. For the baby's healthy development, it is important to have a mother and a father who make possible largely good experiences by being emotionally available, who try to understand their baby's needs, and who are capable of mutual involvement with the baby, that is, a "good-enough mother" or a "good-enough father". At the same time, at points even such parents will be annoyed, will retreat, will not understand the baby and its needs, or will simply not want to know more about it. Sometime parents ask themselves why they wanted to have a baby when it is so exhausting and strenuous to deal with and to satisfy it. It is perhaps reassuring to know that all parents sometimes wish that their baby was gone, and long to return to the undisturbed time of their togetherness as a couple. Life truly becomes difficult if we think we should not have such feelings and thoughts, if we feel guilty or forbid ourselves to have these feelings, instead of understanding that these moods pass and function as an important safety-valve, relieving pressure.

In addition, the idea of being able to or having to "always be there for the baby" misconstrues the fact that the alternation of separation and reunion is a fundamental dimension of life. Experiences of separation alternate with experiences of togetherness. Permanent physical contact is of less importance than whether the contact is linked with the parents' emotional availability. The parents' readiness to consider their baby, to take delight in it, and to accept its "primitive" feelings is then expressed physically: the mother's joyfully shining eyes seeking contact with the baby's, her stroking and kissing its hair, stroking its skin, speaking to it, feeding and carrying it, washing it and changing its nappies—all of these are important forms of communication which give the baby the feeling of being secure and loved. Then the baby can also endure its mother's annoyed look when she feels her everyday life disturbed, as well as the bleary, unfriendly scowls of permanently sleep-deprived parents. A dutiful caring for the child but in an environment deficient in emotional contact and playful affection, singing, or chatter makes the baby perceive the world as cold and hostile, as a mechanical functional exercise, without closeness and joy.

The child itself often intensifies its parents' feelings that they have to put aside their own needs and have to care selflessly for their newborn infant in the first weeks of life. However, it is important that both the father and the mother have time for themselves and their interests, both separately and as a couple. A social network that supports the young parents—for instance, grandparents or friends—is therefore very helpful. If the parents neglect their own needs over a longer period of time, this can result in repressed aggressions, helplessness, exhaustion, or depression.

It should be emphasized again that psychoanalysis does not prescribe any abstract, normative claim of a "correct upbringing" or apportion guilt to the parents. Its concern is rather to describe the latitude and differences of "normal" patterns of upbringing, and to help parents (by means of example) to understand the special situation of a family, to identify the obstructive and beneficial conditions for successful child-rearing, and to offer help in problems with children. Now we shall turn to the question of the development of the body-ego and the perception of separateness.

"The ego is above all something physical, it is not only a surface being but is itself the projection of a surface," one which originates from bodily sensations,[2] Freud (1923: 295) wrote in "The Ego and the Id" ("*Das Ich und das Es*"). The development of a body-ego is based on experiences during pregnancy, in which the growing foetus is held by a warm and soft membrane, which Gaddini (1998: 26) describes as "physiological learning". Building on this experience of a spatial boundary in the mother's body, after birth more differentiated bodily perceptions develop that are dependent on being touched, on skin contact with the caregiver, and other types of sensory perception such as eye contact, the mother's smell, and her voice. If the baby perceives insufficient or no regular stimulation of the baby by an adult, a feeling of estrangement arises, of not being alive, a deficit which can lead to eating disorders and other fundamental personality disorders.

The close connection between body and mind becomes apparent in psychosomatic illnesses. If people cannot perceive their own emotions and cannot express them, then they "speak through their body", producing physical symptoms. Each of us has a psychosomatic potential when problems overpower us and the body expresses mental stress, a phenomenon which Joyce McDougall (1989: 6) has described as "the theatre of the body". If it is not possible to express oneself symbolically, then the expressive form unconsciously chosen is no longer speech but the body, by means of numerous symptoms such as allergies, bowel complaints, gastritis, heart problems, and migraine.

We will proceed from Melanie Klein's assumption that at birth the baby possesses a rudimentary ego-nucleus, that is, it makes a primitive distinction between within and without and already begins to develop active relationships to caregivers (objects).[3] Immediately after birth, babies demonstrate expressive facial reactions that can be ascribed to different feelings such as pain, disgust, joy, and fear. Discomfort is expressed by screaming and flailing, with movements

---

[2] In the English translation a footnote authorised by Freud is added: "The ego is ultimately derived from bodily sensations, chiefly from those springing from the surface of the body. It may thus be regarded as a mental projection of the surface of the body, besides, as we have seen above, representing the superficies of the mental apparatus" (Freud, 1923: 194, footnote).
[3] Daniel Stern's (1985) empirical research on infants confirms both the assumption of an active, competent infant as well as the criticism of the theory of an original symbiosis, as Margaret Mahler (1979) suggested. (See also Dornes, 1993.)

that show that the child wants to be free of something or wants to bring something out of its body. The first sensations are conveyed through the skin and mouth, when the baby sucks on its own fingers or the mother's nipple, and through the eyes which seek eye-contact with the mother immediately after birth.[4] The baby is not only driven by its own needs of hunger and protection, but is also dependent on love, security, and attention, which it expresses physically with fine nuances. Babies are very early able to sense the total mental state of the caregiver through their facial expressions and vocal tone, and react quickly and empathetically. The baby fluctuates on the one hand between feelings of security and satiation, and on the other hand the fear of disintegration and being lost in space. If it is under stress and full of fear, it needs an adult to help it calm down. The fear of disintegration can be lessened by such things as the mother's voice, light, or being held.

Esther Bick has made an important theoretical and clinical contribution to understanding very early experiences via the skin, when she points out that only through the experience of being securely held by the mother does the infant perceive its own skin as a protective boundary that holds the ego together. Perception of skin, in its function as a highly primitive form of personality integration, is closely connected to the experience of external objects (caregivers) (Bick, 1968). By internalizing these experiences, the baby develops a fantasized differentiation between "internal and external space" with the skin as boundary—a concept which will be gone into more in greater detail in Chapter three, where emotional development is discussed.

Through diverse experiences, the baby develops a mental concept of an independent body space that can be regulated, and whose sensitive limits can also be disturbed. Fundamental psychological and psychosomatic problems—such as psychotic and autistic disorders, or eating and development disorders—have their roots in early relationship problems:

> Disturbance in the primal skin function can lead to a development of a "second skin" formation through which dependence

---

[4] The human baby is the only living creature which establishes eye-contact with the mother immediately after birth.

on the object is replaced by a pseudo-independence, by the inappropriate use of certain mental functions, or perhaps innate talents, for the purpose of creating a substitute for this skin container function.

(Bick, 1968: 115)

It should again be emphasized that my remarks must not be understood as meaning that, on the one hand, there are experiences which are exclusively good or exclusively disappointing and negative. Separation and frustration, which are stimulating for development, belong to a healthy development. The unavoidable experiences of pain, limitation, and deficiency are also motors for development. In her book *Die Melodie des Abschieds* (*The Melody of Farewell*), Zwettler–Otte (2006) shows how the psychological preoccupation with fear of separation can be allayed or dealt with in an artistically creative manner. The parents' task consists of helping the infant to learn to deal with such things in small doses. The first mental image is the one of the mother's breast, voice, and warmth being absent. In order to mitigate disappointed expectations, the nourishing memory of a giving, loving breast is activated.

Genevieve Haag (2001) pursued the significance of skin contact for the baby and for the development of the early relationship with the mother by pointing out the importance of the baby's spine contacting a supporting surface. The tactile perception of the body's central–middle axis in the spine conveys knowledge of the centre of the body and its two symmetrical halves. These bodily divisions are experienced by the foetus in its movements in the placenta and uterus.

Joseph Sandler (1960) connected the early body experiences after birth with a "background feeling of security".[5] If this is not experienced after birth, there is a background feeling of threat. Even if the memories of these early years are not conscious, they leave deep traces which significantly influence our perception of the world as a

---

[5] Sandler (1960: 353) writes: "These safety signals are related to such things as the awareness of being protected; for example by the reassuring presence of the mother, I refer only to a simple background feeling which can be compared to a level of tonus in a resting muscle, and which is as different from atonic feelings of death and emptiness as a healthy muscle is from a denervated one."

friendly or threatening place. As a symbol for recording experiences in the unconscious, Freud used the image of the "magic writing pad":[6] "For our psychological apparatus ... has unlimited ways of being receptive to ever new perceptions and creates lasting—and also changeable—traces of them in our memory" (Freud, 1925: 366). Melanie Klein calls this process "memory in feeling" to describe the influence of these early experiences on our personality. The positive experience of being held are relevant both to the physical and emotional dimensions; it lays the foundation for the baby's ability to enjoy things, certain of being gently touched by the parents, of feeling at home in its own body, that is, of accepting its body in an emotionally positive way (cathexis of the body). However, there doesn't always have to be physical contact; language and eye contact constitute symbolic forms of holding and containment. In the following chapter we will try to show how the actual development of a child is influenced by a complex interplay between inner and outer realities—that is, from within, out of the child's fantasies, desires, anxieties, and jealousy, and from supportive or adverse external factors, such as the parents' relationship to the child and the family's living conditions.

Language represents another important medium of communication between mother and baby. Mothers talk to their babies as if they are already able to understand what is spoken. As Norman (2001) describes, infants actually react to the emotional content of what is spoken, to the non-lexical aspect of the language. Little by little, the child can internalize these positive sensory experiences of communicating with its parents, of being consoled and soothed, and can then console and sooth itself by remembering. In doing so, the infant also shows whether or not the parents trust it to soothe itself. If it has had only a few or no positive experiences—because the caregiver was not emotionally available for long stretches of time and it thus feels itself emotionally isolated, or because it was constantly neglected and left alone—then the baby cannot learn to develop its own positive feelings and to experience these as belonging to itself. It is just as difficult for a baby to assume the rhythms of togetherness

---

[6] The magic writing pad is a writing device where the cellophane covering page can be lifted away from the wax matrix beneath, thereby making the writing invisible, which however remains on the wax matrix.

and separation if the parents cannot bear being separated from their baby and are convinced it is necessary to carry the baby around constantly in order to protect it. The parents unconsciously behave as though the baby really cannot manage without them even for a short period of time. A mother who came to the parent–infant therapy with a healthy, happy, and well-nourished baby, described the child's problems in a long letter, and complained that the child could not be without her for even a moment, so that the mother could not even have a shower or get dressed (Diem-Wille, 1999). In the first therapy session it was clear that the baby had developed very well, but the mother had projected onto her daughter her own unsolved unconscious conflicts with her own unmotivated absent father, and therefore her perception of the child's development was distorted. She had not even dared to ask why her father had been so often absent, and no one had ever listened to her. Only after she had talked about these unresolved conflicts with her father in therapy was she able to give her daughter more freedom to develop.

In dealing with parents who are emotionally difficult to reach, one strategy of babies can consist of exaggerating the expression of their feelings in order to gain their parents' attention; or it can injure itself unconsciously to "force" the parents' attention. The parents convey emotion to their baby through words, touch, and body language. Well co-ordinated movements are developed by babies with emotionally available parents who permit it to test its body development independently. Emotionally unsure children whose ambitious parents wanted to anticipate certain steps in development tend to be physically awkward and to injure themselves, continually experiencing what a dangerous place the world is.

It should again be emphasized that our aim is not to condemn "wrong" parental behaviour. What should be pointed out is the close interplay between the actual behaviour of the parents and their baby; this behaviour is also influenced by their unconscious emotions, desires, and anxieties regarding the baby. Observing this close interaction can help us to understand more about the special relationship between parents and their baby.

## 2.2   Psychoanalytic observation of babies

To illustrate the broad spectrum of relationships between parents and their baby, I would like to present and interpret two examples of infant observation. The first example deals with Elias, the first child of a young English couple who had been married for several years. The second example describes a family from Nepal and their fourth daughter, Sushma, whose mother had been suffering from depressive mood swings since the child's birth.

The weekly infant observations based on Esther Bick (Miller *et al.*, 1989; Reid, 1997; Lazar, *et al.*, 1986; Diem-Wille, 1997) aim at recording as exact and detailed a description as possible of the interaction between parents and their baby, as well as body language, facial and verbal expression. Within the framework of a small seminar group led by a psychoanalyst, the weekly observation notes are discussed in detail; then, cautious assumptions about the baby's development and the differentiation of its inner world as well as awareness of itself are discussed. In the following week, further details of the relationship pattern in the family can be accurately observed, which then leads to a modification or consolidation of the hypotheses (see Introduction).

### 2.2.1   Observation of Elias

*In an Infant Observation in London, I observed a baby and its parents. In the first observation Elias was seven days old.*

#### Elias, seven days old

As I arrived ten minutes late, the father opened the door and greeted me. The mother sat in an armchair. Elias lay in her arms and she supported his head with her right hand. He had been breast-fed and had fallen asleep, said the mother. Elias is a lovely baby with full, round cheeks, and a lot of long hair. The mother appears to be tired, but very happy and proud. I congratulate her on her baby and look at it more carefully. While the mother is telling me about the birth, she gently strokes Elias's head, looks at him lovingly, and smiles at him. (There follows a detailed description of the birth, which she was able to manage successfully without painkillers and with the help of her mother-in-law and her husband.) In the meantime, the father has gone into the kitchen to make tea. The mother asks me if I want to hold Elias. I reply that I just want to observe, and remain in my observer role. Without taking her eyes off Elias, the mother talks to me in a soft voice; while she gently touches his forehead and cheeks he sometimes smiles. She adds, "It's a reflex smile." When the father enters with three cups of tea and three pieces of cake, the mother asks him if he wants to take Elias so that she can serve tea. He seems to be happy about the idea, and takes the baby by holding its body in one hand and supporting its head with the other. As he places Elias in his lap, he notices that in this position I would see little of him, and thus turns Elias around so that he is lying on his thighs. Elias opens his eyes once, closes them again, and continues to sleep. Later, he opens his mouth. The father, who has been watching him the entire time, imitates his grimaces and seems to enjoy it all thoroughly. (The father then tells me about the birth in great detail.) … They recount that in the days since his birth they did nothing but watch him daily for many hours. The mother says she is very happy that her husband has taken three weeks off and that they can experience everything together.

Interpretation

The scene quoted shows that body and spirit, psyche and soma, cannot be separated from each other. Elias appears neither psychologically nor physically to have completely accepted the transition from the situation in the womb to the external world. He drinks and sleeps a great deal, and in the first days his eyes are mainly closed, as if he could take in the world only in small portions. The sensations of being held and of being gently stroked envelop him. The parents are building an emotional cocoon around him with their interest, their joy, and their undivided attention. Both are so completely occupied with Elias that it seems that they cannot believe that they really have a healthy, living baby. They adore every part of his body, explore his wrinkles, the shape of his ears, toes, and fingers. In a later observation, the mother strokes Elias's head and forehead while he suckles, examines his chin wrinkles, and thinks that he already has a double chin, no, a triple chin—she is so proud that he has already put on so much weight.

The parents successfully include me as an observer. Although all three are very close to each other, I never feel shut out. I am given tea and cake, the mother offers to let me hold Elias, the father places him so that I can see him clearly. Actually, we three are all observers who marvel at and praise Elias. I received a family photograph as a greeting card, on the back of which were written their three names and "Happy observing".

The realistic description of the stress and pain of birth also can be seen as a good sign. We can understand this as an indication that negative and difficult things are not hidden and pushed aside, but are also to be considered a part of life. Without pain and labour, the transition of the baby from the intrauterine life into the world is not possible, and this is accepted. Her husband and her mother-in-law were important supports for her, and helped her cope with a birth without using painkillers or a local anaesthetic. The birth is seen as a great collective achievement. We assume that a newborn such as Elias has a fine sense for all these positive emotional vibrations and feels soothed by them. We can observe how strongly Elias's facial expression affects the parents by watching the father's reactions, who imitates in an exaggerated manner the wrinkling of the fore-head and the brief opening of his son's eyes: this is an important form of communication with a baby. Through this exaggerated imitation, the baby learns to distinguish between its own imitated expressions of feeling and those of its parents.

By this means a foundation is laid for the infant to see itself as a separate person and, at the same time, a person with whom the mother and father communicate intensively, in order to help it dif-ferentiate feelings and, later, also name them.

Individuation is also stimulated by skin contact. By being stroked, the baby experiences the sensation of the limits of his body through contact with another skin. The contact reminds the baby that it is separate, but not alone.

## Elias, eighteen days old

Elias's mother opens the door with Elias in her arms. Immediately upon greeting me she tells me that Elias has vomited and sprayed milk everywhere. It is the first time that I see how Elias looks at his mother with open eyes. He opens his mouth and groans, and his body contorts painfully. The mother turns him around, presses him firmly against her shoulder, and supports his head with one hand. She says, with a soft, calming voice, "Poor Elias, you feel sick, are you collicy" Elias leans his head against his mother's shoulder, turns his head with a jerky movement, and looks out the window. The mother tells me that he likes to look out the window, that he likes light and sunshine. While she is talking with me, she first turns her-self so that Elias can see better out the window; as he again becomes restless, she walks to and fro with him. Elias looks back and forth between the window and the large patterned Kelim rug hanging on the wall, his mouth is slightly open, and he whimpers continually. Suddenly, he wrinkles his forehead, shuts his eyes, opens his mouth and screams. The mother grabs him with both hands under his arms, raises him high, and peers inquiringly into his face. Involuntarily, she also wrinkles her forehead and closes her eyes in an overdone way, then talks to him. Elias stops screaming and looks at her. She moves him slowly, playfully to and fro, describes what she is doing, and then places him over her shoulder once more. Now she moves more strongly back and forth, a mixture of dancing and skipping. After a few minutes Elias is again restless and starts to cry loudly. With a gentle voice she says to him, "Come on, cry if you will, it's good for your lungs. You will have strong lungs, you upset only me." She seems to want to calm both him and herself, strokes his hair, kisses him on his head and cheeks. Elias reacts to her words and becomes calmer. I am standing behind her and she asks me if Elias is looking at me. I tell her no, he's looking out the window. When he moans again, she asks herself if he could be hungry, but then he would only spit out the milk again. She tries to calm him by persuasion: "What makes you so unhappy? Can you tell me what's wrong? Then I would know what you want. But you can't tell me yet, you're still too small."

She suffers with him, but walks up and down patiently with him. At the same time, she tells me about the previous night. It was a quiet night; he had woken up every hour but hadn't cried. She fed him at 4:30 and 6:00; her husband changed his nappies at 5:30 and 8:00. After that she decided to breast-feed him and helped him to take her nipple in his mouth. Elias made loud noises and closed his eyes while suckling. The mother laughs and says that he made joyful sounds and imitates them. Elias doesn't drink greedily but rather as if he has difficulty in swallowing all the gushing milk. The mother says that there was too much milk, and picks him up so that he can burp.

Interpretation

In this observation Elias is not well. His mother seems to suffer more than he does. She tries to calm him and presses his body close against hers in order to help him cope with the painful colic. Again, the mother's voice, movement, and touch soothe Elias and help him deal with the ache and discomfort. She talks to him as though he can understand her, but at the same time knows that he is still too small to express his needs.

In the chapter on the development of emotions we will go more deeply into the "containment" of primitive feelings, a process taking place on the border between psyche and soma.

## Elias, four months old

The mother opens the door, greets me, and says that they are upstairs "playing". Elias lies naked on a red towel on the parents' bed. As I say "hello" on entering, he turns his head toward me and looks at me. He holds each foot in each hand, draws his right foot up to his mouth and puts a toe in his mouth. As in the previous week when we had all observed his unsuccessful attempt to place his toe in his mouth, all three of us laugh. The father says that Elias has been able to do this for two days now. Elias changes his position, holds one toe with one hand and with the other holds his heel, looks at me and smiles. He continues to play with his body. As he grabs his testicles and penis firmly with his left hand and pulls on them, the father says, "Be careful, don't injure yourself." But Elias continues to pull his penis with enjoyment, and then he again holds his left foot with his hand. Sometimes he is also successful in simultaneously sticking the big toes of both feet in his mouth. The father says that Elias likes to do this, that these are the loveliest times of day … In the middle of playing Elias looks at his father and laughs at him happily, and produces a chuckling "uh" sound. The father laughs back, and then Elias draws up his heels and toes close to his eyes and observes them closely. He starts to urinate, and the father notices it immediately. As no nappies are at hand, he takes Elias's penis and with one finger keeps the urethra closed. Elias stops urinating and continues to play calmly. The father rubs his body clean with a cotton cloth. Then the father plays with him by stretching out Elias's legs; he marvels at how big he already is. The mother, who has been knitting nearby so that his little jacket will be ready before he outgrows it, takes a small romper suit and holds it against Elias's body in order to measure how big he now is. The father says he cannot at all imagine or remember how small Elias had been.

Interpretation

This observation shows Elias's contact with his body, which we see as an indication of his physical and mental development, since his movements are well co-ordinated. Elias begins to examine his body in diverse ways. We see how his feet and hands touch one another and make symbolically clear how things come together—for instance, as he and his mother or he and his father come together. Elias's father responds to every sound from Elias, and it seems as though Elias reacts to this with his entire body. Elias seems to be discovering which parts of his body belong to him. He seems to feel that he is in good hands, so that he can very peacefully and with concentration dedicate himself to carefully exploring his body. He senses his parents' joy over him, and we assume that he has already internalized their happy feelings, which helps him to sense his own body limits and his being separate. He is confident and not anxious, and seems to feel a good, solid skin around himself. We see how strongly the father identifies with Elias: when Elias was wildly pulling his penis, his father told him that he should be careful—an indication of how difficult it is for the father to separate himself from Elias and to let him be independent. He stimulates Elias, plays with him, and shows devoted attachment.

Elias is developing into a cheerful, very agile small child, who crawls about unbelievably quickly and skilfully. It is a great pleasure for Elias to move independently away from his parents, and then to be able to return to them again. Soon, after some training, he will be able to master the extremely steep stairs typical of English houses. I, as an observer, always went closely before or behind him down the stairs, in order to catch him if necessary, at which the mother smiled and reassured me.

The observation of Elias often conveys the picture of a safe world, in which however the breast-feeding remains difficult. In the seminar group, we questioned whether this special admiration of Elias was covering up something; perhaps it was a clue to early, painful experiences of the parents. Somewhat later, Elias's mother told me that she had lost her mother when she was thirteen, and after his birth was especially sad that she would not be able to show Elias to her mother. Elias's healthy development presumably also represents a type of compensation for an unhealed psychological wound (the early loss of the mother).

Let us now turn to another baby, Sushma, whose life began in very difficult circumstances and under unfavourable conditions.

### 2.2.2    Filmed observation of Sushma[7]

Sushma's first years of development in Nepal were the subject of a film by the director Lynn Barnett (2005) during weekly visits. Sushma is the fourth daughter of a desperately poor family; they often did not have enough to eat and lived in a clay hut. The mother, 41, ran away from home at the age of 14 and married her husband when she was 16. She had her first daughter when she was 17, the second two years later, and the third six years afterward. In the advisory centre for planned birth she received a contraceptive injection, but nevertheless became inadvertently pregnant.

---

[7] This is a film, entitled *Monday's Child: A Baby is Born in Nepal* (2005; Artemis Films), from a series of baby observations in different cultures made by director Lynn Barnett. It is an observational video of a Nepalese baby, Sushma, from birth to six months of age. Sushma was born at home, with the support of the mother's midwife, her husband, and her oldest daughter. Although during her pregnancy the mother ate mainly rice and vegetables, because they could not afford milk products, meat, and fish, and she performed hard physical work, Sushma was a strong, lively baby who could drink well from the start, took the nipple by herself, and established eye contact with the mother.

## Sushma, four days old

In the first observation when Sushma is four days old, we see how the mother breast-feeds her with an absent look on her face, seriously, and without saying a word. The moment that Sushma feels and smells the breast, she opens her mouth, turns to the breast, takes the nipple into her mouth, and begins to suck strongly and evenly. She has her eyes closed. As Sushma finds the breast, the mother's eyes stare in front of her absentmindedly; she drifts in her own world and appears unreachable. She grabs her bared breast mechanically and presses on it to make the milk flow more easily. The mother seems lonely and completely alone with the baby. After Sushma has drunk enough, the mother removes her from her breast and slowly, with gentle movements, begins to undress her. In doing so, her face remains serious, she shows no emotion, appearing to regard Sushma rather as an object. She removes the long, colourful cloths that Sushma wears instead of a nappy, and places them on the floor in front of her. She shakes some oil out of a bottle into her palm and begins to oil and massage Sushma's back, belly, chest, and limbs with strong, even, rhythmical movements. One can observe how Sushma relaxes during this process and also how the mother's facial expression becomes more alive.

## Interpretation

Sushma is a baby with a sound constitution, who had a natural birth with no medication. She has a good sucking reflex, drinks regularly, and sleeps well. She was born into a family where there were already three girls, which is why Sushma is rejected by her paternal grandmother:

> Girls represent a great financial burden. There is little room in the small house but also, more importantly, little psychological space in the mother for her baby; she is so preoccupied with her own thoughts and emotions that she has nearly no inner space available for Sushma, to take joy in her, or be able to have contact with her. The extent of the mother's emotional isolation is alarming. Is she depressive? Can she accept the unplanned fourth daughter— in a culture where male children are assigned substantially more prestige and having several daughters is considered a misfortune?

The grandmother's eyes show resentment and blame and leave little chance for hope that Sushma's mother could receive any support from her. Actually, in the six months of observation there was no observable support from the grandmother. When we learn that the mother has become ill in the second week, is running a high fever, and can only take care of the baby in a very limited way, our worries about Sushma increase.

## Sushma, four weeks old

Sushma has put on weight, she looks around her with interest, her arm movements are delicate and energetic, and her fingers move. Next to the mother, who holds Sushma in her arms and only sometimes looks at her, as if by chance, sits her fourteen year-old sister, who radiantly watches Sushma, lovingly follows her movements, and makes friendly comments. The mother places Sushma at her breast. The baby takes the nipple by herself and drinks. With one hand she holds the mother's shawl and moves her hands in the same rhythm as her suckling. The sister is sitting very close to the mother, who appears to enjoy feeling the body of her older daughter, as her friendly glance expresses. When Sushma has finished drinking, the mother holds her on her shoulder, and then passes Sushma to her sister, who has already stretched out her arms toward her. The mother explains how to change the baby's nappy. But first the sister begins to play with Sushma. She moves her face closer to Sushma's face, who looks into her eyes expectantly, and then she touches the baby's hair and forehead with her mouth. Before Sushma's nappy is changed, a black line is painted around her eyes to ward off evil spirits. Sushma seems to be familiar with this procedure already, enduring all this peacefully. While the sister is painting the colour on her eyelid, she speaks emphatically with Sushma explaining why it is so important to receive this protection against the evil eye.

## Interpretation

In this observation we see that Sushma has become a robust, cheerful child and has received a substitute for her depressive mother's lack of attention. The fourteen year-old sister is very devoted to Sushma. Sushma reacts strongly to her older sister, who is almost like a mother:

She seems to enjoy each of Sushma's movements; she laughs a great deal, plays with her extensively, talks to her, and carries her around. With empathy, the mother observes Sushma's cheeriness when her sister is busy with her. She makes no attempt to take Sushma. The ritual of the daily massage seems to ensure a minimal form of physical contact for mother and baby. The massaging also seems to help the mother emerge from her private world. During breast-feeding the mother only stares into space, is barely reachable emotionally, and does not seem to be aware of Sushma at all; physical contact during the massage seems to make it easier for the mother to establish a certain emotional contact to Sushma. In the eighth observation we see that the mother plays fondly with Sushma and Sushma smiles at her.

Sushma aged six months.

Sushma, six months old

A large celebration for the six-month-old baby is being prepared at which the entire family of more than twenty will meet in order to carry out the "social birth", the acceptance into the expanded family, according to Buddhist ritual.

In the film we see the preparation for the festivity, in which the whole house is decorated with colourful exotic flowers and leaves. The ornaments on the walls and doors transform the house into a magnificent dwelling. The mother and Sushma are both wrapped in splendid garments; their hair has been carefully combed and decorated. Both mother and Sushma in her arms seem to enjoy being at the centre of attention. Sushma is very active, and turns her head to look at each new visitor. She grasps towards objects, and smiles at the people who come closer to her. She is handed around from person to person. The mother makes a lively impression and is greeted by the arriving guests with affectionate embraces. Then the established ritual is carried out: Sushma receives a blessed porridge to eat, is anointed with aromatic oils, and is passed around. Blessings are spoken, followed by a delicious meal with many courses. The mother, together with Sushma, whom she again takes in her arms, is treated with respect and reverence. Her face has never shown such happiness; she looks young and very pretty, surrounded by her four children, accepting the guests' attention and good wishes.

## Interpretation

This observation of Sushma shows how important social embedding is. Even under the unfavourable conditions of an initially depressive mother, Sushma can receive and accept other emotional offerings that save her from inwardly "starving" and feeling lost. Even the mother's low spirits seems to be alleviated by Sushma's active, cheery behaviour. In addition, the attentions of the observer and of the cameraman seem to have a stabilizing effect.

## The significance of social support

Severe disruptions of the mother–child relationship arise mostly only if there is a lack of a social network to support the mother or to offer the baby a substitute of emotional warmth and understanding—in addition to a depressive mother who is not emotionally available due to her own massive problems and the baby's fragile disposition in indifferent surroundings. This can be, as in Sushma's case, an older sister, but it can also be a nurse, grandmother, or sympathetic father or grandfather. A physically and psychologically robust baby with a patient temperament, such as Sushma, can benefit from even a small amount of support.

When a depressive mother and her baby (perhaps a very sensitive one) must do without a social network, lasting damage can result. One of my patients describes her mood in the following way: "I don't feel anything then, only emptiness. I get completely exhausted and withdraw into bed the whole day long." If she withdraws into bed, she doesn't have to feel her loneliness and despair, which are concealed behind the emptiness. In order to fill up the emptiness, a "false self" can develop and a person lives a pseudo-life. In "Ego Distortion in Terms of True and False Self" (1965: 144) Winnicott reports of a 50-year-old woman who "all her life long had the feeling that she hadn't even started to exist". At the end of the analysis she had the impression of having arrived "at the beginning of her life". An anorexic patient of mine told me, after a year of analysis: "One waits for life to begin, until one notices that one is already in the midst of it and has wasted many years. I've only felt alive for three months. I am no longer so terribly sad and dispirited. Food means something different now. There is no longer a fight against it—it's just a means to an end." It is very difficult to change this basic pattern of a lack of emotional cathexis of one's own body and a lack of self-esteem. Only "parents who have been emotionally held" can give a baby the necessary emotional security, provided that they themselves have internalized a good, stable, maternal object or that they receive external help from a social support system. Infant–parent therapies produce excellent results in the sensitive first phase. Anderssen-Plaut (1997: 227) describes how, in the therapy of aggressive and jealous Kevin, she succeeded in making the mother aware of her unconscious, destructive fantasies towards her son (connected to the difficult birth); this made it possible for her to gain access to her squandered possibilities of holding her child emotionally.

An important factor for beneficial development is the newborn's temperament. An especially sensitive baby, easily overtaxed by simultaneous stimuli, needs a particularly patient caregiver. It is essential not to overtax the delicate baby, but rather to always offer it only one form of stimulus—either the breast, the voice, or light—to make slow, gentle motions, and to be able to wait until the baby has adjusted to one type of communication. Conversely, a robust baby can take in several stimuli at the same time without problems, or can fade them out with a "protective shield" (against stimuli), as Freud

(1925: 228) called it. Parents of an especially sensitive baby often need the help of a paediatrician, a midwife, or a psychotherapist.

Since we will later go into the emotional development and the development of thought and language, I have limited myself here primarily to the physical dimension of the development of the ego. It is important to understand that the development of the body-ego and the positive or negative cathexis of one's own body is closely connected with the emotional relationship to the important first caregivers.

Different forms of therapy can be offered, even in the case of serious disorders of the body-ego, in order to make contact with the withdrawn child. One observation from a therapy (hippo-therapy) will show how a child with autistic symptoms becomes attentive and even approachable for a moment through their rela-tionship to the therapist and the physical contact to them and to the horse. As the observed child reacted to the observer the mother managed to get him to Horse therapy and he was also observed there. Although Lukas is already older, his autistic disorder and his withdrawal into his private world presumably arose during his first three years of life.

### 2.2.3   Case history of Lukas

In the context of a diploma thesis (Meyer, 2006), a seven-year-old with an autistic disorder, Lukas, was observed regularly for a year. He lives in a foster-child centre and is regularly visited by his separated parents. In the course of the observation, the nurse in charge (and later also the mother) hoped to develop more contact with Lukas. As he started to develop minimal contact with different people, his mother became interested in hippotherapy. Although in Lukas's case we are dealing with an older child, the observation will show how the therapist was successful in establishing emotional contact with him again—a contact that was developed by body experience and which had presumably been disrupted since his first years.

Lukas is the only son in a Persian family that came to Austria ten years ago. The marriage broke up under the burdens both of adapting to a new culture and caring for the difficult, withdrawn boy. Lukas, who had already begun to speak, refused to express himself in words after the emigration. He produces only certain sounds, which can be assigned by his caretakers to certain emotions. Often, he withdraws into his private world. He allows himself to be dressed and guided, passive as a doll.

## Lukas in the eleventh therapy session (excerpt)

Lukas's mother and Lukas, who seems to look through me, enter the hall. I greet both the mother and Lukas who, as before, pays no attention to me.

The therapist takes Lukas—who stands and stares into space—by the hand and says to him that she will now put his helmet on his head. Lukas allows this to be done, and he again reminds me of a doll who is passive and permits everything to be done to it. Subsequently, the therapist explains to him that they would now bridle the horse and have to scrape out its hooves. She needs Lukas's help for this. A leather device, the bridle, is put into his hand. He puts it into his right hand and makes a sweeping motion with his arm. He does this wildly and nearly hits a small kitten which darts past him. I wonder whether he has even noticed it.

Now the therapist takes his hand. She leads Lukas into the stall. Lukas does not especially react. At first, he submits to everything. She shows Lukas how one scrapes hooves clean.

She takes the horse's leg and holds it so that she and Lukas together can clean it. She puts the hoof-scraper into Lukas's hand and he does the work correctly, without hesitation, while she holds the leg. He is praised highly for this. Lukas sometimes accompanies his work with a m-m-m sound … As Lukas appears behind the horse, his facial expression is more lively and his cheeks are ruddy. He doesn't seem uninvolved any longer. The therapist bridles the horse with the leather device which she had given Lukas. She strokes the horse's hide and speaks gently and with quiet words to him. She encourages Lukas to stroke the horse and guides his hand over the horse's hide. Lukas makes the movement rather automatically.

## Interpretation

During discussion of this observation in the seminar group, the observer told of her painful feelings and her disappointment that

Lukas did not seem to recognize her when they met; he seemed to look through her—although in the last two observations he had had made contact with her on his own. This acknowledgement of the observer's feelings is an important resource for better understanding the emotional situation of Lukas's mother. The parents had presumably experienced such painful emotions of disappointment over and over, so that they now no longer had hopes that Lukas would pay attention to them. It is easier to withdraw and "to accept" that the child is different and doesn't establish contact than to hope again and again and be disappointed each time. The "terrible coldness" so often mentioned during the observation is probably not only an allusion to external coldness, but also to the observer's feelings. She seems to identify with Lukas, who lives in a cold, private world. An important positive step is that the mother is becoming open to a possible change in Lukas's behaviour as she brings him to therapy hoping it could help him. Also, the fact that Lukas's mother is in favour of hippotherapy, that she herself brings her son there, and that she remains with him during the session, are evidence of her new quality of taking an interest in her son.

Why are we speaking here so thoroughly about the significance of the observer's feelings when our actual concern is the importance of the skin and the significance of touching as a possible path to psychological contact? This approach should help us understand the emotional sensitivity of Lukas and his parents. Here, transference and countertransference play important roles: with these two terms, we mean the important psychological finding that feelings originating from earlier relationships to the parents are transferred to another person (transference); in this other person, corresponding feelings are then evoked from the unconscious (countertransference). Lukas's unresponsiveness has a different quality than a normal child's temporary inattentiveness; within it are expressed a painful, hopeless seclusion and the baby's failed attempts to make contact, to feel himself held and understood. His first anxieties, which no one contained or understood, lead to a catastrophic anxiety, used as a protective shield to ward off a cruel world and to avoid challenges and obstacles. Observers and caregivers of such children continually experience such shattering disappointments and must ask themselves whether they can cope with the child's pain, hate, and despair.

The therapist, whose greeting Lukas does not react to, takes him by the hand. Only after they have physical contact does she explain to him what is supposed to happen. At first, he is still like a pretty, unresponsive doll who lets everything be done to him—there has not yet been any success in establishing contact, he is emotionally unreachable and very distant. When the therapist gives him the bridle, he uses it as an autistic object, without any meaning, performs stereotypical movements with it, and doesn't notice that he nearly hit a kitten with it.

The therapist again takes Lukas by the hand. He is now so responsive that he is able to use the hoof-scraper correctly to clean the hooves. At this moment there is a minimal emotional contact, which Lukas indicates with a m-m-m sound. His lively facial expression and his ruddy cheeks show that he is emotionally involved. The challenge to stroke the horse is accompanied with the help of the therapist, who takes Lukas's hand and together with him strokes the animal. Lukas seats himself on the horse with the therapist's help.

The therapist walks beside the horse and asks Lukas to slap her hand, which she holds out to him, with one of his. Lukas does so. He is asked to do this several times. The therapist changes sides: first she stands on the horse's left side, then on the right. Lukas follows her instructions and slaps her outstretched hand. In doing so he becomes livelier and makes sounds like eh-h-h-h. The therapist praises Lukas, saying, "Bravo Lukas!" His body is slightly turned to her, but in spite of this he seems stiff.

## Lukas in the eleventh therapy session (continued)

Lukas laughs aloud several times as the therapist brings him and his horse to move more quickly. Lukas is told to hold on firmly. Lukas swings back and forth on the horse's back. His laughter seems sinister and is soon replaced by coughing. The therapist explains to Lukas that they will now do several exercises.

(Towards the end of the session.) The therapist praises Lukas and the horse alternately. She explains to Lukas that he is sitting on a good, well-behaved horse. When the horse comes to rest again, he should stroke it as the therapist is now demonstrating. Somewhat hesitantly, it seems to me, Lukas also performs the movements and strokes the horse's hide.

There follows a round of trotting ... Lukas rides past us at close quarters, and I (the observer, GDW) think that his look has become very inquisitive as his mother begins stroking a young cat nuzzling her ankles. He turns his head completely around towards his mother and watches carefully to see what she is doing. Up to now he has never turned in her direction and shown any interest.

Interpretation

The therapist has shown Lukas, by slapping his hand in hers, that he can do something together with her when he follows her movements attentively. The slapping is also something that they do together, a form of physical contact. Lukas and the horse are both praised; it is clear that together they have achieved something. Lukas can actually perform the therapist's second challenge (to stroke his horse) alone: "hesitantly he strokes the horse's hide". After he has felt what it is like to stroke a horse, and perhaps has had a slight emotional inkling of joy or warmth, he curiously watches his mother stroking a young kitten—an unusual activity—which does not escape the observer's notice. The mother pays no attention because she presumably has experienced Lukas "looking through" her hundreds of times.

In riding, there is a permanent touching of the skin, a sensation of warmth. By caring for the horse, Lukas takes an active role—he who otherwise must be cared for and groomed, dressed and often fed. The exchange of roles is an important experience. In this observation we see how the therapist has succeeded for some moments in advancing into Lukas's private, distant world, and how clearly Lukas shows that the therapist has reached him emotionally.

The skin represents an extensive boundary encompassing the entire body, and is stimulated in many ways from birth on. The interplay between stimulating and being stimulated is shown by birth. The contractions of the uterus cause the child to turn its head to one side, thereby triggering off a series of reflexes which stimulate the uterus. By means of the asymmetrical neck reflex, the so-called "fencer position", the baby turns its head in the opposite direction to the turning of its body, and thus stimulates the mother's final labour contractions—the first co-operative achievement of mother and baby. Touching the delicate "baby skin" of the newborn, the warmth, the snuggling, the relaxed resting at the father's or mother's breast—all these call up strong, loving feelings in the parents and awaken the impulse to want to protect the baby.[8] Through its skin, the baby receives the parents' love and tenderness and their joy over the new living being—voice, eye contact, the parents' smell: all sensory perceptions play a role, and the baby also conveys to the parents an exciting, pleasurable, total body sensation of a special type. However, this only occurs when these adults permit themselves, for at least a few moments, to plunge into their early, primitive feelings, which can be overpowering. Men tend to find this more difficult and to struggle against reviving the passively experienced, unconscious body sensations of the past. Women seem to find identification with the baby's experiences easier, as they can simultaneously feel their active role as givers of birth.

If there are early, fundamental frustrations and a lack of contact—whether because of the baby's disposition and/or unfavourable "environmental conditions" due to the mother's emotional unavailability—psychosomatic or psychological problems can appear. Skin illnesses such as eczema, eating disorders, or self-inflicted injuries in puberty can all be traced back to experiences of deprivation and have strong psychological components. Skin illness is based in problems of setting boundaries between self and object, between child and mother. When pubescent children cut themselves, it is unclear in their fantasy whose skin is being injured, their own or the mother's (cf. Williams, 2003).

Many autistic children cannot stand any body contact and avoid any touching. They seem not to feel their own body and run into objects without reacting. This border area between body (soma) and psyche will be further described in the next chapter on emotional development.

For readers who view psychoanalysis sceptically and consider impulses stemming from the unconscious, repressed conflicts, and inner pictures to be pipe dreams rather than something to be taken seriously, the findings of neurology may be helpful. The psychoanalytic assumptions about the baby come from the psychoanalytic

---

[8] These positive feelings regarding the baby cannot be felt at the beginning by many parents who have not yet disentangled their own ambivalent feelings of fear, uncertainty, and/or wishing to reject the baby. It often takes a certain amount of time to overcome this melancholy and to be capable of having tender feelings.

observation of infants, the reconstruction of play from children's analyses, and dream interpretation and associations from adult analyses.

Neurologists have confirmed these assumptions by measuring the areas of the brain that are responsible for emotions. Measuring and making visible the altered brain areas that react to positive or deficient emotional relationships may have a more convincing effect than reconstructing experience through the analysis of narratives and dreams. The following digression is mainly based on the introduction discussing the interrelationship between love and brain development in *Why Love Matters. How Affection Shapes a Baby's Brain* by Sue Gerhardt (2004), and the writings of Allan Schore (1994, 1997, 2003).

## 2.3    Digression: neurological concepts of the significance of relationships for the development of the brain

Development of a "social brain".

In the late 1970s the function of transfer agents on neurons (neurotransmitters) was discovered. Since then, it has been possible for neurology to localize emotional reactions as neurologically determinable reactions in the brain. Eighty-eight varieties of neurotransmitters have been identified up to now, and more will be discovered in the future. The precise function of the neurotransmitter is only now being investigated. In the brain there are areas whose channels and synapses (connecting points of the transfer agents) have at birth merely a fixed location, to be developed only later. The configuration of the brain in the area of the hippocampus, the tenoral cerebral cortex, the prefrontal cortex (the part of the brain behind the eyes), and the cingular cortex are all immature at birth; the channels are developed only through social experiences. The two hemispheres of the brain are connected by a kind of bridge. Sections of the cerebral cortex, especially from those allocated to the emotional area (hippocampus), constitute links between the reception of sensory perceptions from outside and the association with verbal connections. The prefrontal cortex has a unique task: it connects the sensory perceptions of the cortex with the emotional and survival-oriented subcortex. By investigating patients' damaged cortices it was possible for neurologists to study how a cortex functions. The examination of neurological patients made possible insights into disturbed behaviour patterns and disturbed mental processes. With modern measuring equipment it is possible to relate specific behaviour changes or a condition of mental breakdown to damage in the brain (local brain lesions), an abnormal pattern of electrical activity (measured with an electroencephalograph), or an anomaly in a functional imaging process.[9]

Expressed simply, one can put forward the idea that the part of the brain responsible for the development of emotions is dependent on the number of positive experiences the baby has, as these positive experiences generate biological and chemical reactions which stimulate the connections between neurons, that is, they stimulate an elaborate network in the brain (Gerhardt, 2004). In their research, Davidson and Fox (cited in Gerhardt, 2004: 48) found that in any case a certain amount of unpleasant experiences facilitates the growth of differentiated connections of neuron paths, which, by chemical reaction, leads to "a dose" of the stress hormone cortisol.[10]

Davidson and Fox (cited in Gerhardt, 2004: 31) found that "Babies who see happy behaviour have activated left frontal brains, and babies who witness sad behaviour have activated right frontal brains." Close observation of the baby's physical movements give

---

[9] By "functional imaging process" we mean studies with PET (positron emission tomography) or MRI (magnetic resonance imaging).

[10] Cortisol is the name for hydrocortisone, an adrenal-cortex hormone.

neurologists information about whether the brain is normally developed or whether it has neurological problems. The active movements of arms, legs, and the entire body are never primitive and undifferentiated but rather are adapted to the stage of development and to a given function. From the seventh to eighth week after conception up to two months after birth, the sequence and pattern of movements are unchanged (aside from changes consequent of the force of gravity after birth).

In the first year, the baby's brain more than doubles its weight (Gerhardt, 2004). The enormously increased sugar metabolism (glucose metabolism) of the first two years of life is brought about by the baby's biochemical responses to its mother, facilitating the expression of a genetic disposition. Schore (2003: 45) speaks of the development of a "social brain" and talks about the biological reactions which accompany feelings. This involves the experience of social connections, which are implanted in our body and brain in early childhood. Dough Watt (2001: 18) has referred to these early experiences as "unrememberable and unforgettable". That is, these early experiences are built into our organism and influence our expectations and behaviour and our expectations and behaviour are shaped and organized by social contact, and are not forgotten simply because they are built into our organism. They are not unchangeable but, just as with habits, difficult to change.

Babies are like a raw material of the self, says Gerhardt. They are endowed with genetic equipment and unique development possibilities, but they do not follow an automatic programme; they can only develop as an answer to human attention and care. Therefore, Fonagy (2003: 214) calls the brain a "social organ", as the physical functions and emotional behaviour are shaped by social experiences. "For example, the poorly handled baby develops a more reactive stress response and different biochemical patterns from a well-handled baby" (Gerhardt, 2004: 15).

In each small human organism a vibrating, pulsating symphony of different body rhythms and functions takes place, which are co-ordinated via chemical and electrical messages. These systems communicate through their chemical and electrical signals seeking to remain within the limits of a comfortable range of arousal, adapting to constantly changing inner and outer circumstances. If the tension falls below or rises above a certain range of arousal, the system reacts in order to recover the normal state. However, this norm can be established only after birth and through a social process which adapts to the caregiver. Babies of depressive mothers adjust to low stimulation and become accustomed to a lack of positive feelings. Babies of overactive mothers may remain over-aroused and expect feelings to be expressed explosively. Well cared-for babies come to expect a world which is responsive to their feelings and which helps them to bring intense emotional states back to a comfortable level. Through this they are helped to reduce high states of arousal and learn, little by little, to do it for themselves.

"There are certain biochemical systems which can be set in an unhelpful way if early experience is problematic: both the [biochemical GDW] stress response, as well as other neuropeptides of the emotional system can be adversely affected. Even the growth of the brain itself, which is growing at its most rapid rate in the first year and a half, may not progress adequately if the baby does not have the right conditions to develop" (Gerhardt, 2004: 19). Raw, primitive emotions start at a very basic level: the baby experiences satisfaction and need, comfort or discomfort, but with few nuances and little differentiation, as it does not yet have the mental capacity for processing complicated information. In order to do this, it needs the help of an adult to help reduce its discomfort and distress. With these frequently repeated experiences, patterns of behaviour with the caregiver begin to emerge; the baby gradually absorbs them as images, begins to be able to recognize them, and comes to expect these images, connected as they are with comfort or distress. Examples are the soothing image of the smiling mother who comes to the baby if it cries in its cot, and the image of a hostile face that frightens it. Early images are connected with the desire to draw people closer or to push them away. Physiologically, the baby is in a basic sense connected to the mother (or another caregiver). "It depends on her milk to feed it, to regulate its heartbeat and blood pressure, and to protect its immune system. Its muscular activity is regulated by her touch, as is its growth hormone level. Her body keeps it warm, and she disperses its stress hormone for it by her touch and her feeding" (Gerhardt, 2004: 22). If this cycle is disrupted, there is a change in the natural, normal rhythm. In general, physiological arousal due to some emotional state leads to action of some kind, and once the feeling has been expressed, the organism will return to a resting state. This is the normal cycle of the sympathetic and parasympathetic nervous systems. But the human organism has many other systems that are consistently active: blood pressure, sleep, breathing, and digestion, all of which influence each other and send emotional signals to each other and to the brain (Wiener, 1989). For instance, when small children are very excited, they bounce around on tiptoe like rubber balls, thereby expressing their excitement and releasing their tension. The baby needs the help of a sympathetic adult who mirrors its feelings in a non-verbal form. With facial expressions, tone of voice, touch, and movement, the adult reacts to the baby's emotional expression; the adult, for example, may comfort it if it cries, cradling the baby and smiling at it. An adult can also stimulate its baby when it is in low spirits. Through this, the baby learns to notice its own feelings and to react to other people—something which will be described at length in the next chapter.

If parents are not able to attend to the baby in this way, because they are engrossed in their own problems and therefore cannot notice or regulate their own emotions, this has an influence on the baby. It is especially difficult for many adults to deal with their own more negative feelings such as anger or hostility, and it is especially difficult for them to bear and accept these emotions in their baby. They might feel distressed and may urgently want to reject such feelings, shouting at their baby with such phrases as "Shut up!", "Don't try that with me!", "You make me sick!, or "I can't stand that screaming any more!" Such children cannot then accept such feelings as being a part of themselves. They learn to hold back their feelings—either to deny that they exist, or to avoid expressing them. The parents' varying, permanently dysfunctional reactions can lead to somatic reactions. The normal cycle consists of showing strong feelings through physical action and afterwards returning back to a more peaceful state. However, if the excitement never returns to this state, the cycle is broken, and this can lead to organic disorders such as muscle cramps, shallow breathing, problems of the immune system, and hormonal disorders. The basic result is inner turbulence instead of the experiencing of clear emotions.

Cells and organs regulate themselves and each other. Emotional patterns are acquired in the first year of life. The caregiver's behaviour regarding the baby's feelings is crucial. If feelings (especially negative ones) are experienced as dangerous, they can only be managed through exerting pressure and anxiety. If behaviour always has to please someone, social relationships become only a means to this end. But if feelings are understood as valuable indicators to help recognize the state of one's own organism and that of another person, a different pattern of behaviour arises, in which the other person's feelings count, and the child is motivated to respond to them (Gerhardt, 2004: 30). Trusting and responding to their feelings enables the young child to learn to wait and to reflect, instead of reacting impulsively.

The capacity to empathize is especially connected to the brain's right lobe, which can take in an entire picture—through visual impressions, a spatial sense, and emotional response which convey a general mood. According to Allan Schore, the orbitofrontal cortex controls the entire right brain, which is dominant during the first year (Schore, 2003). The cortex is also larger in the right lobe. Rolls (1999) thinks that our emotional vocabulary and our capacity to identify feelings are processed there, including some of our aesthetic experiences, but also the taste of food, the pleasure of touch, and the recognition of beauty.

Deprivation causes an inadequate development of the right brain. Without sufficient personal attention to a baby, the orbitofrontal cortex will not develop well. Orphans in Romania who had been left for days on end alone in their cots, without regular human care or attention, "had practically a black hole where their orbitofrontal cortex should have been" (Chugani et al., 2001: 1291). In the same way, the cerebral examination of a young girl—she had been locked away without any human emotional contact in a dark room for years by her parents—showed an underdeveloped area in the right lobe.

Up to the development of the "verbal self" (Stern, 1985: 162ff) the right half of the orbitofrontal cortex is dominant, but afterwards the left half becomes dominant. The right lobe can intuitively grasp several modalities simultaneously as a unified picture, while the left brain specializes in sequential and verbal processing—one message at a time (Gerhardt, 2004: 50).

There is a massive number of synaptic connections developing in the prefrontal cortex especially between the sixth and twelfth months, precisely during the time when the emotional relationship to the parents reaches a new intensity due to the baby's differentiated behaviour (Gerhardt, 2004: 43). This growth surge of the prefrontal cortex is reached at an early age when the novelty of being able to walk and the accompanying expansion of independence creates feelings of joy and pride in the child and parents. Here, we can only refer to the intensive discussion and criticism of neurobiology (Damasio, 1995, 2004; Gabbard, 1994; Heintel and Broer, 2005).

*CHAPTER THREE*

# Emotional development
# in the first years

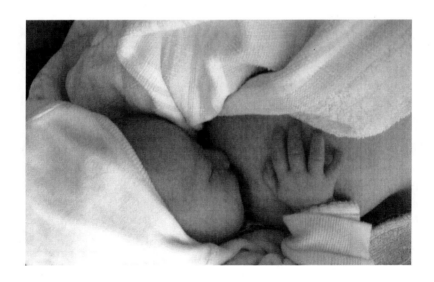

## 3.1    Prehistory of emotional development

All the factors that have an influence on the emotional development of the child I refer to as "prehistory"—even those occurring before birth: they originate in the time before birth, but have consequences later.

The parents' relationship to their baby starts long before the child's birth, as early as the questions of whether or not they want to have a child. In the play of girls and boys aged one-and-a-half years, we can already see how they caress a doll or a cuddly toy and perhaps immediately thereafter toss it away—an indication of ambivalent maternal or paternal images. In addition to the question of whether a child was desired or not, the circumstances of conception play a large role. Was procreation an expression of a loving relationship, where the parents both want to bestow permanence on their love through a creative act? Is the child conceived in order to deliver a successor to a business to the grandparents or to continue a dynasty? Was the child the product of a brutal rape, and used as a weapon against other ethnic groups, as was done systematically and cynically in the Yugoslavian war? Has the child been conceived accidentally from a short romance, without any stable emotional basis of the couple? Is the new baby intended as a substitute for the loss or death of a sibling? Behind the desire for children there are always many, often contradictory, motives, since all men and women also have conscious and unconscious anxieties about this new parental responsibility.

What are the optimal starting conditions for a child? First, it is a deeply caring relationship between the parents and a desire in them both to have a child together. A further important factor is a mature personality of both the man and the woman, based on a successful emotional separation from their own parents, enabling them to recognize reality, above all the reality of the difference between the parents' sexual love for each other and the non-sexual love for a child. A secure social and economic environment is advantageous, as this gives the parents room for a psychological and physical preparation for the new living entity. It is also desirable that there are no losses, crises, or problems to be dealt with during the pregnancy. A peaceful pregnancy and a natural birth with support from the partner, grandparents, and friends are highly supportive.

On the other hand, in early development disorders, or in families undergoing parent–infant therapy, we find that these considerations are overcast with negative signs. Single pregnant women lack the support of the child's father, and shattered marriages make it more difficult for both parents to take joy in the new baby. Unplanned children or children conceived against the woman's (or man's) will can be convinced for a lifetime that they are undesired and a burden, that they have destroyed their mother's life or their parents' marriage. Fortunately, the human psyche is so flexible and multi-faceted that an unplanned child can then become the special favourite of one or both parents. Traumatic events during the pregnancy have a burdensome effect. A shock or a severe upset can even hamper the baby's physical development or make such demands on the mother that she has hardly enough inner room to prepare herself for the new baby. During pregnancy, unconscious and unresolved conflicts with the mother's own parents become actualized, in fact not only present conflicts but those from earlier stages of life as well. If it is not possible for the parents-to-be to work through these problems from their inner world in mutual talks or with therapeutic help, they can be projected onto the baby. Selma Fraiberg (1980: 164) has coined the phrase "ghosts in the nursery" for the unconscious projection of the parents' unresolved conflicts with their own parents onto the baby. Financial worries, uncertainty about the future, or physical stress due to flight or forced displacement can also be burdens, although there are numerous examples of healthy babies being born in incredibly difficult situations if the mother has inner room for the new baby. Psychological and physical difficulties during the pregnancy and a difficult birth can severely encumber the building of a relationship between mother and baby. The death of one of the grandparents, or previous abortions, stillbirths, and miscarriages— particularly if they have been repressed and have not been sufficiently mourned—can constitute a burden on the new baby.

Does this comparison of positive and negative conditions during the pregnancy mean that mothers can develop a positive and sufficient emotional relationship with their baby only under favourable conditions? Psychoanalysis has convincingly shown that the development of a loving relationship between parents and child does not depend primarily upon the external life situation, but far more upon how the parents deal with difficult conditions—that is, whether they have positive, stable objects in their inner worlds from which they can gain strength, whether to mourn a loss or master a crisis, to maintain optimism or maintain hope for themselves and the new baby. Then, even in the most difficult situations such as flight, imprisonment, or poverty, a pregnancy or a healthy baby can convey to its parents the feeling of having done something good by bestowing life on a child, living on in the child and therefore acquiring "a share in immortality" (Freud). In one's own personal history, the fact of having had children and having helped them to become capable of working and loving represents an important and meaningful element in life.

In therapeutic work with parents and infants following the Tavistock model, the "Under Five Counselling Service" (Daws, 1993; Diem-Wille, 1999; Pozzi, 2003), the parents are asked after preliminary discussions what brought them here: How did the baby come to be? Usually the parents start to tell of their desire for a baby, or the conditions under which it was conceived. In Esther Bick's (1964) model of infant observation, most parents also tell the observer how they decided to have a baby. Here are examples from a parent–infant therapy and an Infant Observation.

### 3.1.1    Case study: parent–infant therapy

Mrs K, who had heard my lecture on Infant Observation at a symposium, called me the week thereafter to arrange an appointment for therapy. She suffered from "postpartum depression", she added, as though she were an expert. Her daughter Karin was six weeks old.

In the first therapy session the mother told her story in a very matter-of-fact tone. She had developed a growing inflammation of her kidney pelvis (pyelonephritis) in the thirtieth week of pregnancy and had had to take antibiotics. In the thirty-eighth week, since the ultrasound had showed that the baby was lying crosswise, it was decided to do a Caesarean. She received an epidural, and the father was present at the birth, which proceeded without any complications. In the recovery room Mrs K could hardly see the baby, as the entire family was gathered around her bed and she couldn't assert herself against such a group monopoly. In a monotonous voice, she talked about her breastfeeding problem. Because of the Caesarian and the feeding problem, she had the feeling that she had failed. She couldn't be happy about the baby and sat in her room doing nothing for hours on end, although her husband was very supportive and was delighted in Karin.

Mrs K gave me the impression of near-collapse under a huge burden, but she herself did not dare to recognize this. She was quite capable, she said, of running the household and taking care of the baby, but she felt bleak, as though she were dead. She had very much liked the vivid descriptions of examples from the Infant Observation at the symposium.

In response to my questions about her childhood, her narrative livened as she showed sadness and was able to talk about severe deprivations. When she was four weeks old her mother had left her behind with her grandmother and had relocated with her father to Switzerland in order to work. Her parents came for her when she was seven. Her first pregnancy ended with a miscarriage of the female baby, and afterwards she was unemployed and depressive. When she learned that her mother had lymphoma, she took over her care. Only three months later she noticed that she was pregnant again. A few months after this her beloved grandmother died at the age of 95. She had the impression that no one wanted to know how she was doing. She had tried to manage everything by herself and was now at her wits' end. In the following sessions she was able to talk about her troubled history, to permit herself to mourn, and to accept support.

Mrs K was no longer satisfied to care for her baby merely mechanically, as she had done before the therapy; she now sensed how Karin made contact with her and saw the joy that she displayed when her mother reacted to her. Little by little, she could not only see what significance she had for Karin, but also be delighted in the baby and discover loving feelings in herself.

We see how the pregnancy with Karin was triply encumbered: by the death of her older sister, by her grandmother's illness, and by her great-grandmother's death. Only after Karin's birth did Mrs K really become conscious of her mother's abandoning her when she was four weeks old. She entered therapy in order not to burden Karin with her depressions. When analysing adults we can see what a disastrous influence a physically present, dutifully caring mother has when she is nevertheless emotionally unavailable.

In his article "The Dead Mother", Green (1993) pointed out the effects on a baby's development when its mother sinks into a death-like depression and is no longer emotionally accessible. This results in feelings of insecurity, of pseudo-aliveness, without the satisfaction of a reciprocal, loving happiness. Such a mother has emotional problems and urgently needs psychotherapeutic help.

### 3.1.2    Case study: first interview with the parents in an Infant Observation

I visited Elias's parents (the baby introduced in Chapter Two). I quote from my notes of my first meeting the parents:

> The mother opens the door and lets me in. The mother is a rather small, delicate young woman who works as a teacher. She and her husband live in a small house with a garden in a middle-class district of London. The father greets me and asks me if I would like to have tea with them, which I gladly accept.
>
> As the father returns from the kitchen with the tea, the mother asks me about the procedure in "Infant Observation", and the father writes down my address and telephone number ... Both tell me about their situation without interrupting one another. They say that both of them have always wanted children, and after deciding to have one the mother soon became pregnant. They planned to go together to the hospital for the birth, but to remain there for only a few hours. Afterwards, a midwife would visit them at home daily to care for the mother and baby. The father asks me if this system also exists in Austria. When I answer in the negative, he explains it to me in great detail ... The mother planned to remain at home for a year; the father would be able to stay at home for three weeks after the birth.

There follows a detailed description of their situation. The mother also describes her nightmares of someone taking the child away from her and her being made to go back to work again. They had already chosen a name (Hanna) for a girl, but had not yet agreed on one should it be a boy. The father gave me a tour of the entire house in order to also show me where the toilet was. This welcoming of the observer and the family's descriptions of themselves and their plans gives the impression that this is a case of a desired child and a desired observation.

However, it is important to be aware that no family exists without external or internal problems.

Only much later during the observation does Elias's mother recount that she lost her mother when she was thirteen and that she never could establish a good relationship with her stepmother, who had been her deceased mother's best friend. Her mother-in-law, a warm-hearted woman, tried to substitute for her lost mother, and even the observer was treated like a grandmother. The helpful social network helped Elias's parents to cope with the painful loss and mourning for the absent grandmother. At the end of the observation the mother related that she had already been pregnant once before Elias, but very early on had decided against a baby because she and her husband had wanted to finish their professional training. With Elias's birth, the mourning and guilt over this first lost baby again became painfully conscious. The nightmare of an abducted baby, which the mother had already described in a preliminary talk, often constitutes a visual representation of an insufficiently mourned terminated pregnancy. Only when Elias developed well, and the mother was free from fear that he would die, could the parents talk to each other about their unborn child and mourn it.

## 3.1.3   Therapeutic help before and during pregnancy

Psychological and emotional problems can manifest themselves somatically, by hindering the fertilization of the egg cell by the sperm cell, or when the pregnancy is not carried to full term. If a thorough investigation of the somatic aspects of infertile couples does not indicate any physical problems, therapeutic assistance is recommended. Deeply repressed, burdensome conflicts with her own mother, or hate and guilt feelings due to fantasized attacks in infancy, are often so powerful in a prospective mother's body that "something" in the woman does not permit her to become pregnant—in spite of a perceived, intensive desire for children. A deep unconscious conviction of carrying so much evil within oneself that no healthy baby could originate in one's own body can also lead to infertility. From her therapeutic experience with barren women, Pines (1993: 136) writes that "most had a difficult, conflicted, and frustrating relationship with their own mothers". They are narcissistically wounded and feel just as unsatisfied by their partners as they had felt in their relationship with their mothers. Therapy can help work through these painful, repressed conflicts and often then make conception possible. In the book *Unerfüllter Kinderwunsch* (*Unfulfilled Desire for Children*), Fiegl (2004) addresses the interplay between body and mind and also describes the couple's emotional situation in treating this problem.

Even when a physically healthy mother is already pregnant, unresolved conflicts can complicate the birth or prevent her carrying to full term. Unconscious, unresolved conflicts in the woman can give her the conviction that having the baby is impossible. External problems will then appear larger than life, and anxiety about the baby and its impact on her life will seem overwhelming. In fortunate cases the pregnant woman is able to find therapeutic help towards deciding on a course of action. The experience of being listened to by a therapist who helps her re-experience repressed conflicts and work through them can help diminish emotional obstacles. Below is an example.

### Case study: crisis intervention at the beginning of pregnancy

Mrs S, a thirty-five year-old medical doctor, asks me (as an analyst) to provide "crisis intervention", as she calls it—that is, on a planned termination of pregnancy. She has already received advice from three therapists, but a friend suggested that she also speak with me. Actually, her decision not to have the baby is firm, she says, but she requests two consultations with me.

In the first session she speaks of her strong desire for children, but says that in the past two years her partner has postponed pregnancy for financial reasons. Her parents had a difficult relationship and she, as the only child, was conceived in order to help maintain the relationship. Her father died when she was thirteen, whereupon her mother began to drink and Mrs S had to take care of her. I reply that it was nevertheless her expected baby which had brought her to therapy, and refer to her long-standing wish to have therapy. She is deeply moved that she and not her pregnancy is the focus of my attention. We arrange four sessions in the next two weeks, all still before the deadline for a possible abortion.

In the second session the next day, she begins with the remark that it did her good that I had spoken about her "baby" and not about her pregnancy, as the three other therapists had done. After the session she had become much calmer. For the first time she was happy about expecting a baby; today she had had the first ultrasonic examination, which made the baby real in her mind. Everything looks positive: her boyfriend wants to live with her and the baby and her mother has offered to help her by giving up smoking (she smokes 100 cigarettes daily). She can accept my interpretation that the mother's offer is difficult for her to accept, since her mother is ready to give up something for the new baby that she had never given up for her. Afterward it occurs to her how powerful she feels knowing that she could withhold the longed-for grandchild from her mother.

In the next three sessions the focus is on her question of whether she wants to undergo analysis, fulfilling a long-cherished wish. She talks of her conviction that her problem would be too much for me. It is obvious that she is trying to push me into a hopeless situation— if I say something positive about her wish to have analysis she will either feel trapped or rejected by me. The weekend between the second and third sessions brings back her feelings of abandonment. Almost with relish she tells me how—after a hopeful weekend as a family, buying cuddly toys for the baby, talking about it a great deal and how life would be as a threesome—she had decided against the baby. Both themes—undergoing therapy and the decision of having the baby or not—are closely interwoven. In the interpretation I address her ambivalence concerning therapy. Mrs S is very shy about asking me whether I would accept her as a patient as she is so difficult and completely unreliable. She arrives punctually for the fourth session, pays the fee, and tells me radiantly that she has decided for therapy and to have the baby. The ultrasonic picture shows her foetus, which looks like a fish with wings, it's so alive; she now knows that she really wants to have the baby.

In the same session, as we are arranging the planned, regular sessions for the beginning of May, her ambivalence becomes evident: she wants to go away for one week in May and two weeks in June. She is simultaneously happy that I have time for her and resentfully convinced that I want to get rid of her. Her reactions are nearly panic-stricken: therapy has become a compulsion, she feels herself restricted. The baby is no longer a problem; now therapy fills her with horror. The sessions after the three-week break are marked by excessive acting out; she cancels sessions and again considers completely stopping the therapy. Unconsciously, she wants to find out whether I will keep her on despite her rebellious behaviour or whether I will confirm her conviction that she is unbearable to everyone. Behind her feeling of being locked in during analysis lies her belief that I would not let her have the baby, that I would harm both her and her baby. Instead of an analysis we agree on psychotherapy (two sessions per week). After my agreeing to a reduction of sessions she feels abandoned. In the transference, her rage manifests itself against the analyst/"mother", who never had enough time for her, who did not permit her the new happiness with partner and baby. When she was a child, her mother stuffed her mouth with food instead of listening to her. She thinks her mother was self-absorbed and responsible for giving birth to her four weeks too early because she wedged herself into a sports car, thereby inducing labour. She was frightened by violent death fantasies; her cat had died unexpectedly and she reacted in panic.

She expressed how urgently she needed a third session, but at the same time resisted it vehemently because she was anxious that I could see how greedy she was. She remarked how she made her friend tease her and how she secretly enjoyed her own suffering. All of her problems and ambivalences were no longer projected onto the baby but were acted out in her relationship with the analyst and her wish and anxiety of closeness were acted out via the frequency of her sessions.

She had attempted to master her great fear before giving birth—of being injured or mutilated by the baby's exiting her body—by deciding on a Caesarean. The planned operation represented a dual protection because she thought that her body was capable of killing the baby, and at the same time was afraid that the baby could kill her. On the day of the planned Caesarean her labour pains began; the healthy baby came into the world by natural birth. Working through her equation of separation with death in therapy seemed to make relaxation and a spontaneous birth possible. In therapy I focused on interpreting the transference of her fears, hopes, and conflicts.

This example makes clear how unconscious, unresolved conflicts with one's own mother reappear during pregnancy. As long as Mrs S unconsciously used the baby as a pawn in her battle with her mother and was afraid of her mother's fantasized jealousy and hate, she could not decide to carry the pregnancy to full term.

New experiences are possible when these conflicts are discussed and worked through.

Both of these examples show how therapeutic help is possible with extremely burdensome external situations and internal ambivalences. One can say that all couples who become parents have to overcome smaller or larger problems, all of which can be reflected on and rendered fruitful in open discussions between them.

## 3.2   The first three months as an encounter with archaic fears and loving security (paranoid-schizoid position)

Dealing with joy and sadness.

When we talk of the development from the "archaic" to the mature forms of feeling (in Section 3.3), we do not mean two stages of development but rather two modes of experiencing which remain operative for a lifetime. By mode of experience, we mean the way that impulses, fantasies, and anxieties (as well as defences against them) are related to each other and determine particular ways of relating to people, to the external world, and the self. Melanie Klein coined the easily misunderstood phrase "paranoid-schizoid position" (Klein, 1946) for the archaic form and "depressive position" (Klein, 1935) for the mature form of experiencing. These are misunderstood insofar as they originate in pathology but are also used (here as well) for normal development. During the first three months of life this archaic form of experiencing and feeling is present in all human beings, and little by little develops into a more mature form.

How can we conceive of people who choose exclusively an archaic "paranoid-schizoid" position or a mature "depressive" position to relate to the external world and to other people? In simplified form, one could differentiate between two character types (Joseph 2005:39): one type is touchy, easily hurt, experiences the world as threatening, is distrustful, and always on guard against injustices; this person tends to complain about others, predominantly sees the negative aspects of life, and expects things to go wrong. They cannot bear criticism, can hardly accept their own faults or culpability, looks for the guilty party around them, and is inordinately self-preoccupied and self-centered. They fluctuate between feelings of grandeur and phases of self-doubt and perceived inferiority, and they attempt to control other people by various means. Such anxieties are often manifested in relationships, which are often fraught with disappointment and frustration and are seldom satisfying.

The other character type seems more in touch with his or her feelings—their anger or misery, their pleasure and sorrow. These individuals can take some criticism and blame, can evaluate their own actions critically, are capable of concern for other people, and of putting things right that have gone astray. They are more aware of their own motives and impulses and can make more reasonable judgements about others and the external world. An optimistic basic outlook leads to cordial resonance with other people; life is experienced as satisfying and meaningful.

Each of us has aspects of both these types in us; some people tend more towards one type or the other. At times of extraordinary stress and in crises, we tend to return to the paranoid-schizoid position. In her paper "Notes on Some Schizoid Mechanisms", Melanie Klein (1946) describes her hypothesis relating to very early stages of emotional development from the paranoid-schizoid to the depressive position.

At birth, the baby is born into an unknown world, fundamentally different from the familiar life in the uterus: there, it was never hungry but was nourished by the mother; it could move flexibly in warm amniotic fluid; it heard the mother's heartbeat and voice simultaneously; and followed her movements in its own gentle rhythm. Now it is born and is confronted by powerful needs such as hunger, inchoate impulses, anxieties, and the life and death instincts. In contrast to Freud (1914), Klein (1946: 4) assumed that from birth on the infant was equipped with a rudimentary core ego, a primitive ego which makes possible its emotional contact to another person—an "object", in psychoanalytic terminology. How the baby deals with external reality and its inner world of emotions and anxieties will be shaped by its character and its temperament. From the start, each baby brings into the world a special temperament, a disposition towards impatience or patience, robustness or sensitivity, greater or lesser levels of hostility or envy. This temperament either helps or hinders the parents in getting to know their baby and dealing with it.

The baby's raw feelings and primitive emotional condition during its first three months make impossible its establishing a relationship to a whole person, such as to a mother or father. We assume that it first makes contact only with partial aspects of the person—for example the mother's voice, her smell, her breast, her skin—what Melanie Klein (1935: 262) calls "part objects". We also assume that the infant colours its perception of aspects of the mother by its own moods and fantasies. A baby with colic will at first react with resistance if the mother picks it up; it will scream and recoil, because it momentarily experiences the world and also the mother's arm as hostile and persecutory. Even if the mother regards the baby lovingly and wishes to feed it, the baby will perceive the bottle or breast as an annoyance, will scream fretfully and turn away frustrated and angry. In other words: the baby's anger will be projected onto the bottle or breast and it will turn away from these dangerous and threatening part objects. An important "bad" aspect of the mother is her absence, when she is not available for the baby. There is no negation in the unconscious, thus also no non-presence; the absent object will be experienced as something bad and threatening because it does not satisfy the child's needs at the moment and cannot protect it from dangers. Only the mother's calming words can diminish this stress and make the baby receptive to perceiving the mother's skin contact as positive and accepting the offered bottle or breast. However, the opposite can also be observed: if the infant is in a happy contented mood at feeding time, it will accept the milk and the mother's love as good, discovering goodness in its ideal experience of the mother's breast, voice, and skin. The baby can take up this good, idealized experience in its inner world and thus form the "imago" of a positive inner object that helps it build up a self-confident and warmhearted ego. We call this psychological mechanism "splitting": experiencing the mother's part aspect at first as "only good", as an ideal provider of security, or as "only bad", as persecuting and dangerous. Only later is it possible to understand both these aspects of the mother as belonging to one and the same person.

Other psychological mechanisms, namely "projective identification" and "hallucinatory wish-fulfilment", conceived to explain the function of the ego on a primitive level, will be illustrated by means of a scene where we see how the baby deals with its inner chaos and the external world: the infant is hungry and it cries but no one comes. We assume that the baby cannot yet distinguish between the internal and external, between the feeling of hunger coming from within and a pain inflicted from outside. It registers this pain and expresses it by crying. By chance, it finds its thumb, sticks it in its mouth, and sucks on it. It will eagerly suck its thumb, no longer aware of its hunger, and become quiet for a time, until the hunger breaks through. To explain the inner process in this situation Freud (1905: 179) coined the phrase "hallucinatory wish-fulfilment": when the baby is sucking its thumb, the object it has in its mouth—its thumb—is completely good and satisfying. It no longer feels its hunger, now diverted since the baby has its thumb (or nipple of its bottle) in its mouth; but the hunger is not really gone, it is split off and can for the moment be denied. We assume that at this moment the infant itself is similarly split in its fantasy. A part of its self is a totally contented self and the other part, its hungry, angry self has disappeared—the baby is no longer aware of it. This psychological mechanism works magically and provides the baby with a sense of omnipotence. For a moment, its desire for a satisfactory wish-fulfilment has been realized, it has itself created a moment of consolation, and it has been saved from anxiety and discomfort. This explanation may seem simplistic, but it provides a basis for understanding the elementary psychological processes of splitting. If the mother then offers the breast or the bottle, this will be felt by the baby to be good, ideal, providing love and security. One can see the value of these primitive splitting mechanisms for the personality; however, if such profound mechanisms persist unchanged into later life, they then must be seen as serious disturbances of a neurotic or psychotic type (cf. Joseph, 2005: 40).

In the first months of life the infant has to find its bearings in the unfamiliar real world and also in the inner world of its powerful impulses, accompanied by unavoidable frustrations. To defend itself against this pain and anxiety, it projects painful and confusing parts of the self into an object—we call this defence a primitive form of splitting. If these projections are not contained by an object, then the pressure can be so threatening that the baby feels itself disintegrating, like "an astronaut in space without a spacesuit" as Esther Bick (1986: 296) wrote. Melanie Klein called these feelings and anxieties of falling apart and being persecuted by hostile part objects "paranoid-schizoid"; these effective, primitive modes of functioning exist in every human being. The baby is not aware of its impulses and motives, and therefore is not in a position to consider the effect of its behaviour on its parents. Actually, it is not difficult for the parents to witness the moments in which the baby experiences aspects of its parents as ideal and satisfying. These are deeply exhilarating moments when mother and father feel themselves at the centre of the baby's world, feel their power to make the baby happy and satisfied, and sense the baby's expression of safety and joy. Understandably, the other moments are more difficult: when the baby angrily or in panic turns away from the lovingly offered breast or bottle, screaming its head off, or from the father who wants to pick the baby up and comfort it. It takes a mature parental ego to be able to cope with the frustration, disappointment, and anger over this rejection without paying the baby back in the same manner. These are precisely the moments which often cause the parents to scream back at the child or to shake it fiercely in order to make it quiet. The reason parents often give for physical child abuse and killing their babies is that the baby could not be calmed down, that its screaming drove the parents crazy. In these situations, the parents have to not only bear and accept the baby's projected, powerfully primitive anxieties of falling apart, but to overcome their own reawakened primitive anxieties, inner helplessness, and rage. Their mental balance is threatened simultaneously from two sides. The parents feel that they are being treated unfairly when they get up in the night to feed the baby or pacify it and the child simply does not allow them to do so, turning away from them and making them feel that they are experienced as dangerous and hostile, even though they had the best intentions. The existence of positive, stable objects in the parents' inner world, affording them hope and the ability to contain this rejection and calm the baby, is decisive. The baby's first three months are so strenuous for the parents not only because of lack of sleep but also because of their encounter with the baby's primitive anxieties, rage, and fantasies of hostility, and with their own reanimated primitive emotions.

Luckily, what usually predominates in dealing with a baby are the positive experiences, which give the parents confidence in their maternal and paternal qualities—experiences of being in harmony with the baby, understanding it, and of being able to care for it well. To this end, I now describe a sequence from a psychoanalytical Infant Observation of Felix and his parents, which has been video-recorded for research and teaching purposes.

### 3.2.1   Infant observation: Felix, the "Sunday child"

Felix's mother is thirty-six. He is her first son and she was employed up until his birth. She and her husband have been living in their own house in the south of England for two years. One Sunday she had a spontaneous home birth without any complications (Barnett 2005).

### Felix, twelve days old

The father brings Felix into the bathroom to his mother, who greets them both and takes Felix into her arms. After she has undressed him, she places him in the already prepared baby bathtub.

Felix has his eyes closed and his hands are balled into fists. In a high voice he begins to emit whimpering sounds. In the background the father's voice is audible, although it seems to calm the mother more than it does Felix. The mother starts washing Felix's belly with soap, while uttering calming sounds such as, "Oh Felix, oh dear." His crying becomes louder as the mother lifts him out of the water to wash his bottom, and it increases to a loud, miserable screaming, during which Felix screws up his eyes and with his fists rigidly hold his mother's arms away from him. The mother calmly tries to persuade him, says, "Shhh," turns him around and washes his back while holding him securely under her arm. As the mother has now lifted him nearly entirely out of the water, his crying is of penetrating and frantic volume. He turns his head back and forth, stretching it backwards with increasingly louder screams. The mother turns him around again, dips him into the water, and slowly dribbles water over his belly and chest with her right hand, during all of which his crying diminishes. The mother puts her head close to his and talks to him quietly about how comfortable and warm the water is, asking him if he likes it just a bit. Felix has now opened his eyes a little and looks into his mother's eyes while she smilingly continues talking to him. "Well, you see, it's OK. Now I'll show you something," she says, and begins very gently to move his whole body back and forth in the water, which he seems to enjoy. He has both eyes open now, his fists have also opened, and his stiff bearing has been replaced by a relaxed one. The father's voice also sounds friendly and soothing. The mother now turns to the father and joins him in his soothings. During his to-and-fro movements Felix closes his eyes and lets himself drift, as if this were most agreeable. As the mother continues washing him, he again starts to whine but not as loud or desperately as previously. When the bathing is finished, the mother takes Felix out of the water, wraps him in a towel, and places him affectionately over her shoulder.

## Interpretation

In this short observation we can see how Felix needs protection from the outside world, how he presumably is anxious about falling apart without clothing. An infant's constant complaining and increasingly desperate crying can put an unsure and fearful mother under enormous pressure, making her feel that she has done something harmful to her baby. After bathing and swaddling a frantically crying baby many young mothers feel exhausted. Only when Felix and his mother are in harmony, with her face close to his and making eye contact with him, does Felix no longer feel distressed. With the help of his mother's soothing voice he can actually enjoy the slow movements in the water. The importance of the father's role is also clear. His quiet presence, his confidence that the mother can take good care of Felix, and his calming voice, probably also contribute to the mother's showing hardly any signs of stress or nervousness. The father is able to remain in the background and thereby support both mother and baby. We will see this pattern in the further observations of Felix—how one parent can remain in the background when the other is busy with Felix. Both can also tolerate the fact that each of them has his/her own relationship with Felix and is occupied with him in a special way. There seems to be no competition between the parents regarding their care for Felix.

We also see that both parents comprehend Felix's unhappiness and despair, talk with him, and help him to cope with these overwhelming feelings. In the chapter on "Development of Thinking" we will thoroughly explore Bion's (1963: 90) concept of "container and contained", which relates to the parents' mental processes—how they perceive the baby's raw, disjointed impulses, and how they digest these impulses mentally and then give them back to the baby in a modified form.

In the observations (video recordings) of a baby's first weeks, its development process can be followed. In Felix's first weeks, for example, he reacts in a confused and unhappy manner when he loses the nipple, but several days afterwards he still shows surprise on losing the nipple, but calmly looks for it, which we can interpret as showing his confidence that he will find it again. In numerous short sequences Felix experiences how he can cope with the external world—often supported by warm comments from both his parents—how he seems to grasp onto light coming through the window, how he becomes calm by establishing eye contact with his mother, thus having positive experiences that he can internalize.

### 3.2.2   Learning about human communication

Traditional psychology textbooks describe the ability to express the six forms of the primary or universal emotions, namely joy, sadness, fear, anger, surprise, and disgust. In the first hour of life a newborn can already make facial expressions indicating all of these emotions;[1] they are formed by movements of different parts of the face, for example, the eyes, the mouth, the eyebrows, and so forth. Recent research has shown that it takes a long learning process until the child not only evinces these emotions as reflexes, but also understands their meanings. Secondary or social emotions are: embarrassment, jealousy, guilt, pride, and so forth (Damasio, 1999: 67f). Recognizing and

---

[1] We speak of "emotions" when feelings are expressed which can be seen externally. "Feelings" are perceived internally, by only one person.

understanding one's own feelings and those of others constitutes a highly complex task. It means getting to know oneself and others and reacting adequately. Babies are experts in sensing moods and diffuse tensions that adults are often not aware of. They are equipped with fine antennae that perceive changes in facial expression, intonation, and minimal movements as well as the way they are held, and can draw conclusions about an object's emotional state. The first months of life centre on the baby's experiencing whether the caregiver responds to its needs and can mirror its feelings. The baby needs a special form of communication to help it establish a relationship to itself, to the external world, and to other people.

We can speak of the baby as an expert on social relationships, as a researcher whose specialty is human communication. Later, in playing, the child will express its inner sensitivity, its hopes, desires, conflicts, and fears, and at the same time establish contact with external reality. "Playing is an important means of exploring the relationship between internal reality and external reality" says Caper (1999: 85).

In the observation of Elias in Chapter Two concerning the emergence of the body-ego, we saw how the father imitated each of his son's facial expressions in an exaggerated way, which the baby again responded to. This exaggerated mimicry and the particular way of speaking—"baby talk" or "wet-nurse language"—is a special form of communication between adults and babies; it does not have to be learnt, but lives on in us from our own baby time as "experience in feelings", "intuitively" available. This special "choreography", the interaction between baby and caregiver, lasts approximately to the end of the third or fourth month, up until the development of a lasting inner image of a specific person ("object permanence") or the lasting image of one's self ("subject permanence")—expressions coined by Piaget (2001: 34). This special manner of communicating, if it were between adults, would have an exaggerated and comical effect, as if it were a caricature or bad acting; it is however essential as the first, fundamental emotional understanding between the baby and the caregiving adults. Basilides (2006: 15) writes: "I remember very well how my best friend played with her six-month-old baby in the coffee house, and how absurd the constantly varied "hello, little mouse", "hello sweet little mouse" in different tones of voice seemed to me, but the little child laughed heartily."

Empirical infant research has made video-supported analyses of this complex tactile and verbal early communication between mother and baby in order to understand emotional development and the learning of patterns of social interaction (Stern, 1977). Several sequences described here will show the distinctive character of this reciprocal communication, which comprises a set of signals indicating readiness for interaction as well as the maintaining, ending, or avoiding of interaction. We will then comment on these.

The following sequence lasted four minutes and is a "social interaction" where focus is on the bottle-feeding of a three-and-a-half-month-old baby as Stern (1977) describes.

## Mother and baby in harmony

During the first half of the feeding the baby had been sucking away … and occasionally looking at his mother, sometimes for long stretches (10–15 seconds), at other times gazing lazily around the room. Mother had been fairly still. She glanced at her baby periodically, sort of checking, and every now and then looked at him with a good long look (20–30 seconds) but without talking to him or changing the expression of her face. She rarely said anything when she looked at him, but when she looked away towards me (the observer GD-W) she often talked with much facial animation.

Until this point a normal feeding, not a social interaction, was underway. Then a change began. While talking and looking at me, the mother turned her head and gazed at the infant's face. He was gazing at the ceiling, but out of the corner of his eye he saw her head turn towards him and turned to gaze back to her. This had happened before, but now he broke rhythm and stopped sucking. He let go of the nipple and the suction around it broke as he eased into the faintest suggestion of a smile. The mother abruptly stopped talking and, as she watched his face begin to transform, her eyes opened a little wider and her eyebrows rose a bit. His eyes locked onto hers and together they held motionless for an instant. The infant did not return to sucking and his mother held frozen her slight expression of anticipation. This silent and almost motionless instant continued to hang until the mother suddenly shattered it by saying "Hey!" and simultaneously opening her eyes even wider, raising her eyebrows further, and throwing her head up and towards the infant. Almost simultaneously, the baby's eyes widened. His head tilted up and, as his smile broadened, the nipple fell out of his mouth. Now she said: "Well hello! ... heelló ... heeelloóooo!", so that her pitch rose and the "hellos" became longer and more stressed on each successive repetition. With each phrase the baby expressed more pleasure, and his body resonated almost like a balloon being pumped up, filling a little more with each breath. The mother then paused and her face relaxed. They watched each other expectantly for a moment. The shared excitement between them ebbed, but before it faded completely, the baby suddenly took an initiative and intervened to rescue it. His head lurched forward, his hands jerked up, and a full smile blossomed. His mother was jolted into motion. She moved forward, mouth open, eyes alight, and said: "Ooooh, ya wanna play, do ya ... yeah? I didn't know if you were still hungry ... no ... nooooo ... no I didn't." And off they went.

> After some easy exchanges the pace and excitement increased to a higher level at which the interaction assumed a form of a repeating game. The cycles in the game went something like this. The mother moved closer, leaning in frowning, but with a twinkle in her eyes and her mouth pursed in a circle always on the edge of breaking into a smile. She said, "This time I'm gonna get ya," simultaneously poising her hand over the baby's belly, ready to begin a finger-tickle-march up the baby's belly up and into the hilarious recesses of his neck or armpits. As she hovered and spoke, he smiled and squirmed but always stayed in eye contact with her.
>
> (Stern, 1977: 2–4)[17]

## Interpretation

The baby takes the initiative to interrupt the feeding and commences interaction with the mother, inviting her to play with him. We see how closely interwoven the signals are. The mother's prolonged look is perceived by the baby out of the corner of his eye. The baby's interruption of sucking signals to the mother its readiness to play with her. The mother and baby approach each other in tiny increments, each time exactly observing each other's state of readiness and response. Based on an emotional connection through the long, joyful eye contact, the mother begins a new phase when she says "Hey" and signals surprise in an exaggerated way. The baby's reaction is clear. It moves closer to the mother, letting go of the nipple, and smiles broadly at her—the door to play has been opened. The baby is now more interested in playing than in receiving nourishment. The mother greets it cordially, as if after an absence, and the baby reacts with joy. Again, it is the baby who doesn't want to stop playing; only then does the mother put this fact into words, followed by a statement from her own perspective: she didn't know if he was still hungry. This develops into a game. The mother begins a finger-tickle-march up the baby's belly, which he likes a lot. The playing also contains a dramatic escalation—her words are a mixture of threat and increased expectation, which resolves at the goal—in laughter. Between each cycle there is a brief pause, and then a new cycle begins. The timing is essential: each time there is a short phase of recovery, expectation, until the game starts anew.

Mother and baby are "in harmony" (in tune), as Stern (1977: 5) describes this state of being well-attuned to each other: a fine coordination which has the effect of well-prepared choreography. One notices just how fine such coordination is if it is interrupted briefly, or if the mother doesn't sense the baby's mood correctly or not at the correct time. This is seen in a further sequence.

## Mother and baby briefly "out of touch"

After the finger-march had reached the neck and was punctuated with a final tickle, the mother moved back and away rapidly in her chair. Her face opened up and her eyes wandered off as if she were thinking of a new and even more irresistible plan for her next approach. The baby emitted a just audible "aaah" as he watched, captivated, as she let her emotions pass freely across her face, as if it were a transparent screen flashing the changing pictures in her mind.

Finally, she rushed forward again, perhaps a bit earlier and with more acceleration than the times before. His readiness had not fully settled yet, and he was caught for a split second off guard. His face showed more surprise than pleasure. His eyes were wide and his mouth open but not turned up at the corners. He slightly averted his face but still held his end of the mutual gaze. When she moved back at the end of that cycle she saw that it had not missed somehow—not quite backfired, but missed enough. The pleasure had disappeared. She sat back in her chair for several seconds, talking aloud to herself and to him but without doing anything, only evaluating. She then resumed the game. This time, however, she left out the tickle-march part and established a more regular and marked cadence in her actions. She moved in, more evenly, with her eyebrows, eyes, and mouth in dramatic changing display that promised, but with less threat, to do what she said: "I'm gonna get ya." The baby's attention was again riveted to her, and he began to show an easy smile with his mouth partly open, the face tilted up, and the eyes slightly closed.

During the next four cycles of the renewed and slightly varied game, the mother did pretty much the same, except that on each successive cycle she escalated the level of suspense with her face and voice and timing. It was something like: "I'm gonna get ya! ... I'm gonna get ya! ... I'mmmm gooonaa gétcha!"... "I'mmmm gooooonaaa gétcha!!" The baby became progressively more aroused, and the mounting excitement of both of them contained elements of both glee and danger. During the first cycle the baby stayed captivated by his mother's antics. He smiled broadly and never took his eyes off her face. During the second cycle, he averted his face slightly as she approached, but the smile held. At the beginning of the third sortie by the mother, the baby had still not resumed the full face-to-face position and had his head turned slightly away. As she approached, his face turned even further but still kept looking at her. At the same time, his smile flattened. The eyebrows and the corners of his mouth flickered back and forth between a smile and a sober expression. As the excitement mounted he seemed to run that narrow path between explosive glee and fright. As the path got narrower, he finally broke gaze with mother, appearing thereby to recompose himself for a second, to deescalate his own level of excitement. Having done so successfully, he returned his gaze to mother and exploded into a big grin. On that cue she began, with gusto, her fourth and most successful cycle, but this one proved too much for him, and pushed him across to the other side of the narrow path. He broke gaze immediately, turned away, face averted, and frowned. The mother picked it up immediately. She stopped the game dead in its tracks and said softly, "Oh, honey, maybe you're still hungry, huh ... let's try some milk again?" He returned the gaze. His face eased and he took the nipple. The "moment" of social interaction was over. Feeding had resumed. (This whole episode lasted about four minutes.)

(Stern, 1977: 4–5)

## Interpretation

We see how the mother carefully observes the baby's facial expressions and reactions, but also in what a variety of ways the baby shows his pleasure or his sense of being overwhelmed. The tickling was too much and he was able to make the mother understand this. She interrupted the game, reflected, and then slowly built up a level of stimulation her baby could tolerate, with his tolerance expressed in a beaming smile. Stern (1977: 33) designates this "free play" as being among the most crucial influences in the infant's first phase of learning, in order for the baby to participate in human interaction and thereby develop schemas of the human face, voice, and touch. The baby perceives this momentary schema of human behaviour with its expressive variations. The mother and baby take the initiative alternately. If the expected response is missing, the rhythm has to be changed. The brief discordance is essential for understanding and fine-tuning. The mother's reaction creates attitudes of expectation in the baby as to how its coexistence with the caregiver will be structured and modified. Stern (1995: 21) calls these "schemas of Being-with". A reaction by the baby presumes that it perceives the mother's stimuli and can distinguish them from other stimuli.

The mixture of excitement, joy, and threat in the stimulation is especially interesting; verbal communication also constitutes a mixture of joy and fright. When the mother combines her words with a playful devouring of parts of the child's body, there is a quality of possessiveness, of capture, at times of eating and biting, in this. The expression of ambivalent feelings in games has the same effect as it does in children's songs and rhymes, which deal with love and death, safety and wounding; on the one hand this has a cleansing, cathartic effect for mother and baby, on the other it constitutes a special form of excitement and thrill (Diem-Wille, 2003: 192). It should be emphasized that these experiences of emotionally successful contact, including the limits and variations of the game, are also of great importance for establishing maternal/paternal love. The love for a child and trust in one's own abilities to be an adequate father or mother are built up only gradually. Positive experiences also help the parents or caregivers to overcome their own ambivalence concerning the baby and their new tasks as well as the transformation from their earlier lifestyle. The English paediatrician Winnicott (1947: 73f) speaks of a necessary "hate by the mother", always present to some degree, which also makes it possible for her to leave the baby by itself:

> The mother, however, hates her infant from the word go ... The baby is not the one of childhood play ... The baby is not magically produced ... The baby is a danger to her body in pregnancy and at giving birth ... The baby is an interference with her private life, a challenge to preoccupation ... He is ruthless, treats her as scum, an unpaid servant, a slave ... She has to love him, his excretions and all, at any rate at least at the beginning ... After an awful morning with him she goes out, when he smiles at a stranger, who says: "Isn't he sweet?"

At first we are shocked at the idea that not only a pathologic mother hates her baby, but that every mother does. If we then read the examples Winnicott gives, we may be enlightened. Indeed, we have imagined a baby to be rather like a doll one hugs but then can be laid aside. Indeed, the difficulties of pregnancy and the risks of birth have made us more afraid than we could have imagined. Indeed, the baby's constant demands are exhausting. Grown-up children often ask their parents: Was it also so exhausting with us? Young parents often cannot imagine that their own parents accepted the same hardships and sacrifices bringing them up. Are we not often surprised by our generosity and the sacrifice we are capable of as parents, and yet full of resentment about the endless demands of children? Here, two sentences by Winnicott (1947: 73) are of particular relevance:

> A mother has to be able to tolerate hating her baby, without doing anything about it ... The most remarkable thing about

a mother is her ability to be hurt by her baby and to hate so much without letting the child feel this, and her ability to wait for rewards that may or may not come at a later date.

Acknowledging the father's stronger involvement in caring for babies in recent years, I would like to broaden my observations to also include him. Perhaps "to wait for later rewards" is too strong a statement, when each day there is a reward for the parents' efforts in the infant's thriving health or its smile. However, it is helpful to remember that the parents, in their own paranoid-schizoid frame of mind, also experience a similar, strong oscillation between joy, pride, and an increased self-esteem on the one hand, and doubt, resentment, and frustration on the other. The process of the mother's and father's acceptance of the real baby also means saying farewell to the fantasized baby, the mental image that the parents had developed during the pregnancy. Krejci (1999: 29f) describes this connection as follows:

> The human infant enters the world wrapped in his mother's fantasy. Freud calls this her narcissistic cathexis: the child is a part of her. Even before birth the child's life is influenced to a significant degree by his mother's fantasy. Since the actual child is always different from what she had imagined, and since it is indisputably also the father's child, the birth constitutes a realisation and a differentiation, and makes it necessary to relinquish dreams and the former escape from anxiety in order to get to know the baby in reality.

In early interactions with their babies, parents use "baby talk"/"wet-nurse talk", presumably repeating their own early experiences with their parents. This constitutes a way of passing on early experiences from generation to generation. Accordingly, provided that their envy is ameliorated through love and through identification with their own daughter or son, it is an uplifting experience for grandparents to watch how their children have become loving parents themselves. The particular alternation of delight and joy in play, combined with elements of threat and fear (as we have seen in the play sessions described above) embodies a special quality. Dutiful child care can also transpire without this special emotional connection, but this results in the child leading a shallow emotional life. The intensive encounter between caregiver and baby was characterized by Winnicott (1956: 301) as "primary maternal preoccupation". Bion (1962b: 114) talks of "reverie", the mother's dreamy rapture. We assume that the baby sees itself as the agent and catalyst of these reactions from the adults attending to it. The mother–child relationship lays the foundation for that intense feeling of making another person happy through one's own existence and love. As adults, we experience these intense feelings once again when we fall in love. If we have not had such experiences as babies, we will find it more difficult as adults to become involved in a romantic love relationship—this is not impossible, but it will be difficult and accompanied by painful emotions.

*3.3   Integration of the separated part-objects to an object consistency and a subject consistency (depressive position)*

Integration of love and aggression.

We have described a person's mature mode of integrated functioning in the "depressive position" as follows: The other character type seems more in touch with his or her feelings—their anger or misery, their pleasure and sorrow. These individuals can take some criticism and blame, can evaluate their own actions critically, are capable of concern for other people, and of putting things right that have gone astray. They are more aware of their own motives and impulses and can make more reasonable judgements about others and the external world. An optimistic basic outlook leads to cordial resonance with other people; life is experienced as satisfying and meaningful.

This description refers to a mature person who makes reasonable judgements about reality, is more aware of their own impulses, is patient in satisfying their needs, and can be concerned about others, that is, they can delay their egocentric world view in favour of social responsibility.

How can a baby—who fears disintegration, whose mood oscillates between sudden fantasies of omnipotence and feelings of inferiority, and who is trapped in a magical world—become a mature person? How can mature defence mechanisms such as sublimation be developed from archaic anxieties and primitive defences such as splitting and projective identification? How can social responsibility develop and the child become capable of emotions such as empathy, sorrow, regret, longing, joy, security, and love?

The transition from archaic anxieties and primitive defence mechanisms such as splitting and projective identification (paranoid-schizoid position) to a mature integration (depressive position) does not happen abruptly. These two positions overlap and are never completely resolved—they remain two elementary structures of our emotional life. I will try to describe chronologically some assumptions about the baby's inner development.

Instead of structuring its experiences into only good and bad object categories by means of a splitting process, between the fourth and sixth month the baby—due to its gradual physical maturing and its mental abilities—begins to remember its experiences more clearly and to perceive the world more precisely. These new abilities present the infant with a new experience. It perceives the mother as a whole person who looks after it, feeds it lovingly, rocks it in her arms, and sings songs to it. It can keep her image in its memory and introjects this image as an internal positive object. It notices that it wants to cause this person to come to it when it cries, and that she is not always available and therefore seems inimical and persecuting. Because of its stronger ego it is now able to tolerate the fact that the part objects considered good or bad both belong to one person, that is, that the voice, breast, and smell all belong to the same person, who has good and bad aspects. With the successful mastering of its anxieties—partly with the parents' help, partly independently—the baby bit by bit has created order both in its chaotic inner world and in the external world, by turns threatening and benign. Using the defence mechanisms of splitting and projection, the baby succeeded in stabilizing an ideal object which was only good, which it loved and wanted to retain and, on the other hand, an evil object into which it projected its aggressive impulses and by which it felt threatened. The positive experiences become internalized: it has introjected images of its parents in its "inner world" and identified with them, something that helps it to maintain a constant relationship. Under favourable conditions for development, it will keep its ideal object and ego more stable than the negative impulses and objects. This will lessen its anxieties, with less pressure to give in to dangerous impulses. Thus, the power ascribed in fantasy to the negative object lessens, and the ego, owner of the ideal object, grows stronger, gradually becoming able to integrate both the positive and negative parts. During the first month there have already been moments of integration, which now stabilize. Connected with this is the painful recognition that the mother, the baby's most important caregiver, is a person separate from itself.

This decisive moment in a child's development, when the child recognizes a whole object and constructs a relationship to it—a process Melanie Klein (1952: 72) defines as "the development phase"—is clearly recognizable to any observer. The mother and other observers notice that the child unmistakably recognizes its mother, then its father, and other relevant people in their life. The child can acknowledge that its objects and its self are not ideal—they can accept ambivalence in their objects and in him or herself. This process of integration is extremely painful, and can be seen as a kind of farewell to the desire for having an exclusively good world and a good self, and to the desire for controlling its objects and owning them completely. This wish—to be good oneself and to project evil and badness predominantly onto others—accompanies us more or less throughout life and hinders a realistic perception of the self.

Good parenting and good experiences lessen the ambivalent feelings and will bring out hope and confident feelings. A positive orientation manifests itself in cheerfulness and activity, exploring the world based on a trustful relationship with the parents. John Steiner (1993) emphasizes the importance of both parents in helping the child to cope with painful conflicts. In particular, if the child is angry because of a conflict with one parent, the other parent can help to understand and identify their feelings in coping with the grievance.

The various ways that both parents handle their child and its complaints—including rage, envy, and excessive demands—greatly enrich the child, providing it with familiarity with a wide spectrum of methods for dealing with situations. A lack of understanding and empathy in the parents constitutes an unfavourable condition for development:

> Unpleasant disagreeable experiences and a lack of enjoyable ones in the young child, especially lack of happy and close contact with beloved people, increase ambivalence, diminish trust and hope and confirm anxieties about annihilations and external persecution; moreover, they slow down and perhaps predominately check the beneficial process, through which in the long run inner security is achieved.

> (Klein, 1940: 128)

This also explains the serious consequences that deprivation and the lack of a stable relationship to a reliable caregiver can have. What was actively done to violent or neglected juveniles by their caregivers is actually less important than the juveniles' own overwhelming aggressive impulses and persecutory anxieties, which come from their inner world and which no one contained for them when they were infants. This deficiency has the effect of creating a very limited, unstable inner world and manifests itself through problems in relationships and shallow feelings. When one caregiver is exchanged for another, this not only constitutes a deficiency in the child's external reality, but also means that positive inner objects in the child's fantasy are destroyed, and the world is then experienced as hopeless and empty.

When we speak of "inner objects" what is meant are, for example, images of the real mother, the "external mother", but coloured by the child's fantasies, wishes, and conflicts. Thus, there are different inner images of one person, such as the mother or father, introjected into our inner world, standing in relationship to one another and to the self.

> There is a constant interaction between anxieties related to the "external" mother—as I will call her here in contrast to the

"internal" mother—and those relating to the "internal" mother and the methods used by the ego for dealing with two sets of anxieties are closely interrelated. In the baby's mind the "internal" mother is bound up with the "external" one, of whom she is a "double", though one undergoes alterations in his [sic] mind through the very process of internalisation; that is to say, her image is influenced by his phantasies and by internal stimuli and internal experiences of all kinds.

(Klein, 1940: 126)

This passage from Melanie Klein makes clear on the one hand the significance of the environment, that is, the real mother, on the child's development; on the other hand, it shows how the child's perception of the mother is influenced by its feelings and is thus often distorted. The same is also true of the mother, who has an inner image of her child that is influenced by her hopes, expectations, disappointments, and her optimistic or pessimistic attitude to life—and often prevents her from seeing the real child and perceiving its behaviour. In any case, one positive distortion belongs to any normal motherhood and fatherhood: that they see their own baby as the most loved and as the best in the world.

The parents' attitude towards their child is shaped by their personality and how they relate to other people and to external reality. This affects the child not only by constituting a model of behaviour that the child imitates, but also because it determines the way that the parents relate to their baby: the parents may be relatively fearful and cautious, or they can have faith in the robustness of their child from an early age, thus expecting the child to deal with the world and overcome difficulties without giving up. Here are some short scenes with Felix, the "Sunday child", whose parents expect him to cope with the dangers of the world from very early on.

### 3.3.1    Observation of Felix dealing with obstacles and problems

Felix, four months and two weeks old

With his mother's support, Felix sits on a padded support on the kitchen worktop. In his right hand he holds a rattle which he has been playing with for a while. With his left hand he grasps in the direction of the cupboard, on which a metal, four-cornered grater is standing. The mother laughs and places the grater between his legs. Felix has his gaze fixed on the grater. He stretches out a forefinger, and touches the narrow side with the small, sharp openings. The mother says, "You like that, you like that a lot." Now he seizes the grater, and pulls it toward him so that he can touch the handle with his mouth. The mother watches him. When he gets the handle in his mouth he produces a laborious "ah, ah," holds his left hand on the side of the grater and grabs the upper edge. As the grater slips from his hand and he tries to pull it closer he only pushes it further away. The mother helps him by putting the grater between his out-stretched legs once again. Felix continues to hold the rattle firmly in his right hand. The mother holds Felix securely with her right hand on his back and her left on his leg; her body leans against the kitchen furniture. She moves her head back, looks at Felix, and smiles at him in admiration.

Felix is totally absorbed in his game. On the next attempt to grab the grater, now lying on its side, Felix lets the rattle fall and reaches out with both hands. His mouth is slightly open and some saliva dribbles out. His mother tells the observer that this is his favourite toy and in this way he has learnt to sit. As if in confirmation, Felix leans further forward and beats happily on the grater several times. In the commentary we learn that he remained absorbed in this game for twenty minutes (Barnett 1985).

Interpretation

It is not completely clear just what fascinates Felix about this game. Actually, a kitchen grater is not an ideal toy for a child: it has sharp, different-sized openings and is made of metal. Many people would consider this a dangerous object which children should be protected from, but it is clear that the mother sees it as totally suitable. Felix's long occupation with it is a sign that he is fascinated by it. The mother does not initiate the game but does support it by helping him again and again to take hold of it. When the videos were shown, the audience reacted very nervously, concerned for Felix, and some commented critically on the mother's behaviour.

In the succeeding observations there are also occasionally scenes which were labelled problematic by the viewers; at six months of age, Felix is allowed to play with the contents of the wastepaper basket, and at nine months he was allowed to sit in a meadow and examine the grass, soil, small wooden objects, and so forth. Now, however, we see a different scene at the age of nine months and two-and-a-half weeks, where the mother helps Felix to cope alone with frightening situations.

### Felix, nine months and two-and-a-half weeks old

Felix pulls a wooden newspaper rack up to himself and holds onto it firmly. As he reaches into it with his right hand to pull out a newspaper, he lifts his head and emits a proud, "Ah, ah," and turns his head towards the kitchen where his mother is making noise while cooking. Now he appears to want to crawl to his mother but, as he sits down while still holding on, the newspaper rack falls onto his left leg. Surprised, Felix looks next at the fallen over rack, lifts his head, and pushes the rack a bit away from him. He grimaces and cries out loudly. The mother has obviously heard the toppling sound and comes towards Felix with long steps, already speaking soothingly to him. Felix is in a crawling position and moves towards the mother crying loudly. Now squatting, she stretches out her arms to him, who raises himself up, holding onto her leg and weeping bitterly. "What is the matter with you?" the mother asks. As she picks him up, she joins in with his weeping in a friendly way. She remains squatting and seats Felix on her right leg. Felix becomes quiet immediately, sees the threatening newspaper rack from a safe position, and places his arm around his mother's neck. The mother also looks at the news rack, which the father sets upright, and then looks at Felix again. With a calm voice she tells him that newspaper racks can topple over. She strokes his leg and taps his lower leg gently, then tenderly holds his foot and lays her cheek against his. After the mother has finished, Felix stretches out his hand to the news rack again and signals that he wants to be set down again, which his mother immediately acts on. Her movements and her voice are peaceful and calm.

Felix now holds onto the side of the news rack, remains in contact with it with his body, and reaches for a newspaper with his left hand. The mother remains squatting behind Felix, holds her left hand close below his arm without touching him, and her right hand below his bottom in order to be able to catch him if necessary. Felix stands on tiptoe in order to reach in better, but this time he is very careful about his balance. The mother relaxes, now has both hands behind his back, and observes him carefully. As he unerringly takes the first magazine out of the rack with a wide swing and standing wide-legged and secure throws it onto the floor, the mother rises but remains standing behind him. When Felix reaches into the rack once again, she returns to the kitchen, letting him play on his own without any further comments. Felix has now removed a thick newspaper, placed it on the floor, and sits down instantly, this time at the other side of the rack. This now topples over but in such a way that it does not touch Felix. He looks spellbound, sits up, and turns his head to the kitchen door. His mother remarks that newspaper racks do fall over but that Felix is OK. Felix starts to make sounds of discomfort. From the kitchen, his mother says it's all right, upon which Felix again turns to the newspapers. Before he opens it, his glance falls on the overturned news rack, which is now lying on its side. Still sitting, he stretches his hands out, drums briefly against the rack with both hands, then stands up and goes around exploring it, making "ah" and "oh" sounds as he does so. At the open side he notices that it would be easier here to get to the newspapers. Felix looks at this carefully, reaches inside with his left hand, but then changes his movement. His attention is now on the pictures in the newspaper lying on the floor. With a joyous shout he stands up quickly and with his left hand reaches deep into the horizontal compartment. He straightens up, looks over his shoulder at the kitchen door, gets up on tiptoe, teeters, purses his lips, and then shouts with joy. He crawls to his mother in the kitchen, who picks him up.

Interpretation

At first, the encounter with gravity and the falling over of an object frightened Felix. The interesting news rack changed into a threatening object which seemed to persecute him. It is salutary to see how a baby's interest in exploring objects in the world is closely connected to the emotional relationship to mother and to father. Although Felix is playing by himself, he is emotionally closely linked to his mother, as shown by his glance towards the kitchen and his consolation after his shock when the news rack toppled. He realizes that his mother is there when he needs her—her attention is always slightly directed towards him, with all of his movements in her field of vision. After the first coping with the shock, the mother remains with him long enough to observe that he once more, with fearless interest, directs his attention to the news rack. His trust in a benevolent world seems to have returned and his curiosity been reawakened. When the next problem arises, Felix's mother communicates with her voice that she is there, but also that she thinks he can deal with it by himself—a reasonable assessment. Following all these exciting adventures, Felix returns to the safe haven of his mother, who picks him up and thus rewards him.

With good foresight, the mother has arranged the home so that there as few dangerous areas as possible. In order to master unavoidable difficulties, such as clambering up and down the steep stone stairs in the garden, she practiced with him even before he could walk. Under her supervision, she let him climb down and then showed him the way to climb back up. There are few limits for Felix. We see how, at ten months old, he imitates his mother cleaning the toilet, which he is allowed to do without being urged. Felix is very concentrated and seems to be encouraged by his parents to attempt things on his own; they expect him to learn by himself. A secure emotional relationship with parents is a secure base for exploring the world and for being able to leave the mother while exploring, at least for a short time. In other scenes we shall see how the father encourages Felix, fourteen months old, to go up the stone steps in the garden alone and to help the father with gardening. The father has a special way of whistling for Felix, who reacts immediately to this sound. Felix carries around his father's tools carefully, and drags a heavy hammer about to repair things with. We presume that Felix has internalized his parents' view of him as an independent, competent child, and thus develops self-confidence which is consolidated by each experience that he masters. His view of the world seems to be optimistic as he expects to discover and explore new things. Later we will see him climb up a ladder at the age of twenty months. His movements are sure and calm. It has been shown that children who are allowed to follow their own rhythm of development of movements only get into situations that they can master alone, and almost never injure themselves. Children who are over-anxiously protected are not only fearful and overcautious themselves, but often injure themselves more than the average child. In the chapter on the development of thinking we will go into greater detail into the connection between the quality of the emotional relationship with the parents and the child's desire and ability to explore the world.

It is apparent in the observations of Felix, as well as those of Elias, that father and mother have different ways of dealing with their children. The emotional weave of personality is dependent on the child's thousands of individual experiences, with the parents' differences in personality, in their hopes, preferences, and manner of dealing with the child, representing an enriching or an encumbering opportunity for the child to learn. The complex emotional pattern of a family is also affected by the parents' relationship with each other. In psychoanalytic baby observations we see again and again that not only the child but also the mother behaves differently in the presence of the father.

### 3.3.2    Changing triangular relationship patterns: Child–Mother–Father

The observed baby Tomy was a planned child. The mother had already been happily looking forward to the baby during the pregnancy, and both parents envisioned their life as a threesome, although they could barely imagine quite what it would be like. The difficult and protracted birth was a great burden and disappointment for the mother. In the first six months she told the observer that she "couldn't at all really enjoy little Tomy because I was afraid of doing something wrong" (Basilides, 2006: 4). In the first months the mother gave an impression of being stressed and tired, and dealt very cautiously with Tomy. Now I will describe an observation of Tomy with father and mother.

### Tomy, six months old

The door is open, I enter and call out a loud "Good morning!" It is nine-thirty. Petra calls from the living room, "We've all been up since five-thirty, for us it is nearly midday." She sounds very cheerful. I go inside and see mother, father, and child together with a ball lying on an outspread blanket on the floor. The father (I'll call him George) gets up and greets me. He is wearing a jogging suit, which he immediately apologizes for, saying that it is so much more comfortable for him as he normally has to wear a suit and tie.

Petra is sitting with Tomy on the blanket and George sits down to rejoin them. Tomy is lying on his belly and does not turn to me as he usually does. He is playing with the fringe of the blanket, which he again and again puts into his mouth. This part of the blanket is already quite wet. Petra takes the blanket out of his mouth and George says, "That's fun, the fringe must taste good." He lies down on his belly next to his son, also puts the fringe into his mouth, and says, in Petra's direction, "Mmmm, good." He makes barking noises while he has the fringe in his mouth. Petra and Tomy laugh. Tomy, drooling, looks at his father, the blanket fringe falls out of his mouth, and with a swing he turns onto his back and then onto his belly once more. George and Petra together marvel at how quickly their child can already do that, and they laugh because Tomy looks from one to the other resting on his forearms and with wide open mouth, so that I can easily see his teeth.

He is drooling and his whole pullover is already wet. Tomy laughs and makes a chuckling sound before he lets himself fall onto his back again. His head comes down hard against the blanket. He grimaces for a moment but does not cry, and George says, "You're a very brave lad, nothing has happened." Petra picks Tomy up to look at the back of his head, but George takes him from her hands and says that he has already discussed with his son that nothing happened. Petra laughs and gives each a kiss on the cheek.

Tomy bends forward towards the floor and stretches out his arms to the blanket lying there. George places him there again and Tomy rolls from a sitting position onto his side and then onto his belly, supports himself with both hands, and looks up to where his father is. Today Tomy's skin is completely clear of red spots. George says, in Tomy's direction, "I'll make some coffee for us, then I'll be back," and goes into the kitchen. Tomy stares after him for awhile without moving, pulls his legs up close to him, and seesaws his bottom back and forth, but without moving an inch forward. Petra sits next to him and says that the crawling will still take some time, and strokes Tomy's head.

Tomy, however, still stares fixedly at the door. He starts to grimace and scream. This is not the crying accompanied by tears

I have often seen him do, but just a loud screaming. Petra tries to distract him with the ball and turns Tomy towards her. He resists and lies once again on his stomach. He stares at the door hollering. Petra lifts him up and says, "Well, that will be something—when Papa goes to work again tomorrow, you'll just have to put up with me." Petra stands up and goes into the kitchen with Tomy, where George takes him while she makes the coffee.

(Basilides, 2006: 27ff)

## Interpretation

The mother has occasionally told the observer that her husband deals with Tomy completely differently than she does—"much wilder and not at all anxiously". In this family, the father seems to perform an important relief function. He is less afraid than the mother. He identifies with his son, who puts blanket fringes into his mouth like a small dog might. The father can playfully join in with his barking, so that Tomy and his mother laugh and the mother's warning is neutralized. After this Tomy poses, showing his parents what he can already do, and is admired by them both. In turning over energetically he lands hard against the floor. Now there is a conflict between father and mother about how best to deal with this situation. The mother wants to pick Tomy up and console him; the father wants to encourage him to continue playing and to get over the knock. Later, the observer writes that Tomy's father has three brothers and they loved playing roughly with each other. The father seems to see his son as robust. Actually, Tomy does not cry and immediately wants to be placed on the blanket again. The mother laughs and gives both a peck on the cheek in appeasement and recognition. When the father goes into the kitchen Tomy shows that he will not tolerate this separation and screams. His mother reacts to this and carries him into the kitchen to his father. The observer is also impressed by the change in the mother's behaviour; she seems more secure and less anxious if her husband is present.

Fonagy (1996) has shown, in wide-ranging research with two hundred married couples and their small children, that the attachment between a child and its father and mother can vary greatly. Fonagy (1996: 79) writes: "Surprisingly, early adjustment to father's

IWM [inner working model] is more significant for problem-free development than is the case for mother." He goes on: "As studies of resilient children suggest … even a single secure-understanding relationship may be sufficient for the development of reflective processes and may "save" the child" (Fonagy, 1996: 83). This outcome stresses the importance of fathers for the development of a child.

## 3.4   Emotional education instead of emotional illiteracy

The difficult tasks of parents consist of, first, getting to know their baby's personality, getting in touch with it emotionally, building up a relationship with it, and communicating with it—first in "baby talk", and later in more differentiated ways. The better the parents are able to recognize their own ambivalent feelings towards their child, the sooner they will be in a position to help the child acknowledge its own feelings of love as well as feelings of, for example, jealousy and envy, and to label and accept these feelings. This is a process of several years which demands honesty and patience. We tend to deny our own undesirable impulses and emotions, and attempt either to overlook these in our children or to see them hypercritically. Nevertheless, the parents' task is to help their child to distinguish and to name feelings, not to simplify them but to understand what the child is expressing in a given situation. The truth lies in the details. It is not enough to label a child as "cheerful", "serious", "generous", or "jealous". If one hears oneself saying "you're always saying/doing that", this is an indication that we are destroying the specific moment and its special quality, burdening it with a generalization. The child then doesn't feel understood. It is vital to maintain an inner openness, to look at the child freshly and without prejudice, as it were, in order to recognize its special emotional situation. Heraclites (Patrick, 2006) said that "no man [sic] ever steps in the same river twice, for it's not the same river and he's not the same man". To see life as constantly moving, to recognize one's own and the child's emotional flux, is an important counter-balance to the generalizing tendencies of parents as well as teachers and educators. Above all, this requires not only inner openness and readiness to look closely and openly at the child and its behaviour, but also the ability to pay attention to the details of interaction.

Over and over in parent–infant therapy, it is painful to see how inflexible perceptions prevent the parents from seeing what their child does and what he or she shows in the therapeutic session. They are then deeply surprised when the therapist describes what their child is actually doing at the moment and how he or she has established contact with the therapist. Usually the parents try to dismiss what they have heard, even if it was an accurate description, by saying, "Oh yes, here or with strangers our child always behaves well, but at home it is totally different!"

Remaining open to new, unexpected aspects of a child or of the relationship between child and parents always creates insecurity and doubt as to whether we have understood a situation correctly. Therefore, it is necessary not only to stay emotionally in touch with the child but also with the child in ourselves. Our own feelings do not hinder us but, quite on the contrary, can supply us with important clues for understanding the situation.

In the analytical situation we try to understand something about the inner world of the patient based on the atmosphere during the session and the particular emotional colouring of the interaction. Joseph (1985: 157) writes: "What he [sic] brings in can best be gauged by our focusing our attention on what is going on within the relationship, how he is using the analyst, alongside and beyond what he is saying." We assume that the patient unconsciously tries to draw us into the same relationship patterns as exist in their inner world, that is, that they try to get us to act out with them in a similar way as they experienced their parents relating to them. A forty-year-old patient tended to understand each of my interpretations as either criticism or rejection, which she believed she had to defend herself against. Even if I only repeated something that she herself had just said, perhaps in a harsher voice, she felt I had said something different. Only when we discussed this pattern of our interaction, memories emerged of the critical and reproachful mood in her family. The family was regarded as a model family, a happy marriage with two very successful children; her mother, however, was disappointed with the marriage and felt unloved, as the father had only married on pragmatic grounds, in order to forget an unhappy love affair. He also plunged himself into work: as a "trouble shooter" he reorganized different companies in the shortest possible time. He was attentive to both children as long as they were small, but had no understanding for them as they entered puberty. The patient had always heard only that something she had done was "too much" or was "too little". When she was thirteen, she wrote her father a two-page letter concerning what he thought she had done "too much or too little" of. She never dared, however, to show her father this letter; she believed he would only have shouted or laughed at her. Emerging feelings of having done nothing correctly and of being mainly criticized by both her parents, however hard she tried, made her aware of her hopelessness to ever please.

Sometimes, the child's symptoms which cause the parents to look for professional help do not represent an illness, but rather serve as a shield against the mother's unconscious, destructive projections.

Bernhofer (1998) describes the therapy with a young boy she calls Michael whose behaviour, which appears to be a "perception disorder", protects him from being swamped by maternal projections.

## Case study: Michael

Michael was brought by his mother to a therapist because he rejected physical contact and played alone for hours on end. He withdrew behind a curtain and declined his mother's offers to play with him. The mother was afraid that he could be "disturbed", that is, that he was showing the first signs of a sensomotoric integration disorder (Datler, 1997: 113).

During the first interview with the mother, the early intervention teams had an opportunity to watch Michael and his mother playing. It shows that the mother hardly gives Michael room to discover a toy by him. Here is a description of the observation.

> Michael is now fifteen months old. We are in the therapy room. Mrs D sits down at the card table and sits Michael in an armchair … Michael looks around the room and his eyes remain fixed on an "Activity Centre" (a board with different knobs and levers which move, make noises, and so forth). He points to it with his fingers. Mrs D fetches it for him and places it in front of him. Michael starts to turn one of the knobs. He does it rather slowly and hesitantly.
>
> After a short time Mrs D becomes noticeably restless. She takes Michael's right hand and places it on a different knob. In

touching this knob there is a ringing sound. Mrs D says, "That's how it's done!" Michael does not react to the ringing and seems to be suddenly tired. He no longer looks at the "Activity Centre"; he looks searchingly about the room.

(Bernhofer, 1998: 14)

## Interpretation

First, the observer describes that Michael shows interest in his environment by looking around and pointing at things. His mother recognizes this and can bring him the "desired" toy he looked at. At first Michael shows "normal" behaviour: he touches the knob and turns it. The mother seems to be under great pressure, however; she cannot watch and take part in the way that her child explores the world, but she interrupts his playing in order to show him how one does this "correctly", and thereby interrupts his exploration. Michael experiences that his mother is dissatisfied with him, that his manner of turning the knobs is not the way his mother finds correct. Subsequently, he loses interest and gets tired. I understand his tiredness as a blocked aggressive impulse against the disruption.

In a further observation, Bernhofer shows how the mother can again only join briefly in Michael's game of feeding her—she quickly pressures him into an "adult game", that is, placing the lid "correctly" on the pot, feeding the mother "correctly", and so on. Since Michael is only interested in opening and closing the pot with its lid, he cannot at the same time feed his mother as she expects him to do.

In further sessions with the mother the background of her impatience became clear. She had a younger brother with learning difficulties and problems at school and was afraid that her son could be like her brother. Therapy helped the mother to talk about her own unresolved rivalry problems and guilt feelings regarding her mother, thereby addressing the problem directly. She could become aware of her unconscious rivalry with her mother. Instead of burdening Michael with her unresolved problems with her mother she could begin to see the needs of her child. His withdrawal was a partially successful attempt to protect himself against his mother's irksome projections, into a space invisible to her where he could devote himself to exploring objects without her invasive disturbance.

Datler points out how important it is, when children display behavioural problems, to be able to see not only somatic symptoms, e.g., deficiencies of the central nervous system, but to keep an open mind towards seeing these as symptoms of a problematic relationship with the mother. Such symptoms can be caused by problems in the relationship with the mother and are "to be understood as such in their subjective meaning" (Datler, 1997: 115).

To have a realistic picture of oneself and one's lovable and dark sides also means accepting the injustices and inequalities of life that we are prone to, which takes for granted coping with unavoidable envious impulses. Bion (2005: 10) formulates the aim of analysis, which can also be taken as an aim of successful upbringing:

> I think it is fundamental that the person concerned should be able to be in good contact with himself [sic]—good contact in the sense of tolerant contact, but also in the sense of knowing just how horrible he thinks he is, or his feeling are, or what sort of a person he is. … if you can tolerate yourself as a father or a mother, you might tolerate a mate who is not you, who might be the other parent.

In spite of the constant attempt to see ourselves as an ideal person and to project all undesired impulses onto another person, the process of self-contact and self-toleration is an important prerequisite for accepting another person and living with him or her in such a way that one "becomes complete" and can fulfil the biological function of a couple. In addition to Freud's aim for analysis, to make the patient capable of work and love, Bion stipulates an insight leading to the patient's self-awareness relating to the different qualities of moral judgement of oneself and of the other. We will go more deeply into this later.

### 3.4.1 Tolerance of short-term return to the paranoid-schizoid position

As I have already emphasized, we are concerned with integrating both of the psyche's modes of psychic functioning, which Klein calls the paranoid-schizoid position and the depressive position. They remain effective throughout life and move in the direction of integration if there is a positive development: a movement from the level of the archaic anxieties of disintegration and the primitive defence mechanisms of a splitting into an "ideal—good" and "bad" to the more mature form of integration in the depressive position. Between both positions a continuous movement of tendencies towards integration or fragmentation takes place, expressed in different kinds of anxieties. Particularly in a crisis—illness, separation, or the death of a beloved person—we tend to return to an archaic mental way of functioning which influences our view of the external world and ourselves. Can we assess reality, responsibly recognize the consequences of our actions, and take responsibility for our actions? Or do we tend to experience ourselves as victims, to feel ourselves persecuted by circumstances, to fear other people or to idealize them?

Bion (1963: 3) described this permanent fluctuation between both positions as "dynamic relationship" and made an analogy to a chemical formula which describes two different modes of psychic functioning—"states of mind". Bion used the abbreviation "P/S" for the paranoid-schizoid position and "D" for the depressive position.[2]

$$P/S \leftrightarrow D$$

### Case study: return to the paranoid-schizoid position

I would like to quote a short example from an analysis which describes the especially urgent and threatening quality of experience in the "P/S quality of feeling" of disintegration and panic after a separation, as Pricilla Roth describes it in a vignette from an analysis.

The patient told me that she had not slept at all over the weekend … she kept thinking she heard a child crying, although in fact her daughter wasn't crying, she was fast asleep … She criticized the American troops, which was to be understood as an attack on her American analyst (displacement).

---

[2] He writes in *Elements of Psychoanalysis* (Bion, 1963: 3): "It is a representation of an element that could be called a dynamic relationship between container and contained. The second element I represent PS ↔ D. It may be considered as representing approximately (*a*) the reaction between what Melanie Klein described as the paranoid-schizoid and depressive positions, and (*b*) the reaction precipitated by what Poincaré described as the discovery of the selected fact."

On the following day she reported that she was still not sleeping well, but then went on to complain bitterly about her (three-year-old GDW) daughter (with whom she generally had an affectionate relationship GDW), who had a cold and was "grotty". She said she hates it when the little girl gets like this. She wants her to go back to how she was before she had the cold, and she feels completely hopeless about it. She thinks she will be like this forever, somehow ruined, and not as good as she used to be. The daughter was up with a stuffy nose, and kept my patient up a lot. She was furious with her. She said, "I cannot tolerate it, cannot stand it. I hate her when she's like this ... everything I try to do for her is no good, everything fails. I don't know what's wrong with her—she is sick, cold, and uncomfortable—I do everything and she keeps crying and it makes me hate her. I feel she is getting at me, accusing me, blaming me for not making her feel better. This is not the daughter I wanted to have!" Then, very much as an afterthought, she added that she had left the little girl at a new nursery on that day.

(Roth 2005: 48f)

The patient is a loving mother who has always taken care of her daughter attentively. Why is she now completely unable to respond to the sick girl's needs, feeling herself persecuted and rejected by her, hopelessly convinced that things will never again be harmonious between them? The mother not only sounds annoyed, but in a desperate and threatened state. At the moment she also seems unable to put herself in her daughter's position and to see any connection in her daughter's difficult situation, entering a new kindergarten and therefore feeling lost and lonely.

This return to a paranoid-schizoid state of mind is linked to the current situation in the analysis. At the time of the patient's birthday, the analyst took an unusual two-week break, which actualized early fears of loss and abandonment since the patient's mother had left her alone at an early age. Being left alone in this unusually long break awakened an unbearable resentment in her (and of course also reanimated her annoyance with her mother as a child), so that her hate became stronger than the love for and gratitude towards her analyst, whom she attacked with her bitter criticism of the USA. Unconsciously, she assumed that the analyst would also answer this attack with hatred, would thus retaliate and withdraw her love. At this moment, she felt herself surrounded by hatred on all sides, instead of being held lovingly and being understood. At this point she had lost her maternal skills for her small, three-year-old daughter, and felt herself rejected and criticized by her also.

How did this come about? If we try to understand the inner mental process in the patient, we assume that the pain of being separated from the analyst was overwhelming. Instead of feeling the pain however, it was easier to attack the "bad analyst" and to keep away from the "good analyst". On a conscious level the patient would perhaps say that the separation did not bother her, she knew that the analyst also needed breaks and she also knew that the sessions would continue. Unconsciously, however, an explosive process was set in motion which was then discussed. She attacked the analyst with hate and was then convinced that the analyst hated her and did not want a daughter/patient like her. The guilt feelings at having attacked a beloved person are emotionally difficult to bear. This demands recognition of one's own dependence on the loved one as well as the fact that the loved one is a separate person. With the help of an understanding analyst, such a patient can gain contact to her feelings of being totally thrown off course and experiencing depression at the absence of the analyst.

After this return to an archaic way of experiencing the loss of the beloved object, she could integrate her ambivalent feelings and desires. Roth (2005: 54) summarizes this understanding in the following way: "(she had) an increasing capacity to have a fuller, more inclusive sense of herself and the important people in her life. So she did not simply stay in this paranoid place where she is good and the Americans are bad. She had to deal with her ambivalence." Each regression that is then reflected on makes possible a more stable and tolerant acknowledgement of one's own person and relationships to loved and simultaneously hated persons.

The example of a dynamic balance between the archaic and mature states of mind should underline what Bion emphasizes, that we all continually move between these two positions in a more or less defined manner. Children fluctuate even more strongly between integration and disintegration: their feelings are much more intense and their ego is not yet so consolidated. When they are disappointed or feel abandoned or rejected they can become flooded with rage and scream "idiot mother" or "I hate you! I never want to see you again!" They can hit and be desperately unhappy. It is important for the caregiver to remember that the child—as shown in the previous examples when feeling attacked on two sides—is also overwhelmed by both its inner hatred and the fantasized retaliatory hate of the mother. It is itself in panic because it thinks it has destroyed its inner picture of a good, friendly mother. It is also often difficult for the parents to comprehend what precisely the catalyst was for such an attack. However, it is helpful to know that the utterances of a child in such a state should not be understood as being the sole truth: behind the love for the parents now being attacked there is a schism, and the child is dependent on their help to re-emerge from this crisis and to reconcile with them.

Brenman (2006), in his book *Recovery of the Lost Good Object*, describes how we as analysts feel emotions of hopelessness rising in us during patients' excessive projective identification, and then have to remind ourselves how ill the patient is in order to be able to tolerate and then contain their omnipotent, contemptuous behaviour.

# CHAPTER FOUR

# Development of thinking
# and the capacity to symbolize

When we speak about "thinking" we are generally referring in the everyday sense to the mental functions that psychology deals with, that is to say, attention, perception, thinking in a waking state, judgements, reflection, and acts. In Freudian psychoanalysis, we would call this realm of thought "secondary process". The phrase "secondary process" refers to something on which this psychic mechanism is based—called "primary process" by Freud (1915: 186) since it refers to the primitive functioning of the "system of the unconscious". All perception of reality is, as Freud (1915: 186) argued, informed to a varied extent by fantasies so that memories can be said to not just refer to real events but also to fantasies and thoughts, all of which together constitute an individual's "psychic reality". As opposed to logical thinking, which works with concepts and verbal symbols, the unconscious articulates itself in imagery, which can assume a variety of different meanings. The dream, as Freud (1900: 48) claimed, "thinks predominantly in visual images". The search for clarity and consistency in logical thinking stands in contrast to the attempt to transcend the present, past, and future. In memories events that we find moving are also experienced much later in a similarly intense way. The primary process follows the pleasure principle, which seeks to fulfil wishes and gain pleasure. Both the primary process and the secondary process represent different forms of intellectual (mental) life that function according to certain specific laws. According to Freud (1915: 186f), in the unconscious there is "no negation, no doubt, no degrees of certainty … there are only contents." A juxtaposition of primary and secondary process reveals the characteristics that will be subject to further scrutiny in the following.

*Primary Process*
Adhering to the pleasure principle—deriving or gaining pleasure
Visual representation
Ambiguity (Condensation)
Discharge, gratification—psychic reality
Timelessness
Absence of contradiction
Words as "things"
No connections

*Secondary Process*
Reality principle
Logical thinking, causality
Clarity, logical consistency
Knowledge of external reality
Time consciousness
Negation
Verbal symbols
Connections with other ideas

The human mind is seen as a unity. The higher realms of the mind do not function independently of the archaic ones. The Unconscious is not a rudimentary part but an active system in which mental processes take place. In *The Nature and Function of Phantasy* Susan Isaacs (1948: 73) argues that the original primary mental activity is known as "unconscious fantasy". Even if a conscious thought or an act is rational and appropriate to a situation it addresses unconscious fantasies (Pick, 1992: 25). In Freud's (1900: 601) words: "All thinking is no more than a circuitous path from the memory of a satisfaction (a memory which has been adopted as a purposive idea) to an identical cathexis of the same memory which is hoped to be attained once more through an immediate stage of motor experiences." Rational thought tries to avoid being distracted by something "different" which can be so intense as to undermine this thinking.

The important distinction Freud draws between conscious and unconscious processes is also expressed in the realm of language. In Freudian slips libidinous impulses have an effect over and beyond consciousness. In daydreams the dreamer is aware that s/he is not confronted with real ideas but with wishful thinking. In metaphoric expressions, in creative manifestations and in free association both forms of representation are linked and condensed. Even the speaker's emotional state is expressed in the way that he or she speaks; a mature integrative expression can be seen in coherent narrative which can be followed, whereas disintegration and contradictory patterns of thought are revealed by a stuttering, often fragmentary, contradictory mode of speaking. Intonation in particular can be indicative of a convergence between what is said or meant with an appropriate expression, or by the same token, monotonous or repetitive utterances can point to suppressed emotions or a stilted way of speaking or unclear narrative to divided emotions. This so-called "two layers" of thought, however, should not be understood as implying the existence of two completely distinct systems, since they appear in special hybrid forms. Freud sought to expand the scope of reason. Not just the element of chance comes to bear in dreams, in lapses, or slips of tongue; "deeper" unconscious reason, the "logic of feelings" also prevails over rational thought. Freud has thus been referred to as an enlightener (for instance, by Habermas, 1963, 1968), helping us sound the depths of our psyches in an attempt to attain insight into non-rational realms. The darkness does not conceal chaos but rather an unrelenting order, an unconscious being that can be located in the id. The psychoanalytic method orients itself after a free inner communication that is constantly being modified by the "censorship" of the super-ego. There are "deeper layers" that lie closer to archaic thought and primitive anxieties and "more mature forms of thinking" but generally both mental systems appear in an interrelated form. We thus speak of a "healthy part of the individual" that can enter into a "working alliance" with a therapist and seek a cure as opposed to a neurotic or psychotic part of the personality, which unconsciously resists a cure and does everything in its might to work against it. Alongside the desire to learn more about oneself and one's own unconscious, there is also a sort of recalcitrance and anger over the fact that one is no longer "master in one's own house". Freud (1915: 166) spoke of the "resistance" that works against one's own interest in acquiring new insights. The distinction between primary and secondary process and the hypothesis that the psyche is at work in them in different ways belong to the most important basic assumptions in Freud's work. The term "primary" does not just imply a sort of hierarchical order or capacity but also implies temporal contingencies:

> No mental apparatus exist which possesses only the primary processes ... as they are present from the first outset, while it is only during the course of life that the secondary processes unfold, and come to inhibit and overlay the primary ones; it may even be that their complete domination is not attained until the prime of life.
>
> (Freud, 1900: 602)

The essence of our very being is thus composed of unconscious wishful impulses and anxieties that must be channelled in purposeful paths—through compromises, sublimation, or repression. Philosophers and poets have been aware of the existence of these deep strata of the personality. Friedrich Nietzsche (1886, IV: 68), for instance, wrote the following about this inner conflict in *Beyond Good and Evil*: " "I have done this" my memory states, "I cannot have done this"—my pride states and remains relentless. Finally—my memory yields."

If we now attempt to trace the development of thinking going back to where this capacity emerges in the infant, we will be drawing primarily on the thought of Sigmund Freud, Melanie Klein, and Wilfried Bion. As already noted in previous chapters, the archaic ("paranoid-schizoid") position and the mature position of integration ("depressive position") constitute elements that can also be used to describe the different quality of primitive and of mature thinking. Understanding the mixture of both these forms of thinking and the insight that archaic, egocentric, and magical world views are a normal transitional stage in each child's development, can promote a tolerant attitude in the reader, as described by Alexander Mitscherlich (1954: 12) in the preface to Freud's "Psychopathology of Everyday Life": "We should be indebted to Freud for his leads on how one can gain insight into oneself, laughing, with admiration—instead of uttering a curse."

## 4.1   The beginning of thinking, pre-conception

According to Freud (1911: 218) thinking begins with an experience of lack, a wish that cannot be satisfied. The hungry child who wishes to be fed, feels displeasure and seeks to overcome it by remembering the satisfaction it once experienced when it was fed, producing a sort of "hallucinatory wish fulfilment". Thinking is imposed, as it were, on the psyche by the body's sensations of displeasure. Since the nursing mother is only imagined, the tension must be tolerated long enough, and the external world explored, until a suitable person ("object") appears. Freud (1911: 218) described the "reality principle" as an orientation towards the outer world, which enables the baby to develop an attention span, memory, and sense of judgement in order to find a suitable person. To this end, it is necessary that the child is able to put satisfying its impulsive wishes on hold, gradually learning to be patient and to remember the good experiences of how it was fed, held, consoled, and stroked. Various possibilities of discharging tension are presented until a suitable object for gratifying needs is found. Less energy is emitted in thinking as a trial act than in an action. Freud (1911: 23) wrote that thinking is "essentially an experimental kind of acting, accompanied by displacement of relatively small quantities of cathexis together with less expenditure (discharge) of them". Sensory perceptions are compared with images of recollection and presentation. The resulting images (presentations of things) are closely related to the feelings accompanying them. Only when the images become linked with representations of words is it possible, according to Freud, to conceive of thinking with less expenditure of energy:

> The system Unconscious contains the thing-cathexes of the objects, the first and true object-cathexes; … but the conscious presentation comprises the presentation of the thing plus the presentation of the word belonging to it.

> (Freud, 1915: 200)

Thinking evolves when reality is taken into greater consideration; the pleasure principle is temporarily sacrificed to the reality principle so that a way can be found to satisfy drive wishes in the best and safest way. This primacy of the reality principle only exists to a certain extent. In neurosis, an attempt is made to avoid anxiety-causing aspects of reality, whereas in psychosis these aspects are replaced by a delusional, self-created reality. For Freud, the conception of thinking remains limited to the processes taking place in an individual (cf. Thorner, 1981).

Melanie Klein and Wilfried Bion further developed Freud's concept of thinking by also taking into account a child's relationship with its mother. Accordingly, thinking can only emerge through the mediation of another thinking individual, of a "you" (mother). Proceeding from the concept of projective identification, Wilfried Bion (1962) developed a theory of thinking. The first question he addressed is how it is possible for thinking to emerge. In response to this philosophical question Bion referred to Kant's *Critique of Pure Reason* ([1781]1956) which takes the intuitive forms of space and time as a prerequisite of thinking, and distinction between the "thing-in-itself" and the thing as an object of sensual intuition, as an apparition, as an object of experience. The "thing-in-itself" is referred to as an empty idea, which, as an a priori idea, is inherent in man. In analogy to this "empty thought" Bion (1962a: 179) refers to this innate disposition that is given in each human being as a "preconception" which is different from conceptions or thoughts and also from concepts.[1] Bion says: "Psychoanalytically the theory that the infant has an inborn disposition corresponding to an expectation of a breast may be used to supply a model. When the preconception is brought into contact with a realization that approximates to it, the mental outcome is a conception." Here the issue is not just explaining the sucking reflex enabling the newborn to suck the mother's nipple immediately after birth, but also a mental function. When the preconception, that is the a priori knowledge of the breast, comes into contact with the experience of a real breast, the two merge. The awareness of the real experience allows a conception of the breast to evolve. The fusion of mouth and nipple is seen in analogy to a sexual fusion as a "linking", but here a gratifying sensation is expected to accompany the conception.

In order to proceed from a conception of the breast to a thought, Bion, like Freud, believed that it was necessary to experience and overcome a lack. If the infant wishes to drink from the breast, but then experiences in reality that there is no breast, it will then experience it as the "absent breast". In what way the infant deals with this painful and frustrating experience depends on its capabilities. If it is has the capacity to tolerate the momentary frustration, "then the "no breast" inside becomes a thought, and an apparatus for thinking develops" (Bion, 1962a: 179). He thus addressed Freud's idea of the development of the reality principle, which serves to bridge

---

[1] Daniel Stern (1977: 35) speaks of innate behavioural and motor patterns, of cognitive and thinking tendencies that must develop after birth: "The infant arrives with an array of innately determined perceptual predilections, motor patterns, cognitive or thinking tendencies, and abilities for emotional expressiveness and perhaps recognition. Nonetheless, for the line of inquiry we are now pursuing, none of these innate "orderings" of the world are of enough specificity or fixity to make the new-born encounter the dissonance or confusion described in the newly sighted patients."

the need and the discovery of a suitable act to gratify the need. The capability to bear deprival allows the psyche to develop, which makes the received deprivation more bearable. Through a number of experiences of the returning external breast, experienced as "good" and satisfying, the baby develops the ability to imagine that "the bad feeling being frustrated is actually occurring because there is a good object which is absent but which may return" (Spillius, 1988: 154).

As thinking emerges, Bion (1961: 182) described the relationship between mother and baby in terms of the function of "container" and "contained". This model addresses the question as to how the baby is able to come to terms with unbearable sensual perceptions, with its neediness and fear from which it seeks to free itself. Melanie Klein described how the baby projects these unbearable feelings to rid itself of them. Bion did not see this as a pathological but rather as a normal process of communication in early development. To be able to process its unbearable sensual perceptions—called "beta" elements by Bion—the baby needs another person who assimilates and transforms the projected raw feelings. The mother is capable of "reverie", a receptive organ, which assimilates these projections, "digests" them mentally, and is able to return them to the baby in transformed form, as "alpha" elements:

> Normal development follows, if the relationship between infant and breast permits the infant to project a feeling, say, that it's dying into the mother and to reintroject it after its sojourn in the breast has made it tolerable to the infant's psyche.
>
> (Bion, 1962a: 183)

Bion described the transformation of unbearable sensual perceptions of the infant in the mother's psyche as the result of "alpha elements" or thoughts. If the baby reintrojects these sensual perceptions, now transformed into thoughts, that have been named by the mother, it not only succeeds in assessing its own sensual perceptions and later being able to name them but it will also slowly develop within itself its mother's ability to carry out this transformation. In this complicated emotional process of thinking the infant's psyche is transformed. The ego modelled after the pleasure principle gradually becomes transformed into a "real ego" oriented towards the reality principle, which is capable of thinking. The baby can summon more patience, on the one hand, when it creates an attitude of expectation as a result of a number of satisfying experiences, expecting that the absent mother—her face, her voice, her smell, her breast—will return. However, it can also bridge the lack by means of thoughts; it learns to deal better with its negative feelings and to develop thoughts of the mother.

Bion thus postulated an early first form of thinking that aims at familiarity with psychic qualities, and is the outcome of the early emotional processes taking place between mother and baby, playing a central role for the development—or stunted development—of thought. At issue is not an abstract psychic process but "thinking as a human link—the endeavour to understand, comprehend the reality of, get insight into the nature of, etc. oneself or another" as O'Shaughnessy (1988: 177) writes.

How are we to imagine this complex-sounding process, and in what sense are these developmental steps that can be observed? Particularly in describing the development of thinking, we must rely on conjecture founded in observations, since the baby is unable to say anything about its thinking and we only have access to physical manifestations as data. We thus only have plausible explanations to go by. I would like to illustrate the close linkage of the development of emotions and thinking with a scene taken from the chapter on emotional development; the focus of interpretation is the baby's cognitive performance.

## 4.1.1    Examples taken from the observation of babies

In the following chapters I would like to show the baby developing the capacity to think through its interaction with the mother. Usually containment is described as the mother assimilating painful, primitive sensual impressions that the baby has. Here, however, we shall use a different example—one of a cheerful, playful encounter between mother and baby—in order to illustrate how cognitive abilities are promoted. The first example is taken from Stern, whose observations on baby play during breastfeeding were already cited in the last chapter in connection with the aspect of emotional development. Here we would like to use these observations to focus on cognitive performance.

## Mother and baby in harmony

Let us take a closer look at the detailed sequence of play which interrupts the nursing and try to focus on the mental level to see how the baby unfolds images of the world and the individuals living in it while interacting with the mother. First the baby drinks from its mother's breast, sometimes glancing at the mother or around the room. The mother also looks repeatedly at how the baby is drinking and then lets her gaze wander around the room.

> He let go of the nipple and the suction around it broke as he eased into the faintest suggestion of a smile. The mother abruptly stopped talking and, as she watched his face begin to transform, her eyes opened a little wider and her eyebrows rose a bit. His eyes locked onto hers and together they held motionless for an instant. The infant did not return to sucking and his mother held frozen her slight expression of anticipation. This silent and almost motionless instant continued to hang until the mother suddenly shattered it by saying, "Hey!" and simultaneously opening her eyes even wider, raising her eyebrows further, and throwing her head up and towards the infant. Almost simultaneously, the baby's eyes widened. His head tilted up and, as his smile broadened, the nipple fell out of his mouth. Now she said, "Well hello! ... heelló ... heeelloóooo!", so that her pitch rose and the "hellos" became longer and more stressed on each successive repetition. With each phrase the baby expressed more pleasure, and his body resonated almost like a balloon being pumped up, filling a little more with each breath. The mother then paused and her face relaxed. They watched each other expectantly for a moment.

> (Stern, 1977: 2f)

## Interpretation

Looking at cognitive performance, it is also important to note that the baby takes the initiative to interrupt the nursing process. How is the baby able to recognize that the mother has understood its wish to play? Here we are dealing with a cognitive feat. The baby can surmise the motive from the eye contact with the mother and her behaviour, enabling it to respond.

Crucial, of course, is the point where interpretation begins. As the baby drank, its mother continually looked tenderly at the baby while conversing with the observer. Empirical baby research emphasizes the great important of visual contact. From a psychoanalytic perspective we understand these tender looks as an expression of an internal space in the mother, who has emotional contact with her baby in her thoughts, even if she is speaking with another adult. The fact that the mother is able to perceive the second-long interruption of nursing shows her sensitivity. She keeps the baby at her breast even if it is not sucking, without interrupting the nursing, which an impatient mother might do. She is able to wait to see what the baby is trying to convey to her. She is willing to understand her baby's needs. How does she manage to do this? The mother stops speaking with the observer, looks at her baby with great concentration and opens her eyes wider. We observe this as an imitative facial expression of tension and interest. She may be imitating a possible interpretation of the baby's tension. Formulated from the baby's perspective, it "thinks": What's there? What do I see? Do I see a mother who is interested in my needs? In the following moments of suspended attention when the mother's eyes open wider, she tries to understand what her child wants to convey to her. At this moment she says, "Hey," opening her eyes even wider, pulling her eyebrows up and moving her face towards the baby's. The baby notes that the mother has noticed that it has stopped drinking and has now introduced another form of affection. We read the utterance "hey" as a "linking". Mother and baby have initiated a new form of communication. The baby has reacted in the same moment, that is, it has performed a cognitive act, understanding the changed facial expression of the mother and responding to it. We assume that the baby has solved a complex task, namely, distinguishing the mother's own feelings from the feelings she has imitated.

How does the baby manage to distinguish between its own feelings, conveyed to it through imitation by the mother, and its mother's own feelings? We assume that the exaggerated imitation of its "affect"[2] enables the baby to recognize them as a representation of its own feelings to thus distinguish these facial expressions from its parents' own feelings.

---

[2] Gergely (cited in Fonagy, 1996: 351) describes the exaggerated facial expression as "marking".

The cognitive task is a complex one. We see this as a cognitive process taking place in the baby when it deals with the mother's exaggerated mimic and verbal comments, while she represents the baby's tension, its curiosity, its will to play as a process of trans-formation—analogous to the process of understanding taking place in the mother's psyche. The mother interprets the baby's pause in suckling, the suggestion of a smile and eye contact, as a wish to play, but she gives the baby time to show this. These moments of silence and of concentrated gaze also convey to the observer the intensive emotional quality of two people relating to each other. The mother formulates her hypothesis in words by saying "hey" and then assuming that the baby wants to play. The baby first has no way of classifying the tensions inside it, the physical expression of happi-ness, fear, anger, or boredom. It perceives physical sensations, and then looks to its mother, who shows the affects of the baby in an exaggerated way and then shows her own feelings in an unexag-gerated way. We assume that the baby first perceives this difference between both affects. The empathetic facial expression, the mother's head moving closer, the familiar smell, the face, and the movement, are assigned to the mother. And then the baby "asks", as it were: What is the other feeling shown? Can what is shown match what I am vaguely feeling in myself? Even the naming of the wish—"Do you want to play?", or in the case of Elias' mother "What is making you so unhappy?"—helps the baby to connect the bodily sensations of its own affects with the facial expressions and verbal statements imitated by the mother. We see how the mother repeats the same words, gestures, and movements, often with only very minimal deviations. Brain researchers would probably point out that in these cheerful or painful rituals, neurological pathways or the neuron con-nections are reinforced in the brain. Of course, the baby cannot have such explicit thoughts. But it is true that connections between dif-fuse body sensations with the idea of affects are in development, embedded in the baby's understanding of the mother's (or other caregiver's) feelings.

These rudimentary early experiences associated with one's own way of experiencing the world, distinct from the mother's feel-ings, are also referred to as "referential decouplings" (Fonagy and

Target, 2002: 851).[3] The baby develops thoughts such as, "Am I the person who is surprised and cheerful? Are these my own feelings?" The baby creates an associative connection between its own affective state and its bodily sensations by means of these inner experience patterns (representations). If a similar emotional state appears again, the child will associate it once more with the ascription it has made and ascribe these affects to itself, which Fonagy (2002: 853) calls "secondary representational structure". Similar patterns of interaction follow—a thousand times in different variations. Thus the foundation is laid for the child's ability to grasp itself as an individual distinct from the mother.[4] It is important that the baby learns to distinguish the mother's or the father's feelings from its own, because this mitigates certain negative feelings, primarily those of anxiety.

Next, a quickly alternating, reinforcing exchange of facial expressions and verbal reactions until the mother has formulated in words the baby's wish, which is to play. She also adds a description of her own uncertainty: she hadn't known whether it was still hungry. The well-co-ordinated interaction seems choreographed—this is how closely the processes of perception and thinking relate to each other. We see the mother here as a "container" who responds to and expresses the wish to play. She also, however, shows her surprise and delight at the baby's wish to play with her during nursing. In this process of understanding, a smile can also have an effect on the mother. Several authors (Gergely and Watson, 1996; Rogers and Pennington, 1991; Target and Fonargy, 1966) have referred to this form of interaction with the term "mirroring"; here, however, the level of thinking and also the dynamic aspect are neglected.

## Mother and baby in harmony (continuation)

The shared excitement between them ebbed, but before it faded completely, the baby suddenly took an initiative and intervened to

---

[3] Fonagy (2002: 851) writes: "We refer to this process as "referential decoupling", since the perceived emotional expression is decoupled in the interpretation of the marked affective expression from the usual referent, i.e., the parents' emotional state."

[4] Fonagy (2002: 852) describes the baby's capacity of "referential decoupling" to demarcate its feelings from that of the mother as "organisation of a self-reference".

rescue it. His head lurched forward, his hands jerked up, and a full smile blossomed. His mother was jolted into motion. She moved forward, mouth open and eyes alight, and said, "Ooooh, ya wanna play, do ya … yeah? I didn't know if you were still hungry … no … nooooo … no I didn't." And off they went.

> After some easy exchanges the pace and excitement increased to a higher level at which the interaction assumed a form of a repeating game. The cycles in the game went something like this. The mother moved closer, leaning in frowning, but with a twinkle in her eyes and her mouth pursed in a circle always on the edge of breaking into a smile. She said, "This time I'm gonna get ya," simultaneously poising her hand over the baby's belly, ready to begin a finger-tickle-march up the baby's belly up and into the hilarious recesses of his neck or armpits. As she hovered and spoke, he smiled and squirmed but always stayed in eye contact with her.
>
> (Stern, 1977: 2–4).

## Interpretation

In the following game the baby was subjected to strong physical stimuli through tickling and the mother's head movements, her quickly changing facial expressions in which the baby's behaviour is reinforced and was shown in exaggerated form, and in her "Now I have you." These stimulations are the "raw material" that is needed for the brain's development, so that maturation and development of perception, of cognitive, senso-motor and emotional processes can take place. One could call them "brain nourishment" (Stern, 1977: 5). From the third month on, cognitive-affective stimulations have predominance over sensory ones. Piaget (1999: 34) calls the baby the first active participant of mental work in the expansion of a difficult process of assimilation/adaptation ("effortful assimilation") to the environment, towards creating inner models of the outer world.

In the mother's further play with her baby, excitement grows, along with laughing, intensity of tickling, and greater proximity. Rhythm, timing, and time itself—pauses increase tension within the baby—are of the essence. Time is already required for the mental stimulations to be ordered and implemented, until the baby is receptive again. In the following sequence, the mother loses the level of harmony with her baby. The baby is able to show this: it turns its head away, looks away from the mother, and no longer smiles.

To be able to understand complex human communications, not only convergence and "harmony" are important, but it is equally important to be able to convey the presence of too much stimulation—the baby turns its head away, no longer smiles, signals with its mouth that it is about to cry.

A further example illustrating the development of thinking and exploring the world follows.

## Elias at the age of four months

> When the mother opens the door for me, I can already hear Elias' voice, making cheerful, multi-pitched sounds such as "Uhu". He is lying on a blanket on the floor in the living room. He looks around, sees his mother, recognizes her, and smiles at her. She kneels down next to him, grabs his legs, and kisses him several times on his cheeks, neck, and forehead. Elias opens his eyes even wider and makes cheerful sounds. The mother now plays with him by pressing her mouth on his stomach or breast and then blowing out air. Elias laughs with glee. She tells him what a lovely strong boy he is. It is a real pleasure to watch mother and baby look at each other deep in the eyes. Then she holds a wooden rattle towards him, he moves his right hand, grabs the rattle with two fingers and moves his left hand to hold it. He sticks the rattle and a couple of fingers in his mouth. He sucks on the rattle, on which several small balls are attached with ribbons. He carefully explores each part with his tongue. He puts each ball in his mouth, feels it and studies it with great attention, turns the rattle around, spits it out again and then sticks the next ball in his mouth. Since he turns the rattle while doing this it is not clear whether he is spitting out the balls or whether they are sliding out of his mouth when he turns the rattle, but he is very focused on what he is doing. His mother stays close to him. She keeps imitating the movements of his mouth and his smacking sounds, laughing and describing what

he is doing each moment: "Yes, now you are putting the rattle
in your mouth, smart boy!" "Yes, now the red ball, well done."
"And now the blue one, what a clever boy you are, Elias." Without disrupting his exploration of the rattle, he turns his head
towards me and looks at me with great interest, as if he wanted
to see whether I was paying attention to him. When he lets the
rattle fall his mother kisses him again. He turns his head to
the rattle and rolls on to one side, tries to reach the rattle, but
does not succeed. After several tries the mother gently pushes
the rattle in his direction. He can touch it but not grab it. The
mother observes his attempts, imitates his efforts and his sighs,
then picks up the rattle and holds it so close to his hand that he
can reach it. When the father enters the room and says "Hello!"
Elias turns his head towards the door, looks at the father, and
regales him with a big smile.

(Diem-Wille, 1993: 3)

## Interpretation

At the beginning of the observation Elias is lying on the floor and
his mother is playing with him. We see the mother's empathy and
joy over everything Elias does. She allows him to lie on the floor
by himself, whereas his father usually holds him very close to
his own body, as if he wanted to express his own corporality. The
mother gives Elias more space. Elias has experienced how far he
can elicit joy and enthusiasm in his mother; she strokes and kisses
him, looks closely at his body, his feet. These oft-repeated experiences leave in Elias a hint of memory telling him that he can obtain
her (and the observer's) attention and that she can also express
her enthusiasm in words. Mosaic-like, an inner image of the loving mother emerges, which, however, is informed by his affects
and fantasies as well as by his self-image as someone who sees the
mother as deserving affection. He begins to develop his first ideas
of what happens in the psyche of another person. This stimulates
his biologically innate need for self-discovery and for discovering the world around him. With his own motoric means, stimuli
are produced that are related to perceptions, for example, through
his observing hand movements with his rattle, through acoustic
stimuli during thinking, through tactile stimuli while sucking,

and biting the rattle.[5] Piaget (1999: 45) pointed out the connection between physical grasping and mental grasping, referring to this first phase as "senso-motor learning".

The close connection between the early experience of being "emotionally held in the mind" by the parents and the child's interest in discovering itself and the world are manifested in Elias' behaviour. Elias studies his toys systematically and with great concentration. He undertakes a serious exploration of the consistency of the material, the sounds it generates, and the special taste of the wood. Elias' mother not only partakes of his explorations; she also encourages him by describing what he does and praising him. Elias can see that his mother also remains attentive when he focuses on something else, giving him space to engage in independent action. A triadic relation evolves between Elias, the toy, and the mother who observes his actions and responds with praise. Elias also takes the observer into account. We see the beginnings of Elias' ability to understand emotional states and to associate them with other persons, the ability of so-called "mentalization" (Fonagy and Target, 2002: 842).

How does Elias' mother deal with manifestations of negative emotions? Is she able to endure Elias' pain, to assimilate it, and to enable him to introject her ability to transform his feelings into ideas ("alpha function")? Mental processes are never directly observed; they can only be grasped using empirical data and inferences regarding the parents' ability to take in and to understand their baby's primitive feelings, then returning them in transformed form (containment).This usually involves painful sensations or fear. The following example should serve to show how the mother succeeded in calming Elias.

## Elias at the age of eighteen days

> Elias looks at his mother with his eyes wide open. He opens his mouth and signs, with his body twisted with pain. The mother turns him over and presses him firmly against her shoulder,

---

[5] In experimental studies, Bahrick and Watson (1985) were able to show that infants are already able at the age of three months to use the perceived perfect convergence between their bodily actions and the feedback of adults for self-discovery and self-orientation.

supporting his head with one hand. She makes a face that is just as unhappy as his, briefly imitating his crying, "Uhu", and then saying in a tender, comforting voice: "Poor Elias, you feel sick, you're suffering from flatulence!" Elias leans his head on his mother's shoulder, turns his head with a jerking movement, and looks out the window. ... When he becomes restless again, she walks up and down with him. Elias looks back and forth between the window and the Kelim rug with the big patterns hanging on the wall; his mouth is slightly open and he winces repeatedly. Suddenly he wrinkles his forehead, presses his eyes together, opens his mouth and cries. The mother takes him with both hands under his arms, holds him up, looks at his face with a probing gaze and speaks to him: "That hurts so much, that's so sad." Elias stops crying and looks at her. She moves him slowly, playfully up and down, describing what she is doing. She puts him back over her shoulder. Now she moves back and forth more intensely, a mixture of dancing and hopping. After a few minutes Elias becomes restless again and starts crying loudly. In a soft voice she says to him: "Well, well, just cry, that's good for your lungs. You will get strong lungs; you only manage to get me all upset." ... She strokes his hair, kisses him on the head and on his cheeks. Elias reacts to her words and becomes quieter once again. ... When he begins to grumble, she briefly imitates him and tries to comfort him once more by reassuring him: "What makes you so unhappy? Can't you tell me what's wrong with you? Then I'd know what you want. But you can't tell me, you're still too small." She suffers with him, but walks back and forth with him patiently.

(Diem-Wille, 1993: 12)

## Interpretation

It first appears paradoxical that the parents' exaggerated imitation of expressions of negative feelings can calm the baby. Elias's mother only briefly imitates the crying or his sad, pained facial expression. At the same time, it is also evident to the observer how much the mother suffers with Elias. We assume that a complex process of transformation is taking place very quickly in the mother's psyche. The mother presumably does not merely perceive the observed expressions of pain in Elias but also "receives" raw and primitive sensations not thought by him (which Bion [1962a: 8] calls the "Beta elements"), that is, his inchoate fear that he will perish through those sensations. From her behaviour, we could infer that images from her own experience of a comforting, empathetic mother give her the strength for modifying her baby's raw feelings. Through imitating his crying and sounds of lamentation, she affords Elias the possibility of distinguishing these imitated facial expressions from her purely empathetic facial expressions. She picks him up and presses him tightly against her shoulder; that is, he feels his mother's skin against his body and hears her voice speaking to him as if he could already understand the meaning of her words: "Poor Elias, you feel sick, you're suffering from flatulence." One could have the impression that her voice is not only supposed to calm the baby but also her. Only by way of empathy expressed through imitation does a baby seem to be able to experience its own feelings and understand them. Even the mother's helplessness and pain in her wish to spare Elias his own pain can be understood. Calling this process of transformation and inner processing "intuitive" (Papousek and Papousek, 1987: 672) is only correct if one also takes into account the fact that "intuition"—if indeed available—is based on one's own early good experience. The baby also experiences being held, carried around, and pressed firmly against the mother, which helps it to develop and consolidate an inner structure based on the relation between the mother and itself. Also, there are thought processes taking place in the mother that do not only refer to Elias' feelings but also to her own situation, as when she says: "Well, well, just cry, that's good for your lungs. You will get strong lungs; you only manage to get me all upset."

The mother's irony and the playful way in which she deals with her baby's raw feelings and her own state of being are helpful to Elias, since he experiences in his mother a form of distancing instead of being overwhelmed by the pain. It has even been proven through experiments that babies can be calmed much more quickly if negative affect is exaggerated *ad absurdum* or expressed playfully (Malatesta and Izard, 1984).

Elias learns from these emotional experiences with a mother who shows empathy—something Bion (1962a: 8) calls "learning from experience". Elias learns that he is an "unhappy baby", as his mother refers to him, a baby suffering from pain and flatulence, but he is not subject to overwhelming fear because he has a mother who emotionally takes in his pain and "digests" it mentally. These thoughts are not as explicit as when they are expressed in adult language, but they are somatically and mentally tangible, which prompted Daniel Stern (1985: 37) to speak of an "emerging self" that emerges in interaction with the mother. Neurologist Rizzolatti (2006: 31) discovered "mirror neurons", that is, nerve cells that, upon observing an activity, trigger the same potentials that would also occur if this activity were not just being (passively) observed but (actively) performed. At present an entire system of mirror neurons is assumed to exist (Bauer, 2005).

The difference between Bion's conception and that of other developmental psychologists is summed up as follows by O'Shaughnessy (1988: 180): "Bion's hypotheses disagree with theories which view thinking as merely the emergence of maturation or as an autonomous ego function. According to him, K (knowledge GDW) is hard won by the infant ego from emotional experiences with a nurturing object, functioning normally on the reality principle."

In order to be able to think thoughts and to feel feelings the baby is dependent on a thinking individual who transforms its raw sensual perceptions into ideas that can be thought. Bick (1968: 188) has argued that "this containing object is experienced concretely (by the baby GDW) as a skin".

## 4.2   Magical, egocentric thinking, and symbolic equation

### 4.2.1   Thinking in the paranoid-schizoid position

It is impossible to examine here in full detail the various stages in the development of thinking, especially since our primary aim is to show how affective processes are related to thinking, memory, fantasy, and the development of personality. We will thus focus on the two contrary modalities of thinking in the archaic paranoid-schizoid position on the one hand and the integrated depressive position on the other.

Children's abilities were long underestimated. Until quite recently it was assumed that children were not able to identify complex intentional behaviour in others before the age of three to four (Bates, 1979). At present the consensus is that by the end of the first year of life children have the ability to point to something, to change the direction in which they are looking, and to create social references, that is, they are able to attribute attention or emotions to others (Fonagy and Target, 2002: 841).

Freud linked the desire for knowledge with the question as to the origin of life. Curiosity is directed to fundamental human questions. Where do I come from? Where am I going? These questions involve sexual intercourse, which Freud (1909: 155) called the "primal scene", sexual difference, and questions as to birth and death. Children whose sexual curiosity is suppressed or who are deliberately misled by false information attempt to acquire this knowledge through observation, linking memories with the present and fantasy—or they abandon their curiosity and are then inhibited in their thinking.

Melanie Klein (1930) assumed that the small child already develops an interest in its mother's body. The desire to study her body is always mixed with aggressive elements, since the child wants to penetrate the mother's body either in reality or only in fantasy. Klein speaks of a "yearning for knowledge, the object of which is the mother's body with all its phantasized contents. The sadistic phantasies directed against the inside of her body constitute the first and basic relation to the outside world and to reality. Upon the degree of success with which the subject passes through this phase will depend the extent to which he [sic] can subsequently acquire an external world corresponding to reality" (Klein, 1930: 25). Only gradually is the interest in the mother's body channelled by the related fear of damaging her body to other things in the child's environment, thus mitigating the fear. The desire to explore the inside of the mother's body is then expressed in the child by a shift to other objects. It tries to open the lid of a can, to see what is inside a radio, a drawer, or a piggybank. The child often tears open these things to see what is inside. To yield to the yearning for knowledge requires an ability to overcome the related fear (of damaging the mother's body), which is possible if the child's relationship to the mother is good enough. A child who feels secure in its relationship to the mother can also dare to wander and explore the world. An anxious child, whose relation to the mother is insecure, hanging on her "apron strings", is plagued by the unconscious fear of harming the mother with its aggressive fantasies. The separation fears of children who do not want to go to school or to kindergarten are often related to suppressed, aggressive, jealous fantasies towards the mother. These children suppress their aggressive impulses and worry about the mother, speculating that something could happen to her while they are away.

In its early development a child's thinking is characterized by:

- egocentricity;
- magical feelings of omnipotence (fantasy and reality are often not yet clearly distinguished);
- concrete thinking (concepts remain tied to intuition); and
- symbolic equation.

## Egocentricity

A child experiences itself as the centre of the universe. It sees the world as it would like it to be or as it fears it to be. It wants to be loved exclusively by mother and father, and would like everyone around it to serve only the gratification of its needs. This desire to be able to control everyone around it like an absolute monarch, to "have everyone dance to its tune", is accompanied by strong anxieties of disintegration or death. It tames these anxieties by trying to control others. However, it is not the parents' task to respond to the passionate demands conveyed by a child who is screaming its head off, who locks it knees in a fully stretched position, or employs similar bodily signals.

The parents' task is, however, to help the child learn to tolerate its anxieties and be able to develop patience so as to be able to deal with the frustrations of life in small portions. How well the parents are able to do this depends on whether they were able to develop trust in their child and their own parental skills and are able to help it by containing these painful feelings. As simple as this may sound, it is emotionally difficult to receive these projected primitive feelings of the infant without immediately wanting to take action. The witnessing of this intensive emotional resonance between mother/father and baby is one of the most important experiences of Infant Observation. Even if the observer has learned to assume a clear role, that is, observation without intervention, many observers find it difficult to not pick up the baby or calm it. Feelings stemming from primitive phases are triggered in the observer—the "baby in the observer": a fear of starving, of being alone and helpless, of falling apart.

The ability to contain these primitive feelings is only possible if the parent figure/observer has internalized enough good experiences and had someone themselves who heard their crying and who responded to it.

In psychoanalytic literature, egocentricity is usually described in connection with problematic events, for instance when a child has feelings of hate towards the mother or father due to rejection. If this hated person experiences a misfortune, the child will automatically feel responsible. But even in quite everyday situations, children feel as if they are the centre of the universe. The sun rises for them on the horizon; the moon and the stars follow them on their way home; and they believe that the sun and the moon then stand still. In interviews with children, Piaget (1999) discovered that children believe that the sun, moon, and stars are alive and follow only them. They believe that they can make heavenly bodies do the same things that they do, that this is the reason that they move forward—just as the bear Pooh in Winnie-the-Pooh believes that bees make honey only for him, that an expedition will only take place if he wants to go, and so forth. In later life, this basic attitude persists in a milder or slightly modified form when we wish that "every door should remain open to us", that everyone should wait for us.[6] The phenomenon of seeing oneself as the most important person in the world is also presented in advertising—the customer is king. In aristocratic and royal titles this wish to stand above everyone else becomes explicit. Protocols define who ranks highest in a society, what the seating order is, and so on. The superlative of being most important sometimes results in unintended comic situations, for instance when religious and secular ranks collide. A German master of ceremonies once said at a prince's wedding: "At twelve o'clock the illustrious highnesses shall gather in the castle chapel to honor the Lord on high" (Asserate, 2005: 1,290).

Opposed to the belief of being the centre of the universe, there is the desire to explore the world—the three-month-old baby already wishes to discover the world and itself. The movement of legs and arms produces stimuli that are related to this reaction. For instance,

---

[6] In travel groups this wish that everyone should be waiting for me is often staged unconsciously by the usually shy group members when they come too late and all the other members of the travel group have to wait for them.

the child observes the movement of its arms and then touches one hand with the other one (Watson, 1995). It tries to understand the connection between cause and effect, observes moving objects, follows the movements of its parents and siblings, watches acts related to preparing a meal—all this making the child aware of processes following the reality principle. Contradictory perceptions and interpretations of these perceptions emerge, sometimes following the pleasure principle—the child seeing itself as the centre of the universe—more strongly and at other times with greater weight on the reality principle—grasping cause and effect as independent of each other.

The small child is not able yet to be concerned about the needs of others. It sees their *raison d'etre* as merely serving its own needs and well-being, protecting it against pain and anxiety, always being there when needed.

The other side of egocentricity is doubt—whether the individual has any meaning at all. The small child feels inadequate, it cannot keep up with the adults, it is small, and it cannot do much on its own, feels like a little worm, a nothing. Even the fantasy of being the centre of the universe, one of the "favourites of the Gods" and something exceptional is sometimes retained in later life; this manic over-estimation serves to ward off greater insecurity and doubts about one's meaning, which can quickly topple a sense of grandiosity. Being able to realistically assess one's own meaning and being able to accept that one has both assets and limitations is one of the most difficult achievements of mature integration (depressive position).

## Magical feelings of omnipotence

The ability of the infant to summon its parents, to elicit a response from them through its social smile, to get someone to comfort it, feed it, stroke it, and carry it around, all of this could attribute to a sense of omnipotence. By means of hallucinatory wish fulfilment the infant creates gratification in fantasy, a gratification that it desires and does not receive. Later it will seek to continue the fulfilment of wishes in daydreams. It would like to control its parents and all objects in the world, orders everyone and everything around. For Freud magic represents a technique of animism, that is, objects in an environment are perceived as living and are instilled with consciousness.

It (magic) is "the practical for controlling the world around them" (Freud, 1912/13: 74).[7]

The counterpoint to fantasies of omnipotence is the recognition of reality, of one's own dependency and neediness. A life-affirmative attitude entails tolerating the pain of dependence and the satisfaction of one's needs by another person. To this end it is necessary to recognize that another person (mother) has something (milk, love, tenderness) on which the child is dependent. The capability to recognize these gifts derived from the mother culminates in gratitude (Klein, 1957). Another way of dealing with one's own neediness is to deny the experience of painful dependence and to turn to a grandiose fantasy. In an Infant Observation a father commented on the inertia/passivity of his son in sucking the nipple as follows: "He only takes hold of it if he thinks he has come across it by accident. I don't think he likes to feel that he really needs it" (Spillius, 1993: 1,281). It was clear that the parents had understanding for the baby's attitude. The father interpreted and probably projected his own feelings onto the son, namely that a child does not want to have much to do with this "other", this "non-I" thing from which it gets its milk. The more difficult it is for the child to accept its dependence and concede to the parents their control over what it needs, the more difficult it is for the child to accept what is offered. Melanie Klein's assumption that babies from birth on have a tendency to express envy or display outspoken envy provoked a storm of disagreement. This perspective focusing on the baby's temperament, however, constitutes an important dimension in assessing whether a baby is "easygoing", whether it accepts what is offered and is then satisfied, or whether it is possible only with great effort to make a "difficult" baby accept affection, milk, and care. How well a child manages to accept all that the parents offer it depends also on the child's temperament. It must be acknowledged that the parents are a source of good, of food, of love, and of support, and that they have something the child needs and on

---

[7] Freud distinguished between three world views—the animistic (or mythological) one, the religious one, and the scientific one. "They people the world with innumerable spiritual beings both benevolent and malignant, and these spirits and demons they regard as the causes of natural phenomena and they believe that not only animals and plants but all the inanimate objects in the world are animated by them" (Freud, 1912/13: 75).

which it is dependent. If patience and sufficient positive conditions of care and love prevail, the child will succeed in accepting this good and also be grateful for it (cf. Spillius, 1993).

"Magical thinking is the most original way of thinking in the world before the emergence of words." writes Fraiburg (1980: 79). Rational thought processes can only evolve with the development of language. At the beginning of language acquisition words have a magical meaning, but at the same time the child is introduced to the new laws of language, the rational meaning independent of the child.

Until the age of four, recognition of reality is accompanied by pre-conceptual, intuitive thinking, as Piaget described. From observations of his own children he elucidates the mode of explanation typical of the age of four with the following example: "At the age of four-and-a-half, J. said: "The clouds move very slowly, because they have no feet or legs. They make themselves as long as worms and caterpillars, which is why they move so slowly"" (Piaget, 1969: 317). Even animistic thought remains active to the age of six, as Piaget (1969: 317) illustrates with an example: "As the wind slammed shut the door of the chicken coop and she screamed out of fright: "It is evil, the wind, it frightens us." "But not on purpose?" "Yes, on purpose. It is evil, it said that we were evil." "But doesn't the wind know what it does?" "It knows that it blows.""

## Concrete thinking and symbolic equation

Hanna Segal (1991: 41) calls the primitive form of symbolization "symbolic equation", since this is linked with concrete thinking. We understand concrete thinking to mean that a symbol is equated with the object symbolized. The symbol, that is, a word, and what it stands for are not yet differentiated. In proper symbolization, the word is felt to represent the object. The word for the object is seen as something distinct from the object. The speaker then knows that "bear" is the word for a real bear.

Adult patients or children who are caught up in concrete thinking perceive spoken words to be objects or actions. A child who has heard the story of a crocodile and perhaps has an unconscious anxiety that (in its fantasy), a crocodile will destroy its mother's babies in her womb, will be afraid when going to sleep because it believes that a crocodile or a robber is lying under its bed. It is helpful for the parents to know that they must look under the bed with the child to make sure together that there is no monster lurking below.

If an analyst or other person speaks of the fear of witches or crocodiles, the child or other disturbed patient may see it as confirming its fears, that is, that there is really a crocodile or witch in the room. A patient, for instance, experienced his analyst as "black Indian" after he had become annoyed with her during a session and "saw" her face turning black (a hallucination) in his anger. A writer who underwent analysis because she suffered from writer's block could not write when "she began experiencing words as fragments of objects". Another borderline patient often could not read because she believed that "the words would jump out of the page and bite her eyes" (Segal, 1957: 51). These examples may first seem unsettling because they show a completely deranged psychological state, which differs completely from "normal thinking". Freud (1905: 40) makes clear that the boundary, assumed to be absolute, between "normal" and "mentally ill" differs in its intensity, and he was able to show that adults in a crises sometimes regress to hallucinatory wishful thinking, delusion, or concrete thinking, all of which are part of the normal development of a child. In healthy children there is also a potential for further development in the case of developmentally related symbolic equation—for instance, the word "crocodile" being identified with an actual crocodile hiding under its bed. When children rely on their parents to help them to sort this out, their anxiety can gradually be diminished. However, if the idea remains or becomes consolidated—for example, if a child is convinced that there are evil spirits in the cellar caused by unconscious inner conflicts—a childhood phobia develops, prompting the child to avoid that place.

Klein (1926) understood children's play as a symbolic expression of unconscious conflicts and was thus able to explore the early development of the inner world in infancy. The idea of one child—that it could come to embody an object's qualities by eating that object—was illustrated by a scene from a child analysis: "The four-year-old boy made snowflakes out of pieces of paper which he tossed about in the room and pretending to eat them. Then he suddenly stopped and asked worried whether people who swallowed snowflakes would become real snowflakes and would melt" (Caper, [1988]2000: 165). In the child's mind the symbolized snowflakes became concrete snowflakes, and they would then take revenge for being swallowed by giving him their own qualities—so that he, too, was in danger of melting.

The child is not yet able to see early symbols as a substitute but perceives them as the equation of the object. According to psychoanalysis, a child's ability to shift the interest from its mother's body and its own body to other objects in the environment always depends on the quality of the child's relations to its first caregivers, usually the mother and the father. In accordance with Charles Morris (1938), we can speak of a triadic relation (three-term relation), that is, a relation between the thing symbolized, the thing functioning as a symbol, and a person for whom the one represents the other. When given affectionate care from its parents, the infant experiences considerable attention given to its bodily excretions, that is, it is cleaned, bathed, and oiled and its nappies are changed. It follows its bodily excretions with great interest, is attentive and concentrated when urinating or defecating. If it has the opportunity to observe what comes out of its body, outdoors or in the bathroom, it will not just want to look but also touch to get a better idea of the substance and the smell. Parents of course try to keep the child from experimenting directly with its excrement and provide it, for example, with different containers in order to play with the bath water instead of its urine. The child thus transfers feelings of bodily products to ersatz materials. On the one hand, the child associates these excrements with positive feelings, with something that it produced, for instance, a large puddle or a pile, and on the other, it gives them aggressive connotations, as tools of attack or defence, for example, urine and faeces as projectiles or weapons. The ray of water, the sand, the kneading mass, putty, clay, and so on are used in both dimensions, either as material for playing, studying, and creative representation or as weapon, when clay balls are thrown, other children are splashed with a ray of water or driven away. In her short story "Making Poison", Margaret Atwood describes how all poisonous things merge to form a dangerous venom:

> When I was five my brother and I made poison ... we put all the poisonous things into it that we could think of: toadstools, dead mice, mountain ash berries which may not have been poisonous but looked it, piss which we saved up in order to add it to the

paint can. By the time the can was full everything in it was very poisonous ... Why did we make the poison in the first place? I can remember the glee with which we stirred and added the sense of magic and accomplishment. Making poison is as much fun as making a cake. People like to make poison. If you don't understand this you will never understand anything.

(Atwood, 1997: 11f)

Atwood can stay in touch with her childlike magical thinking where toadstools, berries, and urine are gleefully mixed into a poisonous drink. Old magical potions, alchemical concoctions, work with these symbolic analogies.

Even in normal development, the close relation between the ego and symbolized objects remains intact, for instance in the pleasurable activity with water or clay. However, this is only possible if the anal pleasure in toilet training was not replaced by disgust. If the child is not able to experience the affectionate response and empathy of the parents or caregivers, it will hardly develop interest in its own body and in objects of the world, and will remain disinterested and passive. Fraiberg (1980a: 46) wrote:

> Small children in clean homes where they have experienced no maternal love do not feel attracted to objects, they feel no pleasure or excitement in their discoveries ... Since people cannot give them any pleasure, there is also no pleasure outside of their bodies.

If the relationship of the child to their important caregivers is deeply disturbed, the problem of inhibited symbolization can also appear: the child then is so anxious that its development is inhibited in play, language, and relations to the persons around it. This will be addressed in greater detail in Section 4.4 "Mental and Emotional Disturbances".

The early form of symbolization is closely related to language development. Language establishes a special connection between the individual and the given linguistic community. Between the child and its mother, language acquisition also constitutes something that separates them but which also links them on a new level.

Here we cannot go into more detail regarding the various theories of language development (cf. Gori, 1977; Greenson, 1954; Pelikan, 2004). We can only explore this to the extent it affects the process of symbolization.

The small child first develops sounds that have a dual meaning. The ability to produce various sounds with the lips, the tongue, and the larynx is part of the child's exploration of the body and its possibilities. In addition to crying, which expresses states of tension, pain, and unease, there are sounds of pleasure and well-being. The child then experiences that its parents can attribute meaning to these sounds and receive them as a form of communication, so that the baby is able to link its—probably innate—desire to establish contact to the real contact it experiences, as well as reaction to this real contact. The first "words" such as *mamama* and later *papapa* are understood in many languages as referring to "mother" and "father", but they are initially used by the baby to also name a variety of objects and activities. Objects the baby sees have an imperative character—it does not distinguish between animate and inanimate objects. As in fairytales, objects "speak" to the child—"Touch me," "Shake me," "Put me in your mouth." The child's attention is initially only short-lived since it is attracted to every object, especially if brightly coloured—even if the child was occupied with something else beforehand. Up to the age of eight months, an object that disappears from the baby's sight is also emotionally gone. The saying "out of sight, out of mind" refers to this phenomenon, which later primarily serves as an unconscious defence against psychic pain. If the father hides the glasses the baby is reaching for behind a pillow, the baby, up to the age of eight months, will only look surprised. From the ninth month on it will try to find the glasses behind the pillow. It has remembered the object. If the father then hides the glasses at a different location it will look for the glasses again in the same place where they were first hidden.[8]

---

[8] Piaget (1999: 110) describes this behaviour of a child at the age of eight to eleven months as the "A-not-B mistake". Even though the child has seen that an object was first hidden at place "A" and then at place "B", it looks for it at "A", as in the first successful attempt to find the hidden object. Piaget argues that the child still sees the object in a more comprehensive sense as part of its own action. The modes of action, that is, the fact that it found the object at "A", counts more than the perception of having seen it disappear at "B". Dornes' book *Early Childhood* (2001) deals in greater detail with Piaget and his followers (see especially pp. 107ff).

Only a few weeks later is it able to remember two or more hiding places. It knows that the object continues to exist, even when it is gone—something Piaget (1999: 56) called "object permanence". The baby begins to develop constant concepts of a real world (cf. Fraiberg, 1969: 9f.). The absent object or human being is only then fantasized by the baby, for instance, as the "bad" mother, if it wants at this very moment to be fed, comforted, calmed by this mother/breast and this wish is not fulfilled.

Here we can only mention the extensive discussion on the question of whether a baby develops "inner images" and if so whether the expectation of the mother triggers a visual image of the still absent mother (cf. Dornes, 2001a). Melanie Klein (1952) assumes a "remembering in feelings", by which she does not mean the sum of all real experiences that this person (object) can trigger (as Piaget argues) but also the loving and aggressive contacts experienced by this person in their fantasy. At the age of eighteen months, the small child develops a higher form of thinking—logical thinking. It discovers that it is not the creator of all things but that the causes of certain events are located outside. How do all these complex and often contradictory developments come to fruition in the small child? How can we imagine this development of thinking in close association with a caregiver? In the following passage, I would like to describe and then interpret a scene from an Infant Observation.

## Observation of Felix at the age of sixteen months

Felix is sitting on the floor in the kitchen, while his mother is cooking. In his right hand he holds a longish, empty paper box and in his left hand he has an empty towel roll. He looks at both in alternation, and then throws away the box and takes the roll with both hands. He holds it to his mouth like a wind instrument without blowing into it. Then he holds it only with his right hand and sticks the fingers of his right hand in his mouth. The mother has watched him doing this; she sits down on the floor across from him and imitates the sound of a trumpet: "Tiri-tiri-tri!" (In one octave.). "Do it." While the mother is making these sounds, Felix looks at her with interest, and then puts the roll to his mouth again. "Yes, do it, right," the mother urges him. The mother has gotten up in the meantime and clears away the father's clothes. Felix now does "Tiri-tr-tri" into his roll and laughs mischievously. The mother says: "Yes, that's right," and sings once again in response: "Tiri-tri-tri." Felix has turned to the side, lifting his "wind instrument" high in the air like a jazz musician and laughing. Since he is sitting close to a writing board that is hanging on the kitchen wall, he bangs on it twice with his kitchen roll, all the while laughing. He then turns to the front, glances as if by chance at his mother who keeps watching him, and beams over his entire face. Now he moves his fingers as if he were playing the clarinet, his gaze fixed on his mother, and emphatically blows his "Tiri-tri-tri." "Very good," his mother says, full of admiration. Felix smiles, turns his eyes away, takes the "trumpet" from his mouth and bangs with it on the paper box next to him. The mother says to him: "Please put your bottle up." His bottle lies next to him. Felix looks at his kitchen towel roll, moves it farther away and then says: "There!" The mother repeats her request, asks him to stand his bottle up. Felix does not let the towel roll out of his hands, but he directs his gaze to the bottle. The mother repeats in a friendly voice: "Please put the bottle up." Felix places the towel roll on the ground, points his left hand to the bottle, and says: "There!" while he looks at his mother with his mouth wide open. She now says emphatically: "Put it up!" Felix now unintentionally moves the bottle further away with his towel roll. Then he moves the towel roll standing on the floor back and forth and watches closely what happens when he bangs it very hard on the floor, making a loud sound. "Put it up, sweetie," his mother says imploringly. Felix looks at her only briefly to then continue banging the roll and looking at it, then he turns his gaze with curiosity towards his mother as if he wanted to find out what she will now do. He takes the bottle with the nipple facing downward and presses the towel roll and the bottle closely to his chest, presses his lips together and looks at his mother full of expectation. "Good," says the mother, "I did not say pick it up, but put it up." While the mother is saying that, she moves closer to Felix and sits down across from him, with Felix observing closely. She says twice: "Put it on the floor!" gesturing what she has just said with her hands. Felix stares stiffly at the floor and holds both objects pressed against him. The mother laughs, crawls on all fours, reaches for the bottle and pulls it slowly towards herself. Felix looks at the bottle, while the mother takes it slowly and places it in front of him on the floor. She puts the bottle on the ground demonstratively, saying, "Put it up." Then she says: "Now it is standing." Felix looks at the bottle and notices some milk drops that have dropped onto the ground next to the bottle; he points at it with his finger and says, full of awe: "There." The mother puts the bottle away and passes a towel to Felix with which he then energetically wipes the floor, never losing sight of the milk drops. He also wipes his shoes. The mother has come closer, laughs at him and points at a further milk drop between his legs. She points to it and asks: "And what about this?" Felix bends over with concentration to also wipe away these drops. Then he lifts the towel up high and looks at the spot where the milk drop had been. The mother has stayed with him, observing his cleaning and commenting on it with "good boy". Felix thrusts himself forward and crawls around the table towards the mother, the towel in one hand and the towel roll in the other. He turns around so that he touches his mother's knee with his back, bends forward and once again wipes the floor, letting the towel roll fall. The mother points to further milk drops and says: "Look there, look, there is a bit more."

> Since Felix sits and does not react, she takes the towel out of his hand in a friendly way, saying, "I'll show you." She wipes the floor around Felix with a large circular motion, and then puts the towel on the table. Felix observes her movement, but when his gaze falls on the towel roll, he picks it up with both hands. The mother puts the bottle on a chair, saying: "Look, I'm putting it here now." Felix immediately scuttles to the bottle, grabs it after briefly glancing at his mother, turns it around and lets milk drip out of it. "No, no, no," the mother says in passing and takes the bottle out of Felix's hands. Felix observes the milk drops that have fallen on the floor and he touches the ground— with a gleeful squeal. The mother stands up with the bottle in her hand and goes away. Felix also stands up and follows her.

(Barnett, 1985)

## Interpretation

In this short sequence lasting less than five minutes, complex interactions and complex cognitive processes take place. First Felix focuses on two objects, throwing one away and concentrating on the empty paper towel roll. He studies its weight, holds it in his hand, and points it to his mouth but then ends up sticking his finger in his mouth. The kitchen roll seems to keep becoming a greater part of him, which he can move and control as he likes. Only when his mother sits down across from him and imitates the sounds of a trumpet does the interesting kitchen roll become something different: a symbol of a trumpet. A process of communication unfolds between Felix and his mother. She has observed how he holds the towel roll against his mouth; she sits down next to him and introduces something new with her "tiri-tri-tri", namely, a symbolized trumpet. With her praise and recognition of Felix the mother gives him the incentive to distinguish between the towel roll as such and towel roll as a trumpet. The playful interaction culminates in a rhythmic musical performance, which is something both Felix and his mother can enjoy and laugh at. He makes this perform-ance for his mother, and in so doing experiences how he can gain her love and recognition. It becomes an act of joint music-making. When Felix uses the towel roll as a percussion instrument, he learns that he is supposed to make sounds with it. The exploration of the towel roll, its material qualities and its symbolic use as a trumpet, is interrupted by the mother's asking him to set the bottle down in an upright position. The mother patiently repeats her request, she tries to prompt him to act first with her words. His looking at the bottle shows that he can link the word "bottle" with the correct object. He also points to the bottle and associates it with a "there" in the sense of recognition. However, it is the affects associated with the move-ment of the towel roll that dominate. Felix uses the roll to move the bottle, but does not let it go. Even though Felix shows that he can understand his mother's words, the appeal of the "instrument" gen-erating sounds is stronger. The bottle probably reminds him of milk and perhaps also nursing. Felix grabs the roll and the bottle and presses both firmly to him. The mother stays in contact with Felix and his actions; she smiles at him and praises him for actually hav-ing grasped the bottle. His gaze seems to express that he somehow "knows" that he is not doing what his mother expects of him. With his reaction he "draws" his mother closer to him. She sits down to him and speaks emphatically. With great empathy, the mother tries to convey to Felix the meaning of her request; she not only repeats her sentence but also shows with a gesture how to place the bottle, showing it by doing it herself and then showing Felix what it looks like when the bottle is standing.

In the third part of the scene Felix once again takes the initiative. He sees the milk drops on the floor, they attract his interest and he communicates this new theme to his mother by pointing to it and saying "there". Felix seems to be falling back on earlier experiences. When his mother gives him a towel he immediately begins wiping away the milk drops. The focused gaze reflects the "scientific" interest in whether the wiping and the disappearance of the milk drops have something to do with each other. The mother helps him wipe and tries to return to the issue of placing the bottle, but with no success. Felix seems to want to continue his exploration of the hypothesis that milk drops come out of the bottle. He turns the bottle upside down and observes how milk drops emerge from it. Even though the mother says "no" and gently pulls away the bottle, he squeals with glee when he touches the newly created milk drops on the floor.

In this brief sequence important foundations are laid for learning language, the first experiences made with symbolization and communication. The child repeatedly hears the same sentences from the mother and learns how it can make the mother laugh or how it can annoy her, how he can draw his mother closer, or how she alternatively reacts to it. The objects are no longer just objects but also begin to assume a symbolic meaning. The child begins experiencing the reality principle by noticing how milk drips from the bottle and that it can repeat this process by holding the bottle upside down. His movements and sounds have meaning, causing things to move and generating sounds. Just as the mother is interested in Felix, Felix is also interested in things, moving them or holding them firmly pressed to himself. The drops have such a great meaning that everything else recedes into the background—they must be touched, looked at, wiped away, and created anew. In the entire sequence Felix's exploration of the world takes place in close contact with his mother who comments and encourages his movements and cognitive achievements. It is clearly visible how elements of magical thinking blend with the reality principle, namely the study of how things relate (letting milk drip out of the bottle). When we next focus on the mature mode of thinking we will again recall that the modality of thinking in the paranoid-schizoid position, the special constellation of anxieties, magical thinking, and animism in a deeper layer of our personality remains alive and more or less strongly influences not only our attitude to the external world but also the matrix that governs our way of thinking.

## 4.3    Logical thinking based on the reality principle (thinking in the depressive position)

Mature thinking is characterized by the knowledge of the difference between self and object, and that between internal reality and external reality, an accepting of the reality principle and causality, and having the ability to symbolize. The fantasized omnipotent control of other persons and things is replaced by knowledge of being a separate person and having the capacity to endure the grief connected with this knowledge. The child can also accept the different quality of their sexual relation and their parental love.

The emergence of logical thinking based on the reality principle takes place slowly and continuously alongside the primitive, magical thinking based on the pleasure principle. We assume that from the beginning of life there exists a rudimentary perception of what is real. The experience of pleasurable drinking to satisfy hunger has a different quality when it is combined with love and affection or accompanied by an emotionally unavailable and absent-minded mother. Hearing the mother's voice, smelling her specific odour, constitute for Bion (1962a: 91) an important link between preconception and real experience which enable a concept of the breast, of the voice, of smell to emerge. In addition to the egocentric idea that the movement of an object is caused by one's wishing or acting, we think that there are also traces of another perception, an awareness of the movement of objects or of individuals caused by themselves. Both of these forms of thinking can exist parallel to each other for several years. The intense attention and concentration shown by small children in observing and exploring things and connections takes two directions: outwards, to observe and perceive, and inwards, where models are formed for processing perceptions. Various basic "hypotheses" are examined as ways to explain these phenomena. When we speak of "hypotheses", then these appear in the first years of life as unconscious fantasies of objects or contexts that must first be examined on the basis of perceptions in the external world—in this way, the small child is able to learn from its experiences or, in Bion's (1962: 92) words, to acquire "living knowledge". Caper (1999: 73) writes: "Unconscious phantasy is an essential component of learning from experience, since one of the major ways in which we learn about reality is by posing hypotheses about it in the form of phantasies, then testing them against perception."

In normal, healthy development, encountering reality leads to a modification of hallucinatory wishes and those hypotheses that follow only the pleasure principle, and to an acknowledgement of reality. The one-a-half year old Ella, for instance, observed how someone who put his clothes in a travel bag then went away. When she watches her father packing clothes in a bag before he leaves for the hospital to have minor surgery, she carries the travel bag into her bedroom and begins to pack her clothes, toys, and sleeping blanket. With this, she is saying that she wants to travel with him.

In order to express this wish, she uses her rudimentary knowledge about cause and effect. Her emotional message—namely, that she does not want to be separated from her father—moved the father every time he found her small socks or stuffed animal at the hospital. For Ella it was a painful but important learning process that her father had removed almost all of her clothing from the bag and that her magical ritual could not save her from the painful separation. Her almost inconsolable weeping seemed to emerge from two sources—one of them being grief over being separated from her father for three days, and the other the grief that her overreaching fantasies could not be fulfilled. The parents helped her to deal with both psychological problems and to learn from the experience.

In psychoanalysis, the ability to symbolize is an ability of the ego which, with its anxieties, develops to symbols instead of continuing to focus on the mother's body and its contents. In her "Notes on Symbol Formation" Hanna Segal (1957: 52) writes:

> Symbol formation starts very early, probably as early as object relations, but changes its character and function with the changes in the character of the ego and the object relations.

> Not only the actual content of the symbol but the very way in which symbols are formed and used seems to reflect precisely the ego's state of development and its way of dealing with its objects. If symbolism is seen as a three-term relation, problems of symbol formation must be examined in the context of the ego's retaliation.

The ability to think in a mature, logical form and to symbolize thus depends on emotional maturity and on experiencing not only oneself as an individual separate from the mother, but also the caregivers as individuals in their own right with their good and bad qualities— as "whole objects" and not just as "part objects". At the same time, ambivalent feelings, those of love and hate, envy and gratitude, can be felt, and fear of the possible loss of the both loved and hated person perceived. These intensely ambivalent feelings trigger grief and the wish to "repair" the damaged person in fantasy. Under favourable, normal developmental conditions, the awareness of internal and external reality will grow. Instead of wanting to completely control people important to it, the child focuses on the question of how it can protect the loved parents from its aggressions and its wish to possess them. It also begins to consider the parents' situation and their needs—something Winnicott (1963: 73) has described as the "ability to show concern".

How quickly, however, the mature form is given up in favour of an egocentric perspective is illustrated by the following scene. A girl who had just started school sometimes vomited in the evening because of her nervousness. She complained to her grandmother and said that she would prefer to still attend kindergarten. She said that she would rather be only three years old and be starting kindergarten. The brother, two years younger, listened attentively, briefly reflected, and said that he would then be two years older than she— she would be three and he five. The sister didn't want that. "No," she said, "then you would be only one year old." The girl was able to express her wish to be younger. However, in response to the idea of being two years younger than her brother, she replaced logic with an egocentric perspective, letting him become younger just as herself.

Winnicott (1951: 229) used the phrase "transitional object" or "transitional phenomenon" to refer to the transition from symbolic equation to a symbol proper. A child's stuffed animal or soft blanket stands for the mother's warmth and her protection, helping it to sleep. This object stands, as it were, halfway between a concrete identification with a stuffed animal and mother—it is not the mother, but instead recalls her. The child in part knows that the blanket is only an ersatz for the mother, but denies this in order to be able to find the blanket just as good as she is. If the transitional object, for example, a bottle, is more important or even better than the person to be replaced, then there is a symbolic identification or it becomes an "autistic object":

> When these transitional objects slide over into becoming all-important, just as good as—or better than—the real human mother, enabling the child to ignore permanently and chronically this mother and the need for a living human being, they become symbolic equations, or autistic objects.

> (Alvarez, 1992: 44)

In this way children can keep the illusion of having control over their object, and they avoid relationships with other persons, love and pain, frustration and happiness, rejection and exclusion—that is to say, psychic pain. Such an autistic retreat only takes place in the face of massive frustration, painful experiences, and the simultaneous lack of even minimal gratification over an extended period of time. If an adequate emotional foundation has been laid, it might be difficult to get the child away again from its "possession" of a transitional object, for example, its bottle, but this can succeed if the child is provided adequate psychological and physical contact with its parents. It is thus not advisable, from a certain age, to let the child always drink alone with its bottle—on the one hand, the feeling of absolute control can emerge, whereas the linking of feeding with the psychological availability with the mother or father is weakened.

Language can also serve as a transitional object, as when the child tells itself a story before going to sleep, babbling this story in the intonation of the parents' narration. The child talks to itself, it seems: in its imagination it is both one parent and the baby to whom the story is told (cf. Cavell, 1997; Pelinka, 2004). It can thus lull itself to sleep with the help of melodic rhythms.

I would like to use a scene with Felix and his parents to illustrate the close connection between the child's emotional bond with its parents and the learning of a language as a medium of symbolization.

## Felix at seventeen months looking at a picture book

Felix is sitting on his father's lap, his mother is sitting next to him and is holding a picture book towards Felix. She points at a picture. Felix says: "(C) at." The mother repeats: "Yes, that is a cat." Felix says: "P(r)etty." The mother nods and says: "Yes, that is pretty, it's a flower." Felix grabs the book, points at something, then takes the book from his mother's hand and thumbs through it. He leans back, resting on his father's chest, holding the book in his hands. The mother reaches for Felix, and the father moves his face towards Felix's face. Felix smiles at his father, sits up, and the father smiles back. In the meantime the mother has taken the book again and moved to the next page which she holds at Felix, even though he is still looking towards his father in the opposite direction. Then Felix quickly turns around, points to the picture and says clearly: "Baby." The mother says smiling: "That's right." While leafing through the book Felix already forms a "u" and looks with great concentration at the next picture. Felix says: "Yes." The mother waits a few seconds. Since Felix says nothing and continues to look at the picture, she says: "Brush." Felix immediately touches his hair. The father observes the two of them and gives Felix the freedom to move on his lap.

The mother says: "Yes, the brush is for hair, to comb." On the next page there is something that Felix calls "Uh". The mother says: "Shoe—that's right." Felix first points to the mother's shoes, then bends forward, from where he can see the father's shoes. With an extended index finger he points to the father's shoes; the mother also looks at the father's shoes. In the meantime Felix's attention is directed to the father's wristwatch. The mother also points to the shoes, in response to which Felix briefly turns his attention back to the mother but he then bangs on the father's watch and says: "Ticktack." The father says: "That's a ticktack, a watch." Felix directs his father's hand with the watch to his ear and listens with bated breath. While Felix listens, the father imitates the sound of a ticking watch. Felix's mouth is wide open with tension and he listens with great interest. Suddenly he bursts out laughing and the father joins his laughter and puts his arm down again. Felix leans back with pride and joy, producing sounds of enthusiasm, such as: "Ah, oh" and laughing. The father now takes the book. Felix has put a finger of his left hand in his mouth and leans on the father who has turned a page. Felix's head rests on his father's shoulders. He takes his finger out of his mouth and sits up, with his gaze remaining tethered to the book.

(Barnett, 1985)

## Interpretation

Felix lives in two worlds, the magic world in which he is the centre of the universe, and the real world, in which he is a child among a million other children. He is a small child who still has a lot to learn—right now, the first abstractions of learning a language that he will then be able to use in communication. Felix feels and knows that he is the central focus of his parents' attention, although he might have a faint idea that the way his mother and father spend a night together could have a different quality. He can leave these thoughts in the background even if in the morning when greeting his parents he wildly shoves himself between father and mother to move them apart. He feels his father's skin touching him, his arms with which he holds him, which leaves a memory trace or a "somatic sensation" (Caper, 2000: 162).

Klein (1957: 180) describes these early experiences as follows:

When these pre-verbal notions and phantasies are revived in the transference situation, they appear as memories in feeling, as I would call them, and are reconstructed and put into words with the help of the analyst. In the same way, words have to be used when we are reconstructing and describing other phenomena belonging to the early stages of development. In fact we cannot translate the language of the unconscious without lending it words from our consciousness.

The picture book is an object Felix loves, with which he associates many positive, happy experiences he has had while looking at it. In fact, a love of books is already established in these early years of life. A child who in the first two years of life already makes use of a picture book in order to understand the world with the help of its parents will also be able to build on this positive experience in later life.[9] The first image, namely that of a cat, is familiar to Felix, since he lives with a large black cat. Before he could even say "mama", he could at six months mimic the meow of the cat so precisely that his parents had to laugh. Referring to a flower, Felix first did not say "flower" but "nice"—he was probably able to remember his mother's countless references that taught him to smell a flower instead of pulling or picking it, saying "nice flower". Felix then takes the book; he wants to decide when the page is to be turned. The mother leafs back, and before Felix says "baby" he quickly becomes a small baby, cuddling up on his father's chest. Felix succeeds in establishing a link between the individual images and the concrete objects named, and also making his first abstractions.

> The concept "brush" is associated with hair that is combed with the brush. The image of a shoe does not imply a certain shoe; it refers to all shoes, both the father's shoe and the mother's shoe. While looking at the picture book Felix trains logical, abstract thinking. At the same time he is the centre of both of his parents' attention, who respond affectionately to him and confirm all his words—which could be seen as confirming his egocentric world view. He is the one who prompts his parents to act this way, and at the same time he accepts his parents' love and pride which help to strengthen his sense of self-esteem and his ego, which in turn helps his orientation to reality and reduces his libidinous wishes, since he experiences a real confirmation of his efforts. In these playful interactions, these everyday actions, Felix also learns about the meaning of words: brushing hair, putting on shoes. When Felix bends down and moves close to a ticking watch, his attention is drawn to it. Felix grabs his father's arm

---

[9] Early promotion of reading lays the foundation for the love of books. In the German province of Saxony parents are given information about the importance of reading books out loud to children to promote their linguistic development. Together with the foundation *Lesen* (Reading) a campaign with the name "Bookstart" that was started in Great Britain is carried out. One book is given to parents as a gift along with recommendations on reading to children. Even paediatricians are to be made aware of the dual importance of reading to children—strengthening a good, deep emotional relation to the parents and also promoting a child's linguistic development (Die Zeit, 2006: 45).

and thus moves the watch closer to his ear—a gesture that the father has probably already often made with Felix. The question now is what makes the ticking sound. Is it the watch that Felix presses to his ear or is it the father? In Felix's and his father's laughter it becomes clear that Felix does indeed notice that his father too has imitated the ticking. It is a complex process, a cognitive, emotional, and social one. Felix then puts his finger in his mouth, something which he himself can do and control. He has briefly regressed to an earlier form of soothing himself, but then he is again the seventeen-month-old boy—he sits up and takes his finger out of his mouth.

## 4.3.1    Linguistic development

Since words can replace elements of magical thinking, words can be used in the transitional phase like "magical formulas" (Fraiberg, 1980a: 83). The word replaces an act (Fraiberg, 1980: 85) and can establish a new contact. When Felix said "nice" when looking at the flower, we can assume that he used this word instead of touching a flower. In place of physical contact, he created contact by means of words—a unique human achievement. The child can communicate with others in a new way, but in so doing loses, as Stern noted, a quality of immediacy. Learning to speak is a double-edged sword. On the one hand, messages become clearer and easier to understand for others, but on the other hand, what is termed with language as "abstract understanding" overlaps with original experience. Certain realms of feeling, of subjective states and physical manifestations, recede into the background when a child is able to express itself with language. Thus, as Stern (1985: 173f) emphasizes, the acquisition of language presents both "a new way of being related to others" and also "has an alienating effect on self-experience and togetherness".

For parents and educators, it is important to understand that in the first three years of its life a child lives in two worlds at the same time—what we call the magical one and the real one. It is important to make things and processes that are called by name also visible and tangible or to let the child experience them. It is not enough, for instance, to tell the child that its parents will go away and that a babysitter will take care of it. A recurring ritual of parting is necessary in which the child, holding the babysitter's arm, watches the parents say goodbye, receives a kiss and wave from them and is able also say "goodbye" and to wave back. Just as important is the ritual of greeting the parents when they return, in order to give the child the possibility of processing the separation and the return in an emotional and cognitive way. Even when the small child cries when its parents leave and shows that it would rather stay with the mother or father, it is especially important for the adults to tolerate this pain. The alternative that many parents, kindergarten teachers, and educators opt for— namely, advising the parents to sneak away—is unhelpful. On the contrary, it is very confusing because the child constantly lives with the fear that the parents could simply disappear. Often the small children begin to cry when they see the person who is supposed to look after them in their parents' absence, the babysitter or the grandmother, and cling to their mother. The mother's assurance—"I'm not leaving yet" is irrelevant for the child. It only truly comprehends the situation when it knows that it will be waving goodbye when the parents leave, and that it will be present when the parents return.

## 4.4   Mental and emotional disturbances

Although it is obvious how intimately linked emotional development is with thinking, it is difficult to say how psychic disturbances can evolve. Certainly, a problematic relation with the parents does not automatically have a negative impact on the child's capacity to think. An intense preoccupation with inanimate objects or, later, with images and books can have a compensatory effect. Even in such severe manifestations of psychological deprivation such as autism and Asperger's syndrome, special abilities can evolve, such as the ability to calculate with great speed, a photographic memory, or mathematic talent.[10] By

---

[10] At a meeting of the Psychiatric Association in New York, psychiatrist Dr. Horwitz presented the twenty-four year-old twin brothers Gela and Uscht who were mentally retarded, spoke like six-year-olds, and were also incapable of doing the simplest calculations but were able to perform extraordinary memory feats. They were, for instance, capable of immediately in split-second time saying the right day of the week for each date, be it in the past or future. Even though they had had no history lessons, they instinctively knew the birth dates of famous figures and, if asked to do so, they could also immediately say how old these individuals would be today. They could also say what the weather had been like on a certain day for each day of their life (Sacks, 1985: 185ff).

the same token, in the analytic treatment of seemingly unintelligent children, blocked mental faculties disappeared once the underlying anxieties were interpreted. In the first analysis of a psychotic boy, Dick, treated by Melanie Klein (1946), she was able to eliminate his inhibitions in thinking and playing through revealing his underlying anxieties and making them comprehensible. In other cases, children in analysis proved to be excellent in school, to show an interest in sophisticated subject matter that went far beyond that of their age group, but also to be lonely and to suffer from anxiety and nightmares.

Freud (1923: 19) showed what psychic efforts are required in order to protect thinking from the influences of primary processes so that it is not distracted. At the same time, archaic thinking was later referred to by Freud (1923: 45) as the "id"—the seat of creativity. Every metaphor draws for its figurative thought on the id. For artists, the unconscious is a source from which themes and expressive modes are derived. In children, play is an important means for expressing unconscious wishes, ideas, conflicts, and anxieties.

How can a boundary be drawn between normal development and developmental disturbance? Wishes and the need to capture all attention can be so strong up until the age of seven or eight that a child's narrated stories tend to reflect more the wishes than actual reality. Anna Freud (1965) emphasized that it is important to describe this phenomenon not as lying, but as spinning tales, expressive of a child's wishes. It helps such a child when adults do not get angry over its "tale-spinning" but instead help the child to understand that these fantasy stories are an expression of its wishes. For example, a seven-year-old boy, whom I will call Karim, told a "fisherman's story" after he had been fishing for two hours at sea and had not caught any fish. He said that he had caught three fish and in each time he told the story his tale became ever more elaborate. When catching the second fish the hook had become so twisted that he had to cut it and his friend Max had given him a new fishhook. He demonstrated the size of the fish and tried to make his story credible. The next day, he asked his grandmother to go fishing with him, which she did. He then succeeded in actually catching a fish, which made him happy. On the way home he admitted that he had invented the tale he had told the previous day, "just for a joke", since he had wanted to catch a fish. Without adults explicitly doubting his story, after his success in actually catching a fish he could recognize his wish to have caught one already the first day and was able to correct his fantasy story tale.

The important difference between the normal primitive mode of thinking and feeling (in the paranoid-schizoid position) and the mature form (in the depressive position) is whether there is a development, whether the child can learn from experience and bear the psychic pain linked to giving up its omnipotence, magical thinking, imagined control and oneness with the principal caregiver. Is there a healthy instance in the child that allows it to distance itself from its primitive wishes and defence mechanism and to learn from experience, that is, to compare its infantile illusions with reality, and to modify them? Karim, for instance, knew in the back of his mind that he had not really caught three fish. Even though he did eventually manage to increasingly believe the tale he had spun, it did not become a fixed idea.

To cite another example describing a more normal occurrence, Sybil Gräfin Schönfeldt, translator of many children's books, tells the following story about something she experienced during the Hamburg children's book week:

> The little boy sat under a trestle table, on which we displayed the books, and was engrossed in Catweazle, a story about a magician from the Middle Ages, who ends up in the modern age where, of course, he encounters a number of problems. "How nice that you're reading that," I say, "I translated that."— "Oh," he answered with eyes wide open: "That's my favorite book. Catweazle—that's me."
>
> (cited in *Gaschke*, 2006: 48)

The equation of a figure from a book with oneself corresponds to the little boy's wishful thinking. He also wants to master adventures with the same courage as Catweazle the magician but at the same time there can be no doubt that he knows his real name and knows who he is. By contrast, with a psychotic child or adult the idea of being Napoleon, Hitler, or God becomes an inner certainty that cannot be destroyed by external reality. Perceptions of reality become so alienated, inverted, or modified that they reinforce the delusional idea, for example, seeing other people as spies who want to topple or kill them. Thus people experiencing psychotic phases cannot learn from their experiences. The reality principle is relinquished in favour of the pleasure principle and wishful thinking.

A child's normal development comprises mental states such as omnipotent fantasies and magical thinking, which in an adult are taken to be a symptom of illness, delusion, or hallucination. However, as a result of the primitive perception of reality at work from the beginning, they are usually transformed into spontaneous unconscious fantasies and allow learning through experience. To master this transformation, a child nevertheless is dependent on an adequate containment to be able to deal with overwhelming anxieties. If the child's destructive forces against itself, its caregivers, and the perception of reality are not answered by affection and transformed (from beta elements into alpha elements), the child can turn away from reality either completely or partially. The perception of the self and of the external world becomes so strongly distorted that reality confirms megalomania or delusional ideas instead of modifying them, so that no learning from experience is possible. Caper (1999: 144) underscored Freud's opinion that adult neurosis is largely based on child neurosis which, in the meantime, has perhaps been concealed by seeming normalcy (Freud, 1909: 1918). Adults suffering from illness thus do not produce symptoms that occur in a normal primitive development but rather primitive versions of the experiential modes of children suffering from illness. "Illness in the adult is not a regression of a fixation to a normal primitive state, *but a non-progression from an abnormal one*" (Caper, 1999: 72; emphasis in original). Neurotic and psychotic symptoms are thus already visible in children and babies if one is open enough to notice them. A referral to a psychoanalyst who can make clear whether an emotional disturbance exists that can be treated through therapy certainly makes sense. With early intervention it is possible to help a child of preschool age if the problems have not become too strongly integrated in the personality. Parent–infant therapy or psychoanalytic child analysis can also provide quick help to a small child and its parents, whereas for adults analysis over a period of several years is typically necessary.

I would now like to present in detail the case of an eight-year-old boy in order to show how developmental disturbances are manifested and how they can be dealt with in child analysis. But first I would like to describe the "setting" of child analysis according to Melanie Klein.

## Setting of child analysis according to Melanie Klein

In 1908 Freud carried out the first child analysis, which was known as "Little Hans". The child's father told Freud about his son's development and later about his phobia of horses. Freud encouraged the father to talk with his son about his thoughts and feelings concerning his fears, dreams, and actual experiences. Melanie Klein's model of child analysis follows principles of treatment similar to Freudian adult analysis. Instead of free association and discussion, analytic work with children revolves around playing, drawing, and telling stories. At the beginning of the analysis the child is given a set of toys that is placed in a closeable drawer at the end of the session. The therapy room is simply furnished, with warm and cold running water, a table with chairs, a couch with a few cushions, and washable walls. Toys include small, wooden figures, animals, and small cars, material for drawing and creating things, glue and tape, a small ball and modelling clay.

Playing with the child provides access to its inner world, conscious and unconscious patterns of relating to its parents, siblings, and other important figures of identification—relationships that are all reactivated in the transference to the analyst. Interpreting the transference and the resistance thereto helps mitigate the patient's fears. Much emphasis is placed on observing how the child reacts to an interpretation and not just whether the child agrees but also how effective the interpretation is. If an interpretation reduces the fear, enables the child to play more freely and to tell stories, and helps it to establish deeper, more realistic relationships, then this interpretation was "right" (Klein, 1926; Joseph, 2003).

### 4.4.1    Case study: child analysis of Ferdinand

Initial situation

Ferdinand was eight years old when he began analysis with me. The elementary school teacher had recommended that Ferdinand's parents seek psychological help since he was very timid. He did not want to take part in group activities and neither played ball nor sang. He usually withdrew into a corner and observed the other children. He didn't have any friends, neither at school nor in his neighbourhood. He got excellent marks at school, indisputably the best student in his class. He was very reserved and serious.

His parents had also noticed that he usually was self-occupied, that he hid when their friends with children came over, and spoke with no one. His mother said she had already accepted the fact that he was an intellectual type, who avoided any form of physical contact and athletic activity. In Christmas photographs he was the only one who looked sad, while his three sisters smiled cheerfully. In the first conversation with his parents, the mother said that Ferdinand had never been jealous of his sisters who were one year, two and three and a half years younger; she had accepted his early independence. Throughout her pregnancy and during his first period as a baby, the boy had been unproblematic, and she and her husband had very much looked forward to their first child.

Ferdinand attended a computer course for which he had to travel through the entire city. He was, however, capable of infuriating and maddening his mother by acting as if he did not hear her and did not react to her. The mother's brother, who had also been timid and inhibited as a child, had also undergone psychoanalysis as an adult and urged her not to wait so long with Ferdinand. The teacher's recommendation had then prompted them to take action.

## Therapy process: first year

In the first session Ferdinand was so frightened that he remained standing there almost glued to the spot in the therapy room and stared ahead of him. Only when I addressed his anxiety and noted how difficult it is to speak with an unknown person in an unknown situation was he able to sit down, cowering like an embryo on the chair. He did not touch any of the toys that were spread out on the table for him, and told me in a high-pitched voice about the traffic accident in which a schoolmate had almost been killed. The analysis represented to him a dangerous traffic situation in which something terrible could happen to him. After this interpretation he told me how much a pack of gummy bears, a bar of chocolate, and so on, cost. Whenever he was overcome by anxiety he told me in a compulsive way the price of sweets, which calmed him. Sweets to gratify his oral longings and to ward off his anxieties played an important role during the analysis. He knew that he needed help and he wanted to undergo analysis. The parents finally gave their consent even though the mother was very sceptical and could not imagine him changing.

His father was more optimistic and hoped that he could become a happy child who could play and laugh instead of being so serious and reserved.

In the next sessions, Ferdinand told me what he had learned in school, and drew pictures relating to the national holiday. He created dozens of highly complicated folded paper planes which he sent gliding through the room. He gave small lectures and tried to convey the impression of a schoolchild who knew everything, was on top of everything. However, hidden behind this façade was his fear and loneliness, concealed behind his "omniscience" and paired with contempt. Once he understood his loneliness and his jealousy of other children who came to therapy he seemed to become much more relaxed. Before the first Christmas break he drew a picture of himself living in a fortress.

Ferdinand's drawing of a fortress.

After he had looked at his earlier drawings and wanted to know if I could remember them, he added two doors to his fortress. It seemed to please him that I understood he could open up a tiny way in for me when I wanted to use these doors. He smiled to me and then drew two ominous-looking maelstroms. I had not grasped the intensity of his feelings correctly so that he had to correct me by drawing intense maelstroms for me to grasp how dangerous his fury and anger was, how these feelings brewed behind the walls, waiting to erupt. He ignored the end of the session by simply continuing to draw and acting as if I had not spoken about the session being over. Only when I understood how hard it was for him to go was he able to leave.

In his drawing Ferdinand showed me how he had withdrawn into an almost inaccessible fortress. By being alone and being able to do everything best himself, he did not have to admit his jealousy and his pain at being pushed into the background because of the birth of his sisters. He lives in a world where he needs no one and thus need not be jealous or hurt by his siblings, or the separation from his mother. After a number of "tests" to see if I would also give up entering into contact with him or understanding him, like his mother, he drew the secret doors that probably depict the two therapy sessions. (For scheduling reasons I could first only offer him two hours; from Christmas on he had three sessions.)

In the calendar that I drew for him he only enters the dates that are important to him: Christmas and his birthday. He wants to be the first and only child. He is irritated by the other drawers in the cabinet for three other therapy children, and he tried to open them as if by chance. He acts as if he did this by accident. He wants to erase the birthday dates of his sisters, and wipe away the other children. When I understand that he believes he receives too little in life, he begins to express his feelings with greater clarity. He does not just want to play in the therapy room but wants to take possession of the entire apartment. He explores every corner in the therapy room carefully. When I then interpret to him that he wants to take possession of the entire room and also of me, he extends his explorations to the waiting room and the side rooms. I tell him that he wants to show me that the playing room is not enough, that he wants to take possession of the entire house and of me. The theme of taking-into-possession and completely-merging-with-me also appears in the way that he devours sweets, which he brings to the session in great quantities. Very concretely, he wants to take me in, to swallow me, so that he is no longer separated from me. Behind his indifferent façade, his greed and his wish to completely possess me, emerge. His longing to not have to share his mother, the jealousy he felt towards the new babies appearing each year, was deeply suppressed and only emerged in the transference in analysis.

At first I underestimate the intensity of his desire to destroy, to smear, and to ruin all other babies and children, since he has such a well-behaved façade. But then he corrects me by the way that he plays. At the end of each session, noted by *him* by looking at his watch, he begins to ransack the entire room. After I interpret the jealousy he feels towards the next (child) patient, he intensifies his actions. He develops an entire repertory of tricks to trip the next child: he plans for it to slip in a puddle of water next to the door; to get stuck walking on a glued spot. With great precision he creates an almost invisible trap by mounting a piece of perforated tape to the faucet so that it will splash when a child turns it on. When I address his desire to be the only one with me he smiles in agreement and is surprised that I understand him. His great inhibition and his self-control lessen; he is now able to show feelings he has hidden until now, such as jealousy, curiosity and rivalry, affection and pain. His movements become more co-ordinated, his stiff, awkward movements quickly vanishing. He shows delight in wreaking havoc in the room.

His curiosity, his desire to penetrate things, emerges from behind his indifference. Looking and observing assume for him a great importance. He once brings a camera, which he seems to be using to photograph everything, but then it turns out to be a squirt revolver with which he leaves his traces on the wall, on the floor, and on the window. In his fantasy, water stands for his urine, with which he wants to gain access to important figures (his mother, me, his father). He tries to penetrate my mind, and my thoughts, with his eyes. He does not wish to learn from experience, to feel psychic pain, but to steal my thoughts. He gives proof of these interpretations by making the stream of water even bigger, correcting it as it were, and showing me that I first underestimated the violent nature of his fantasies and desires.

After six months, his parents tell me in a meeting with me that Ferdinand has changed in a very positive way. He has become more trusting, now lets himself be touched, and even allows his father to give him a goodnight kiss. He speaks more, is no longer so withdrawn, and even plays with his sisters. The aim of child analysis is to help children to express their unconscious problems in the therapy sessions, so that they can be experienced and discussed. By working through the problems in the session the symptoms in the external world often quickly disappear. This, however, does not mean that they have really vanished; they have only been shifted to the sessions of psychoanalysis.

After sessions in which he has made emotional contact with me, there are sessions in which he completely withdraws and provokes me. He brings an entire package of sweets and a comic book, which absorbs him the entire session without his even glancing at me. He seems to accept with satisfaction my description of the situation that he wants to exclude me today, and to make me as furious as his mother. Indeed, this behaviour triggers strong countertransference feelings in me, making me feel useless and out of place, painful feelings of being excluded. I am supposed to feel as he did after the birth of the new baby, when his mother had no time and psychic space for him. When he feels understood, he touches me as if by accident. If, however, I start to discuss this physical contact, he immediately jerks back.

In the following phase he demonstrates his superiority towards me and brushes off my "silly" interpretations. He laughs at me and subtly mocks me. He sits on a chair on top of the table and thrones over me. He climbs from one window to another, climbs up the doorframe. He avoids touching the floor, as if he wanted to show me how he avoids coming into touch with frightening and threatening feelings and making contact with reality. A physically clumsy boy has become a skilled climber. He climbs in parks on monkey bars and attends a mountain climbing course in the spring on his own. When he has access to a new area of expertise, he also wants to be the best there.

He has become less anxious. At home he begins bumping into his sisters, as if by accident, when they take something away from him. He leans onto his father when he watches TV, even though in the morning he prevents a good-morning kiss by turning away his head. But he does not mind his father putting a hand on his head. Ferdinand writes excellent essays in school and now reluctantly does participate in school activities. The teachers at school notice a change. When other children ask Ferdinand to help them, Ferdinand explains the material to them and helps them with their tasks so that he is well liked. He now often spends more time with the worst boys in the class whose mischievous feats he admires. In therapy he wants to do everything on his own and only rarely asks me for help. He makes sure that the hour ends on time, and leaves abruptly. He draws the following picture:

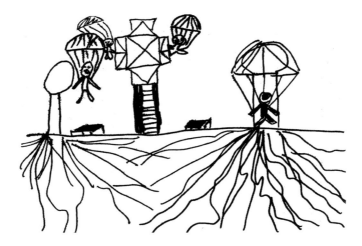

Ferdinand draws a scaffold.

In this drawing he uses me as a scaffold which he can climb up in order to be able to jump down. He uses analysis as an instrument to rid him of his anxiety, like gliding down to the ground with a parachute.

Second year of analysis

In the second year after summer vacation, Ferdinand showed me how happy he was to be back. He also showed his jealousy of my husband, with whom, in his fantasy, I spent my holidays and excluded him. With the modelling clay he forms two rolls that he bends into a "U" shape before putting one on top of the other, which I, in my fantasy, associate with my husband being "on me". Then he throws both of them over, which I see as an indication of his anger that he wants to knock me over, because I left him alone for so long. Then he tells me in a quiet voice that they are now rebuilding the house and that he is getting a room on the attic floor. I interpret that this as a sign that here, too, he also feels returned to "his place". He builds a boat, which he floats in the water. He demonstrates how his eight-week vacation was: sometimes gently swaying along but oftentimes threatened by waves and almost capsizing. When I offer this interpretation he builds a stable boat out of a box, on which he places a bottle with glue and lets it float. I understand this as a picture of him, now that he has grown more stable and robust and does not sink so easily since he is back in analysis.

In the following session he brings along a toy periscope with which he can peek around the corner or see what is happening behind or next to him. He shows me his curiosity regarding what I do when he is not there—with the other children, or at home with my husband. He observes me very carefully when he thinks I am not looking at him. He looks at my body as if he wants to make sure that I am not going to have a new baby.

In the countertransference I sometimes feel completely lost and out of place. He can dismiss my interpretations and triumph over me. When he wants to gloss over this in the therapy session he tells me how in building the extension on his house, everything is screwed together with plaster boards. He oscillates between disparaging behaviour—not taking note of me and my words—and a readiness to listen carefully. Being absent is an important form of defence for him. He pretends not to notice how his parents spend more time with his cheerful sisters than with him. He uses the same tactic when he wants to anger his mother, which he easily succeeds at doing. Instead of feeling how painful it is when the mother does not focus on him, he projects these feelings onto her and is capable of evoking these feelings in the mother (and his analyst). He can devote a good part of the session to stuffing himself with sweets, which not only reflects his greed but also gives him the illusion that he could feed himself, could do everything on his own, that he does not need anyone. At these times, he does not use his mouth to speak and to enter into contact with me but only to eat, and he does not want to give me any attention. He distances himself mentally and is lonely but without any needs, as he can provide everything for himself. It is painful to watch him retreat, at the same time aware of how I feel excluded. He listens to my interpretations but acts as if they were irrelevant. He blows up the package of the sweets and then bursts it, just as he lets my words explode.

At times he shows his anxiety about himself and his health by tearing things apart, sinking and breaking them. He smears with crayons, takes apart the felt-tip marker and concocts dangerous, poisonous liquids which he mixes with glue. Once he begins to be aware of and understand his aggressions, these excesses diminish and he can deal playfully with his aggression in reality. He has become friends with the most poorly behaved child in his class. He tells me that he made a large snowball together with this friend. The two of them were unable to lift it to put it on top of the snowman. So they let it roll down the slope and they were delighted when the girls reacted with shock and laughed. This was the first time that he had done something "bad". His unconscious desire to kill his sisters had been so great before he began analysis that he did not dare play with other children for fear that he could do them harm. Once this unconscious anger lessened, he was able to express it through play in reality.

In the analytic session he can talk about threatening events in the family, about the death of his favourite aunt who passed away very suddenly. He is confused but can speak about it.

Slowly he develops trust and feels more secure. This is illustrated by a sequence in a session where he played like a much younger child and was able to make up for the experience of something he had been unable to express earlier in a playful way: he came and discovered with a glance that he had gotten a new roll of tape. He filled the roll of tape with water and coloured it red with the ink of a felt-tip marker. He constructed a communicating receptacle with the tape and the empty bottle representing him. In it the red liquid is coloured more intensely each time he presses it in and out. Playing, he shows how he sucks everything in without reflecting on it. At my description of this, he reacts and becomes very sad. I speak about the coming weekend and his fear that his bad ideas could become real. He washes his hands and goes to a small black table which he turns around and sits down in. I ask what the table is and he says in a matter-of-fact way: "A boat." He moves around the entire room in his "boat". I tell him that he can build a boat once he understands his feelings. He moves to his drawer, affixes the boat to it with his tape and climbs up the chest of drawers. "Now you are much bigger than me and you think you can do everything; then you are not sad." When he climbs back down again, he avoids touching the floor, gets into his boat and once again moves about the room in his boat. "You show me that you can now move around in the entire room and you are sure that you have a place here with me, with your friendly and bad thoughts." I ask where he is going but he does not answer. When he comes back to his drawer he says: "Now I am back. That is my port." He tapes his boat to the drawer. When he climbs up on the drawer he touches me, as if accidentally, since I am sitting next to it. He is relieved that I gave him the tape. "You show me how good it is for you to go back home, to come back to me." (This session took place in the first week after the Christmas break.)

In my conversation with the parents at the end of the second year, both are cheerful—they seem much younger—and they have come to see me on their bicycles. They tell me how much Ferdinand has changed, how cheerful he has become. He could now defend himself and showed humour, was truly witty. When his cousin kept calling him by the wrong name and said that Ferdinand had simply confused him by correcting him, Ferdinand said "goodbye" to him the next time he greeted him. When the cousin asked him whether he should go, Ferdinand said calmly that he had simply gotten confused. Everyone had laughed at this.

Ferdinand now played so much with his sisters that it seemed as if he wanted to make up for what he had missed. They build sandcastles for hours with copious quantities of water, and also make "mud castles". His interest in science had been whetted, he read "Geo" magazines and asked clever questions. He now enjoyed coming to the analytic sessions. At a party, he had actually mustered up the courage to play the piano to an audience—something he had refused to do until then. He still had fears of the dark cellar. When he put his bike in the garage, he preferred to make a detour instead of going through the cellar. He was very interested in his little sisters' tadpoles but he still did not touch any animals.

Ferdinand was helpful; he would fetch something for his father even if not asked to do so. He also stated his wishes and was able to attain them, for example, he wanted to go the pool on his own and managed to do this. He learned how to swim well and he enjoyed swimming with his sisters.

## Third year of analysis

In spite of these positive developments, Ferdinand's parents understood that a third year of analysis was important in order to stabilize the progress that had been made. Ferdinand was now better able to understand why he isolated himself. At the Carneval party he wanted to dress up as a box, but then changed his mind and went as a traffic light—with three openings: red, yellow, and green. With this he expressed that he had now established various forms of contact with the world. His three weekly analysis hours enabled him to reveal hidden problems and concealed feelings and to reflect on them.

At the next meeting with the parents, Ferdinand's mother was occupied with thoughts arising from Ferdinand's new ability to say what actually bothered him. He had said to her: "You are constantly worrying about Flavia (the little sister). Why don't you do something with me as well!" But he could still accept his parents' "no" as an answer without withdrawing into his shell again.

In the therapy sessions he began playing with me—"sinking ships" and basketball, using a basket he constructed himself. He tried to beat me, to be better than me. At the same time, a battle was waging inside him—between his sensitive side that wanted to understand more, and his narcissistic side, that wanted to be superior and to cheat me instead of learning from experience. Often he hid his recognition of our work together, how much analysis had helped him, and used his intelligence to beat me. His acknowledgement of how important the sessions were for him and how stable the relationship was that he had built up with me, conveyed sometimes through physical touch, apparently had to seem unwitting. He used his charm and intelligence to tell funny stories and to hide his fear. For instance, when he spoke about various kinds of dogs and their babies, he made me laugh and at the same time hid his fear of contact. He didn't dare touch any dogs because he was afraid of being poisoned. Ferdinand could accept my interpretation that he told me funny things so that he did not have to discuss what he was afraid of.

## The end of analysis

In summary, we can state that Ferdinand realized how much he had eluded maternal care and deprived himself by fleeing into pseudo-independence in order not to feel his deep jealousy and his immense hate. He fled into a fantasy world in which he did not need anybody. His high intelligence and his ability to do things on his own were conducive to his defence. However, it was not a well-founded independence but one that was based on an eruptive blend of jealousy, narcissistic injury, envy, and loss of control, which could have exploded at any moment. To protect himself and other children from his internal explosive mood he was inhibited and avoided contact with them. His body became rigid and clumsy. Ferdinand fluctuated between recognition of the great meaning of analysis for himself and the maintenance of his narcissistic megalomania, his sense of not needing anyone. He was, however, capable of showing that he experienced analysis as a secure place where for the first time he was able to reveal his inner conflicts.

Esther Bick (1968: 115) has called this ersatz form of pseudo-independence a "second skin" which develops when children do not receive or are not able to accept containment and emotional understanding and then try to fend for themselves. It was possible to reduce the basic thrust of Ferdinand's emotional withdrawal and his isolation, and he was then better able to show his sadness and to articulate his needs to his mother. The parents also showed more sensitivity in responding to him and did not let a negative answer deter them from undertaking some activity alone with him. The father, for instance, went to ethnological exhibitions alone with Ferdinand, which greatly interested both of them.

An early intervention enabled Ferdinand to better integrate his split emotions and to become more self-assured, without simply pretending but actually developing authentic feelings and being able to enter into relationships. At school he now had friends who played with him and visited him at home. He also used his excellent intellectual performance to help friends and classmates in solving difficult tasks. Ferdinand would have probably led a limited life if he had been isolated and inhibited; he would have shut himself off even more and would have compensated for his loneliness by excelling academically. In puberty or once he was a university student he would, however, probably no longer been able to keep up this defence structure and would have perhaps suffered a psychic breakdown. It would then have been immensely more difficult to gain access to the early problems and to have helped him.

## 4.4.2   Thought disorders and their causes

The question as to the causes of severe psychic problems remains controversial. There is, however, a general consensus that a baby's special disposition and unfavourable environmental conditions—the way parents treat a child—are equally responsible. For a particularly sensitive child who is quickly inundated with stimuli, scared, and bears frustrations only with difficulty, an average family situation can be insufficient. Such a child cannot concentrate on drinking when it experiences other stimuli, may develop eating problems, sleep poorly, cry a lot, and thus burden the mother so that she reacts by becoming nervous and high-strung. The result is a vicious cycle. These children, so under the influence of their anxieties, then cannot accept the positive aspects of their relationships with their parents in order to mitigate their fears, which results in their suffering from psychic problems. A robust and patient child can, by contrast, also develop in a below-average family since it accepts every form of attention, is able to comfort itself, and can calm itself by sucking its thumb: with its cheerful nature and positive development, it may even take an active positive influence on a mother who tends towards melancholy.

Even the "overprotective", spoiling behaviour of parents who want to keep unpleasant experiences away from the child may actually make it more difficult for a child to develop:

> A certain amount even of unpleasant experiences is of value in this testing of reality by the child if by overcoming them, he [sic] feels that he can retain his objects as well as their love for him and his love for them, and thus preserve or reestablish internal life and harmony in face of danger.

(Klein, 1940: 127)

Coming to terms with frustration strengthens the child's trust in its own abilities even in the face of dangers from the outside. Bion's (1963: 27) concept of the "container and the contained" does not merely refer to the successful form of acceptance and transformation of overwhelming primitive elements (beta-elements) but also to two possible forms of maldevelopment—when the mother is unable to assimilate the child's beta-elements and these rebound to the child or, in another possible variant, "parasitic containment". This happens when the mother is so overwhelmed by her own problems that she projects these onto her child and the child is then swamped with its parents' unconscious conflicts. As was shown in the examples cited above, a normal baby can assess the emotional state of its caregivers and remember this interaction—in short, it can learn to think. The infant relies on its caregiver to love it and to recognize its moods and feelings. Bion describes the infant's knowledge of the reality of its emotions:

> ... a sense of reality to the individual in the way that food, drink, air and excretion of waste products matters. Failure to eat, drink or breathe properly has disastrous consequences for life itself. Failure to use the emotional experience produces a comparable disaster in the development of the personality; I include among these disasters degrees of psychotic deterioration, that could be described as death of the personality.
>
> (Bion, 1992: 42)

In accepting and understanding projective identifications, irrespective of whether the child sees them as good or bad, the foundations of both emotional development and the ability to think are laid. These are the innumerable small playful or oppressive sequences already illustrated with examples. The state of mind a mother requires for this, which Bion (1962: 35) has called "reverie"—"the mental state which is open to the perception of all "things" of the loved object"—is not always possible to achieve. However, if such a "reverie" exists to a certain degree, then that is sufficient. Children are robust and can bear not always being understood if they have mainly positive experiences.

## Insufficient containment

There are difficult life situations, oppressive crises, and psychological problems suffered by the mother, such as depression or anxiety, which make it permanently impossible for the parents to assimilate the child's primitive anxieties and wishes. One indication of the fact that a child or an adult had no "container" as a baby who helped it to assimilate its "raw" feelings and transform them into "alpha-elements" are massive identifications that put another person under pressure to act and induce guilt feelings in that person—for example, the analyst (Caper, 1999: 134).

Here I would like to use an example to trace a baby's mental state. Its mother was unable to assimilate its beta elements and to digest them emotionally. A mother dutifully cares for her baby but without relating to it harmoniously. She cannot decipher what the child's crying means at different times—whether it is bored or in mortal fear. Bored crying would demand of an empathetic mother that she pick up her baby or offer it something stimulating, give it something to hold or to look at. A baby crying out of panic should trigger fear in the mother if she is capable of accepting the projection that the baby might die, and then capable of reflecting on how she could communicate with the baby. If the latently simulated mortal fear is too threatening for the mother, then she distances herself from it and almost always asks herself: "What does the baby want?" to which she answers: "I don't know what's wrong with it." In such a case the baby experiences the failure of normal relief in which his primitive fears are assimilated since it had no container. It then develops into an adult who massively projects its feelings onto other persons, as if seeking to compensate for these childhood experiences. In analysis, and only in analysis, the analyst may succeed in understanding the feelings projected onto them, to digest them and to make them accessible to the patient by interpreting the phenomenon of counter-transference.

Another example: A sensitive child might learn to adapt to its mother's emotional state and to guess what kind of child the mother would like. It will then not show its authentic feelings, wishes, and needs but rather orient itself to the mother's expectations. It will behave so that it causes no trouble or will try to cheer up the mother when she is sad. At the same time it will develop the feeling that it is not really connected to the mother. In milder manifestations of this, there are adults who first reflect what their partner, their child, or boss want and then express and formulate these wishes as their own. This person feels like their "mother's servant", pleasing her and divining her every wish. The emotional price is that this person is convinced that they do not deserve to be loved when they reveal their true qualities, good and bad, love and hate. They will probably suppress their aggressions, projecting them onto others, and then quickly feeling persecuted or idealizing others. Winnicott (1960: 140) speaks here of a "false self", and Jacobson (1964) of a "as-if personality". These persons feel that they themselves do not know who they are. They try to play the role of spouse, father, and the good colleague, as well as they can, but without truly attaining emotional contact to others. If they fall in love, they worry about losing themselves, becoming dependent or being devoured, and then distance themselves. One form of keeping others at bay is to not enter into any real relationship, for example, to remain married but parallel to this having a love affair—a form that is destructive for all three persons involved. A danger is especially given if a child is very intelligent. The mind then becomes the place of the false self, its preoccupation with things, theories, and experiences does not become alive, but rather a dead knowledge, as Lazar (1999: 215) describes:

> A one-sided, unproductive accumulation of knowledge which always resembles a collection of dead, ultimately useless stuff ... this, as we know, is the goal of many pseudo-scientific activities for hoarding knowledge that are driven by unconscious fantasies which basically remain non-gratifying because they have lost their actual meaning.

## Parasitic containment

Parasitic containment is destructive either for the baby's capacity to think or for the mother's. Bion illustrates this with examples of ailing mothers or strongly disturbed babies. In this case the mother is not only incapable of "detoxifying" the feelings projected onto her, she also functions as a negative object that robs the projections of their meaning and lets the baby introject them as "nameless dread". Or the mother projects her own fears and unresolved conflicts onto a baby that is thus swamped with undigested fears, resulting in physical symptoms. Bion speaks of "nameless dread" (*Bion*, 1992: 30–36; *Grinberg* et al., 1993: 53; *Lüders*, 2002: 96f; *Green*, 1993). An alarming sign of a deeply disturbed relationship with the mother is when a baby does not establish any visual contact with the mother during the first year, or there is no playful activity between the mother and the baby.

An example I would like to cite is the parent–infant therapy with a small girl named Jane, described by Selma Fraiberg in "Ghosts in the Nursery" (1980b: 167ff). In the initial therapeutic situation we learn that the mother would like to give up Jane for adoption, while the father is against this and seeks therapeutic help. In the first contact, the "therapy in the kitchen", the mother makes a disinterested impression. Conspicuously, she does not seem to hear or react to the crying of her five-and-a-half month old boy.

When the mother tells the story of her own life in an apathetic voice, it becomes clear that she herself was an undesired, neglected child whose crying was never heard. Her mother had suffered from postpartum depression and had made a serious attempt to end her life which had left her permanently mentally scarred and unable to take care of her own child. For the first five years Jane's mother was cared for by an aunt, and then she was sent to her grandmother who lived in the country in great poverty. There were crimes, sexual abuse, promiscuity in the family, where she remained an outcast and unloved. She later met and married her present husband. Because of a short affair with another man, she had doubts whether Jane was her husband's daughter. She saw Jane as the consequence of this misstep and wanted to give her up.

Jane showed signs of her neglect. While she was properly clothed, she lay passively and disinterestedly in her crib and seldom had any contact with her mother. She hardly smiled and only made a few spontaneous sounds. In sum, she conveyed the impression of desperately needing help. Nevertheless, it would not have made sense to urge Jane's mother to take more care of her daughter. This probably would have only increased her feelings of guilt about being such a mother. She may have sensed something in her daughter's unconscious, aggressive stance against which she wanted to protect her by surrendering her for adoption. The therapist's intervention consisted in listening to the mother—perhaps for the first time in her life, to assimilate her painful feelings that she was never wanted and to give her permission to feel and to remember her feelings, that is, to give Jane's mother a containment. This made dramatic changes possible. The mother could turn to Jane, accept her, and speak to her about her trials and tribulations while holding her in her arms. And, as the therapist noticed, Jane gave her mother a special smile.

In the first months of a child's life, therapeutic support is particularly important, since the threatening disturbances in the interaction between mother, father, and baby are still only beginning. The presence of the infant in the child–infant therapy has a sort of catalyst effect which, by virtue of its action (for example, intense crying at a particular moment in the story), helps make the unconscious problems of the parents and the forms of parasitic containment visible and tangible.

## 4.5   Final remarks

The theory of thinking that was described here in very broad lines is based on the further development of Freud's ideas by Melanie Klein and Wilfried Bion, certainly "the most potent, productive and creative pair that the history of psychoanalysis brought forth" (Lazar, 1999: 220). This can give the reader only a glimpse and cannot replace the reading of the original papers. Observations have provided ample evidence for the close connection between the development of a normal capacity to think and the ability to establish an emotional relation of love and hate, fear and joy with a person (the mother). Only the experience of the psychic reality of a loved person with all the concomitant primitive feelings and fears forms the basis for normal development. The discovery the child makes—that one and the same person has both good and bad qualities—is integrated in its conception of one single reality. The realization that much of what is desirable and real does not originate in the child and also cannot be influenced by it, instead depending on another person—and that the child requires another person to attain gratification—is something Klein (1957: 177) calls "gratitude". In the next chapter on psychosexual development, I will deal with another important dimension of "triangular" space in thinking, since it is related to the Oedipal conflict.

Psychoanalytic understanding of thinking must seem strange to conventional theory, since it seems to describe a threat to the mind and to logic. However, it actually expands our understanding of thinking, which is actually based on two different types of logic. The psychic unity of man has proved to be a fallacy. Green (1994: 92) once said: "The subject was not longer one, but two." The point is to cultivate the creative use of the coexistence of primary and secondary process so as to be able to deal with these confusing types of thinking. The goal is "to recognize the existence of subjective logic of the primary process without giving up all claims to the objective logic of secondary processes" (Green, 1994: 94). Thus the realm of rationality can be expanded when we try to understand ourselves and children on a deeper level.

*CHAPTER FIVE*

# The psychosexual development
# of a child

185

When we speak of the psychosexual development of a child instead of "sexuality", this implies a broader understanding of sexuality also including seemingly asexual forms of behaviour. The development of infantile sexuality, as described by Freud in his "Three Essays on the Theory of Sexuality" (1905a), is a significant addition to the understanding of intra-psychical connections. Freud situates sexuality in the unconscious, which he sees as the liminal area between soma and psyche. Since it is a central notion of psychoanalytic understanding we will take a closer look at sexuality.

## 5.1    A broader understanding of sexuality

Freud (1917: 320) uses the notion of sexuality differently than it is commonly employed in everyday language. He not only uses it to refer to the differences between the sexes, the sexual act, and procreation but to describe every form of pleasure and satisfaction which can be derived from its objects—that is, also eating, playing, and much more. Most of our thoughts and acts are based precisely on these acts—and they are also activated in sleep. Sexuality is meant in a much broader sense, and Freud (1917: 320) uses the term "libido" to refer to it. This broader understanding of sexuality is linked to the development of personality (Nietzschke, 1988). Freud himself suggested using the term "psychosexuality" in psychoanalytic theory, since the psychic factor is decisive in connection with the relationship to parents and siblings (Freud, 1910: 119). Here the issue is the individual's capacity to love, linked with an intense, emotional, and affective experience during the sexual act and not an erection or ability to achieve an orgasm. The personality is the product of the development of infantile sexuality into the mature psychosexuality of the adult. Psychosexuality thus cannot be identified with sexual behaviour measured by experimental means (Kinsey, 1948, 1953). It can be influenced by psychic factors such as anxiety, hate, and guilt feelings and be intensified by tenderness and love. Thus a technically successful sexual intercourse without tender feelings can leave behind a shallow, even repulsive feeling, in lieu of happiness and fulfilment. Freud was able to attain an understanding of the unconscious roots of psychosexuality by studying abnormal behaviour, perversion, and sexual aberrations. Freud (1905: 170) assumed that "normal" manifestations of sexual drives could essentially not be separated from "abnormal" ones:

> The extraordinary wide dissemination of the perversions forces us to suppose that the disposition to perversions is itself of no great rarity but must form a part of what passes as the normal constitution.

Nietzschke (2005: 6) wrote that Freud thus "strongly opposed the degradation and degeneration theorists of the 19th century who ... distinguished strictly between sexual perversion and so-called normal manifestations of human sexuality".

In place of such a strict distinction, Freud offers the idea of healing disorders, eliminating sexual fixations through remembering and working through them. A further important insight of Freud had to do with the plasticity of sexual cathexis. Fights, masochistic relationships, humiliations, or even the overcoming of dangerous situations, are rooted in perverse sexual wishes and, given a certain inner predisposition, they could even be preferred over the "normal" sexual satisfaction, as we will see later in our discussion of perversion.

The Freudian study of sexuality and discovery of the unconscious is based on the psychoanalytic work with patients, Freud's own self-analysis, and the study of myths and artworks. In explaining our suffering, inhibitions, and scruples Freud made recourse to mythological figures and stories; he put the terrible violent and anarchic gods of Olympus and their irreconcilable struggles, harking back to antiquity, into perspective with our own actions. "Psychoanalysis" refers to the ancient saga of the proud nymph Psyche who was held captive and tormented by Cupid. The notion of the psyche, or what Freud called the "psychic apparatus", goes back to the nymph Psyche, who in Greek mythology was identified with an intangible, inscrutable soul. The god of love had initiated her in divine pleasure, but it was forbidden to speak of these pleasures. The child Psyche bore Cupid was named "pleasure" (Hedone). Freudian analysis has set itself the goal of freeing her from the dictate of silence Cupid sealed by laying his finger on Psyche's lips. In his patient Dora, Freud observed that while failing to mention her sexual seduction she touched her small moneybag with her fingertips—symbolic for her invisible genitals. "When the lips are silent, the finger tips become eloquent," Freud (1905b: 55) noted ironically.

In literature, sexuality is described as a polarity between pleasure aiming at eternity and as a burden. Friedrich Nietzsche (2005: 284) wrote: "Yet, all joy wants Eternity—wants deepest, deep Eternity." Samuel Beckett in contrast mocked sex as "reward frenzy" and an "ingenious PR-idea" on which the idea of creation is based (cited in Kümmel, 2006: 49). The Janus-headed nature of sexuality is revealed both through its connection with love as the source of the greatest happiness and also through its aspect of frenzy—a drive to commit acts conflicting with moral and reasonable considerations.

A ten-year-old girl had a dream affording metaphorical expression to both of these aspects. She told her parents about this dream at breakfast: "Today I dreamed that I could fly. I am standing on a mountain and there are problems. I extend my arms and can simply fly." (As she is telling this story she extends her arms and shows, with a mischievous smile, how she can fly in huge curves like a swallow.) "It is wonderful. Then I sit on a large horse that is resting by a deep gorge, the horse shirks back and throws me off in a huge arc. I land on the back of Martha's horse (Martha is her best friend with whom she had gone riding the previous day) and we both ride on, tackle all obstacles and make good headway."

Interpretation: In the dream the girl enjoys her ability to fly elegantly like a swallow—a symbol for taking off sexually. She is then thrown off by the horse which can be seen as standing for libido. This alludes to her fear of whether she will be able to handle this new inner power. The deep canyon alludes to dangers. Her rescue comes through friendship of the same sex, symbolized by her good friend. On the back of her friend's horse they are able to overcome all obstacles together.

Freud compares the experience of orgasm with the "oceanic" memory of the mother's limitless womb. But it is this very sense of losing oneself in sexual surrender that also instills fear, which in the dream is expressed by being thrown off the horse. It is also frightening to become dependent, and to feel overwhelmed by one's own sexual wishes.

## 5.2    The concept of bisexuality

Freud posits his complex model of bisexual impulses as an alternative to the seemingly simple and clear division of the sexes into male and female for the purpose of procreation.

Femininity and masculinity first seem to be defined biologically. Freud gave a new slant to this definition by borrowing Weinberger's (1903) concept of "human bisexuality" and by emphasizing the importance of the psychical cathexis of the body as either male or female. Freud (1905a: 218 footnote) wrote: "It is essential to understand clearly that the concepts of "masculinity" and "femininity," whose meaning seems so unambiguous to ordinary people, are among the most confused that occur in science."

The notions of "masculinity" and "femininity" are confusing in science because, according to Freud (1905: 120), it is impossible to understand "normal" sexuality without understanding the pathological manifestations of sexual life. This is because "normal" and "pathological" can only be quantitatively distinguished; they cannot be grasped in purely qualitative terms. Some homosexual men experience sexuality as female and some lesbian women experience theirs as male, a phenomenon Freud (1905: 116) describes as an "inversion" (and not as "perversion").

Freud defines three meanings for understanding the male or female dimension:

* The first meaning refers to activity and passivity. Freud attributes the active side (male) to libido and the passive (female) side to the drive object.
* The second meaning—biological significance—is characterized by the presence of ova or of semen and the function ascribed to each. Activity and its concomitant phenomena—more powerful muscular development, aggressiveness, greater intensity of libido—can only be linked with biological masculinity in general principle, since there are animal species in which these attributes are assumed to a greater degree by females.
* The third meaning, sociological relevance, refers to the "observation of actually existing masculine and feminine individuals" in a historical context (Freud, 1905: 120).

From this Freud (1905a: 218 footnote) concludes "that in human beings pure masculinity or femininity is not to be found either in a psychological or a biological sense". This means that in a psychoanalytic understanding, mature sexual identity can only be achieved when the bisexual and incestuous wishes of childhood are integrated. Only after mourning over the loss of these wishes can mature mono-sexuality be accepted, with homosexual and incestuous tendencies remaining at least in a latent form. Freud argued that a mature sexual identity required identification with both sexes:

> A man develops not only on the basis of his male identification but also on the basis of feminine identification, and a woman takes on masculine identifications, as from her father, as part of her normal psychological development—independently of anatomical differences.
>
> (Laufer, 2005: 135)

There is also the more colloquial notion of a "masculine woman" and a "feminine man". Nonetheless, in "normal" development one gender identity prevails—either a female or a male "core gender identity" which need not converge with biological endowment. We know that most people have a certain fear regarding the extent to which they are seen by their environment as male or female. How the parents and the environment define gender identity also plays a significant role. In studying the early biography and psychological functioning of transsexuals, Stoller has noted that their sense of reality is entirely intact in various realms of life and that they do not have a greater anxiety regarding their sexual identity than heterosexuals. Male-to-female transsexuals have always believed that they are female and were actively reinforced by their mothers to believe this (Stoller, 1968). Stoller concluded that the core gender identity that develops at the age of eighteen months emerges in the early mother–child relationship and that maternal fantasies and wishes play a central role.

We thus see the male stereotype of a "muscle man" or the female counterpart of a "bimbo" as being indicative of a disturbance. A macho stance can indicate a fear of unity with the mother (Birksted-Breen, 2005: 1,499). If the integration of male and female aspects, that is, passive and active impulses, has not succeeded, because they are too threatening, one aspect—the male or female aspect—becomes over-emphasized.[1] If a man's fear of his female aspects—the assimilation of tender, nurturing impulses—is too threatening, he reacts by over-emphasizing everything male, with disdain for everything female; emotions are experienced as weakness, and crying as a disgrace.

## 5.3  Infantile sexuality

The concept of "infantile sexuality" was already very controversial in Freud's time. He was accused of endorsing a "pansexuality", and the church in particular accused him of soiling the "innocence of children". Even today, while his basic ideas find wide recognition, he also still has critics. For instance, empirical infant researchers—for example, Martin Dornes—have called his ideas into question. In his contribution on "Infantile Sexuality and Infant Research" (2005: 125) he writes:

> Mother and child constitute less drive objects for one another than resonance spaces for a diversity of corporeal and psychi-cal needs: physiological regulation, sensual pleasure, curiosity, attachment, communication, aversions and perhaps also recog-nition … Thus greater emphasis must be laid on these aspects as opposed to the traditional perspective, and the formerly central issue of sexuality recedes into the background.

Dornes' multi-layered relevance of the mother–child relationship is often confirmed in the following passages. The broader notion of psychosexuality does not only concern a purely pleasure-oriented satisfaction. Instead, it encompasses a holistic experience of love, security, and pleasure, mixed with ambivalent feelings of frustration, envy, and abandon. The uplifting sense of security and the mutual bond between mother and child are associated with pleasure. Freud and many analysts after him, however, have shown that disorders in early relationships are reflected in sexual experience and in the entire personality structure. Every psychical disturbance is at the

---

[1] With violent boys in therapy, it becomes clear that violence constitutes a divergence from an internally experienced helplessness, for instance when they draw themselves as a rabbit seeking protection, in an "enchanted family" (Diem-Wille, 2003: 156).

same time a disturbance of psychosexual experience, even without visible manifestations in sexual function or gratification.

In normal psychosexual development Freud distinguished three consecutive phases: the "oral phase", the "anal phase", and the "phallic phase". Today we assume that these erogenous zones also convey pleasurable excitement, with the focus changing in each case. These erogenous zones, which also include the skin as a large and pleasurable "sensory organ that is vital for survival" (Brosig and Gieler, 2004: 12) can remain receptive to pleasure throughout one's entire life if development has been largely positive.

### 5.3.1    Oral, anal, and phallic phase

An infant's early relationship to its first caregiver—usually the mother—is the first love affair and lays the ground for its later experiences of love and pleasurable satisfaction. The first "pair of lovers" is the mother–child couple. Survival as a goal encompasses not only feeding and body care, but also the development of an emotional, mental, and psychosexual relationship. Only when the child experiences love and satisfaction and achieves emotional contact with the mother and the father will it be capable of loving and entering into relationships as an adult. It is impossible to love without having had the experience of being loved oneself. If a child is deprived of this early experience, it will have trouble as an adult engaging in a satisfying love experience and will experience more painful, unfulfilled relationships. In therapy or analysis it is possible to work through deprivation and anger concerning deficient early love experience and to allow the patient, to a certain degree, to experience a new quality of relationship. The natural feeling of security, safety, and optimistic pleasure in life resulting from these early experiences can, however, never be fully replaced.

In the first mother–child interactions we can note analogies to later experiences as adults in romantic love. In my book *Das Kleinkind und seine Eltern* (*The Infant and his Parents*) (2003: 88 ff) I studied in detail these analogies that can be seen in body exploration, prolonged eye contact, and the language of lovers. Parents explore the baby's body, learn every inch of it, and touch all parts of the body when they caress, bathe, and cream their baby—often accompanied by playful kissing and fondling. This is similar to a couple that has just fallen in love and are exploring each other's body erotically for the first time, looking, commenting on it, kissing, and experiencing it with pleasure in being the centre of attention for someone else. This pleasurable experience also entails memories of early experiences. If a partner has no positive experiences to draw on, s/he will not be able to engage in the same way in an exploration of the body, and perhaps will not be able to bear constant physical contact, only able to fall asleep alone, for example. Extended physical contact in the phase of falling in love is a reactivation of the early experience of being touched as a baby. Prolonged eye contact without words is an expression of aggression or intimacy for adults: two persons stare at each other before they attack each other or fall into each other's arms like two people who have just fallen in love. Lovers even unconsciously imitate "baby language" when they assign each other tender nicknames—even a tender pronunciation of the other person's name is experienced as a caress. The harmonious "choreography" of mother and child described above, and the exaggerated imitation of the infant's facial expression by the mother, are linked with pleasurable feelings and happiness for both.

## Oral phase

The primary erotogenic zones at the beginning of life are the mouth, the mucous membranes, and the gums. When drinking the child experiences a sense of pleasure that is not just limited to the mouth but extends to the entire body. Sensual sucking—be it on the thumb, the tongue, or the big toe—calms the child even if it is not hungry. This insight prompted Freud (1914: 76) to speak of "autoeroticism". The infantile sexual fantasy of the oral phase consists in fusion through assimilating, ingestion, and being fully absorbed in a state of security. This is also closely linked to aggressive fantasies of incorporating, biting, and destroying (Freud, 1905a). The mouth and the sensitive parts of the gum do not merely stimulate the erogonetic; the mechanism of incorporating, biting, digesting, and expelling also represents a basic mental and emotional pattern, which expresses love or aggression. "I like you so much I could devour you," is an allusion to this connection, just as the expression: "I don't like the taste of him." The first kiss conveys the intensity of early pleasure, with one person seeking out another in order to gain pleasure.

## Anal phase

For Freud, the "anal phase" did not begin until the second year of life:

> Like the labial zone, the anal zone is well suited by its position to act as a medium through which sexuality may attach itself to other somatic functions. It is to be presumed that the erotogenic significance of this part of the body is very great from the very first.

> (Freud, 1905a: 185)

Pleasure can be derived from the mucous membranes of the anal zone, the stimulation on retention, and excretion. To increase the excitement, some children retain their stool. Manual stimulation of the mucous membrane of the anus is not at all uncommon among older children. The child's faeces represent the first gift to the parents, expressing its active compliance with its caregivers, while withholding expresses disobedience. It thus makes sense to not begin with toilet training until the child has good control over its muscles. It is possible to see when a child has reached this state by observing if a child can walk up and down steps with one foot placed after the other (cf. Diem-Wille, 2003: 230). A number of neurotic disturbances are established through the power struggle in toilet training if the parents use humiliation, shame, and coercion in this process instead of helping the child to fulfil its wish to go to the toilet like adults through letting the child take the initiative or encouraging it to do so.

During play, water is also used in a pleasurable way as a symbol of urination. Materials similar to bodily excrements such as water, mud, Play-Doh, and the like serve to satisfy a desire to knead and smear with substitute materials.

Verbal expression of the body's excrement production gives small children great pleasure. Anal jokes of children are an expression of primordial humour. Two examples to illustrate this (Titze, 1995: 45):

> "The coachman laughs so hard it makes him poop in his pants. The woman in the carriage cannot bear the smell." (Boy, almost five years old).
>     "Grandma and grandpa sit on the sofa, grandpa shits, the sofa splits." (Girl, five years old).

In both examples the powerfulness of the bodily excretions are fantasized. In the first, this means the stench that the coachman's excrement produces; in the second, it is grandpa whose excrement is so powerful that it splits the sofa. Melanie Klein (1930: 24) once pointed out that in a child's fantasy, the body excrements are powerful weapons or important gifts for the parents. Children are armed, as it were, with their bodily functions, the oral weapons of biting and screaming, vomiting and devouring and the anal, violent destructive fantasies of mutilating, gassing and drowning, vacating and robbing.

## Phallic phase

The phallic or infantile-genital[2] phase has as its erogenous zone the external sexual organs—in the boy the penis and testicles and in the girl the clitoris and labia. The anatomical location and stimulation

---

[2] Tyson and Tyson (2001: 68) have shown how problematic the term "phallic" is since Freud was primarily referring to a boy's psychosexual development.

during cleaning indicate their later importance, as Freud (1905a: 188) points out: "It is scarcely possible to avoid the conclusion that the foundations for the future primacy over sexual activity exercised by this erotogenic zone are established by early infantile masturbation." A girl often achieves excitement by pressing together her thighs and making rhythmic movements, often accompanied by stimulating fantasies, whereas boys prefer to use their hand for stimulation.

## 5.3.2    "Polymorphous-perverse disposition"—infantile sexuality

In his study of infantile sexuality, which Freud (1905: 191) saw as beginning with birth, he coined the term "polymorphous-perverse" infantile sexuality. For this term Freud elicited criticism mainly from church circles because he was seen as undermining the ideal of infantile innocence and purity. What did Freud really mean? That all children were perverse? That they were evil and bad and that we are all guilty of all manner of perversions? The answer to these questions is, of course, not so easy since this term encompasses several basic assumptions. First, there is the assumption that a child strives for pleasure and wishes to avoid displeasure and pain. This is relatively understandable, even though there are several phenomena such as masochism, repetition compulsion,[3] and self-inflicted injury that seem to contradict this assumption. Small children do not yet show shame, disgust, and morals; these emerge in the course of an individual's upbringing—in the "process of civilization" (Elias, 1939: 25). Behavioural modes that would be deemed "perverse" in adults appear in the normal development of children. Small children love to show their bodies naked; they run around naked and are happy to be seen doing so. An adult who strips to attract onlookers is seen as an exhibitionist. Perverse curiosity connected with observing sexual acts is referred to as "voyeurism"; in the small child, it is seen as a healthy reaction to view intimate acts with curiosity. Children watch other children, adults, and animals with great interest while they are emptying their bowels, just as they are also stimulated by strong

---

[3] Psychoanalysis sees the compulsive-obsessive disorder as being a phenomenon where an individual voluntarily selects and even seeks out the same acts, relational patterns, or forms of interaction that, in the past, caused pain, unhappiness, and suffering, with the effect of an inner urge or maelstrom, forcing the individual to adopt this self-destructive behaviour even if he or she knows better.

emotions or controversy to take a closer look. Through the process of civilization and in our upbringing, adult curiosity is seen as invasive; we are taught to look away. But there are certain situations—such as serious road traffic accidents—where morbid curiosity wins out; we know how difficult it is to make onlookers drive away.

The wishes for satisfaction ("partial drives") in childhood remain important in one's later life, even if they become subordinated to the primacy of genital sexuality. They become important sources of pleasure in the so-called foreplay preceding sexual intercourse. If someone is able to maintain access to these sources of pleasure through visual means, smelling, caressing, self-exhibition, and so on, then s/he will be able to experience pleasure in the creative shaping of a sexual encounter and also be able to generate pleasure in his/her partner. If these acts are no longer accessible, that is, inhibited due to a strict upbringing, if they are covered over by shame, disgust, or guilt feelings, then playful exploration of the beloved and the erotic encounter will be limited. By the same token, a certain degree of taboo can increase pleasure when boundaries are transgressed.

Infantile sexuality is often evident in children when they exhibit a seductive, solicitous behaviour to the parent of the opposite sex. The child cuddles up, wants to sit on its parent's lap and often appears rather flirtatious, dancing, hopping and thus attracting the gazes of its parents or of other adults. It is up to adults to respect boundaries. In the sexual abuse of children this boundary is not merely transgressed, but the child is seduced or forced to let an adult perform sexual acts with it. Children often offer little resistance to these transgressions, since they are often seduced by persons they know and love. When adults initiate such a transgression extreme confusion follows, which can weigh heavily on a child's further development.

Here it should be noted that the phenomenon of the "plasticitiy of sexual cathexis" can also undergo a reversal: the wishes and feelings of pleasure originally related to the erogenous zones can be withdrawn, "desexualized", and find expression in an oral or anal character. The "oral character" is characterized by an emphasis on the mouth, the mucous membranes, and the desire to incorporate something, to dissolve boundaries. Eating and drinking play a central role and smoking and drugs may be used to transgress boundaries.

Anal eroticism can be sublimated and then lead to related characteristics such as orderliness, thriftiness, and obstinacy. Thriftiness can become so intense that it assumes the form of stinginess, and stubbornness can become defiance accompanied by a proclivity to break out in fits of rage and revengefulness (Freud, 1908, 1917). The symbolic meaning of money and faeces that are manifested in mythology and fairy tales (shitting money, and so forth) can often not be experienced subjectively by the stingy adult: saving, hoarding, and accumulating money is then rationalized as an "economical attitude" instead of being linked to pleasure.

Psychosexual development proceeds through various dramatic stages that have an effect on the entire personality, the way the body is experienced, feelings, thinking, and relationships. Initially, the psychosexual relationship is more strongly focused on one person (the mother), but then it becomes expanded to a three-person-constellation (father and mother as a couple and the child) which is accompanied by a conflicting internal development. Freud (1905: 207) referred to this developmental stage as the "Oedipus conflict" in reference to the classical Greek saga, which Sophocles treated in the drama "King Oedipus".

## 5.4   The Oedipal conflict

The drama of King Oedipus describes the tragic fate of Oedipus who unwittingly kills his father King Laios, solves the riddle of the Sphinx, and is thus able to defeat it. He is rewarded for this with the hand of widowed Queen Jocasta.

This was predicted by the Delphic oracle the moment that Oedipus was born. King Laios tried to evade his fate by giving his son Oedipus to a herdsman who was asked to kill the son. The compassionate herdsman could not bring it upon himself to murder the small baby and brought it to the childless king of Corinth. Oedipus did not know he was not growing up with his real parents. When he left his parents he reached Thebes where he performed his act of patricide without knowing it. Jocasta and Oedipus lived happily as a married couple for many years and had four children until Apollo inflicted a plague upon the city because the king's murderer lived there in impunity. Sophocles shows the painful dual struggle inherent in not recognizing the truth. Oedipus tries to avoid recognizing what the blind seer Theresias related, but at the same time he rejects Jocasta's attempts to pacify him. Sophocles describes Oedipus as the captive of a terrible prophecy. Precisely this sense of being forced to act against all moral laws and conscious motives may have prompted Freud to use the Oedipus saga to name all unconscious impulses at work in us, impulses we cannot evade.

## 5.4.1   Early stages of the Oedipus conflict

In her further development of Freud's ideas, Melanie Klein (1928, 1945) discovered signs of the early stages of the Oedipus conflict in the first year of life. The mother, or partial aspects of the mother (part objects), was given pleasurable cathexis by the baby in the satisfaction of hunger, in sucking, and in being stroked and carried around. The mother as the first "love object" seemed to possess everything that could account for the baby's pleasure and happiness. We assume that the baby experiences this early mother as omnipotent. At the same time the experience of helplessness and neediness as described by Freud in "Inhibitions, Symptoms and Anxiety" (1926) represents the prototype of all traumatic situations, and the theme of nightmares. The intermittent absence of the mother triggers in the baby strong rage and feelings of being deserted—as an experience of frustration. It is as if everything becomes negative and threatening. The baby feels persecuted by the mother's part aspects (voice, breast, mouth). How intense the feelings of being abandoned are and what fatal rage they can trigger can be seen not only in the many cases of women being murdered when they leave their husbands but also the threatening inner reaction when relationships are dissolved. Even mature adults often show the tendency to split good and evil, to denigrate their spouse, and to re-edit their past. One often hears from married couples who are separating that they actually never loved their partner, that they had known from the very outset that it would end badly. It is difficult to simultaneously keep alive good and bad memories. During separations, people often assume the behaviour patterns of a baby, for instance, only nourishing themselves with fluids, for example, drinking only coffee, alcohol, and milk or eating little, which expresses the unconscious fear of having to starve. It is very difficult to bear the narcissistic injury of being abandoned without devaluing and destroying all the good experiences in a relationship. Even mature adults have trouble seeing that they loved each other and that this love has changed to the point that it is simply too weak to base a relationship on.

We assume that the small child also has an interest in its parents' relationship. If parents have a good, secure relationship, this is a source of security for the child, if also a situation that can trigger feelings of envy and jealousy. These negative feelings can be directed against one parent or against the couple. If the parents' relationship is bad, this can sometimes be welcomed by the child since it affords him or her emotional access to the frustrated parent, but can also be a source of insecurity, triggering anxiety and feelings of guilt.

The Austrian writer Peter Turrini (1996: 176) described the threatening quality of his parents' sexual intercourse in a poem:

> My older brother slept in a cot in the kitchen;
> My younger brother and I slept with our parents in
> The same room.
>
> Sometimes a noise woke me up,
> It sounded like sobs and whining,
> Like crying and shoving,
> Like gasping and pulling;
> it always got louder and filled the darkened room.
>
> It sounded as if my father hit,
> It sounded as if my mother was being hit;
> This struggle ended with a sudden stillness.
> I held my breath and pressed my hand on my
> chest,
> so the pounding of my heart
> wouldn't give me away.

In this poem not only the uncanny sounds that the parents make during intercourse but also the child's excitement is described. The impression given is that Turrini was unable to talk to anyone about this.

Freud (1915: 266) assumed that everybody has a primary fantasy about the parents' union—the so-called "primal scene". In the early phase the child interprets sexual intercourse as an aggressive act performed by the father who penetrates the mother either orally or anally. The child can develop the image of a combined oedipal couple whose aggressive union is dangerous for both. Even the insemination fantasies or the theories of birth that emerge in this period are either oral or anal. The child assumes that babies are created either by eating, vomiting, or kissing. Or it fantasizes the birth of the baby as being similar to stools expelled from the anus, and thus often studies its own stools with great interest and wonders what forms can be recognized in them. Unconscious wishes of boys and little girls are often responsible for the retention of stools since children believe that they can get a big belly and then press out a huge baby in the form of a "giant sausage". The reactivation of these early infantile fantasies is often responsible for the anxieties pregnant women have when they believe the baby could tear them up and destroy their body (Raphael-Leff, 1993: 109f). The infantile fantasy of the parents' sexual union includes the idea that the father's penis remains in the mother or fills her abdomen with countless babies and excrements, as many as the "sand grains in the sea" or the tadpoles and the spawn of fish. These images often appear in the dreams of pregnant women. The child's fantasized jealous attacks on the mother's body and the destruction of the babies assumed to be there are often very distressing to it, since it is afraid of being punished by the mother or father.

In one of Melanie Klein's important contributions, she directed our attention to the emergence of a cruel, strict superego that remains hostile to a child's ego and can still be active until the child grows up. This early superego is cruel, never satisfied, and "works" with hate and condemnation of the entire individual. A patient once said: "I have said to myself hundreds of times a day: "I hate myself, I hate myself, I hate myself," because I was never good enough." Or she thought: "I ought to be locked up until I am normal; I cannot expect anyone to tolerate me." The early, terrifying superego consists of internalized versions of the parents which attack the ego as strongly distorted, persecutory internal figures (Hinselwood, 1991: 61). The transformation of the early, cruel superego into a benevolent, moral conscience is crucial for society and the individual.

### 5.4.2   Case study: child analysis of Leo

The case of Leo shows how difficult it is to resolve Oedipal conflicts if the first emotional separation from the mother was not really possible—for instance, due to difficulties during weaning. The emotional separation from the mother is influenced by the possibility/impossibility of the child being able to distance itself from its bodily excretions. The early manifestation of the Oedipal conflict takes place at a time in which concrete, magical thinking predominates and the word is often equated with what it symbolizes. Since these early manifestations of experience are so difficult to retrace, I would like to elaborate on this subject by using material from Leo's playing in his analysis.

### Initial situation—family background

At the age of two Leo came with his parents to a parent–infant therapy. The parents were at their wits' end, they said, and had no idea what they should do with their son. He had sleeping problems, would not let himself be undressed, did not want to walk, and did not eat properly. He bit small children, had temper tantrums, and could hardly be controlled. Both parents seemed unhappy and desperate. The pregnancy and the birth of Leo had not posed any problems. However, the mother had fallen ill several weeks after the birth of her child and took only homeopathic medication because she was nursing. She reported that she had to lie down for the most part during the first months of Leo's life but in spite of that she had fully nursed Leo, which had been an enormous burden on her body. Since she herself had not been breastfed as a baby she was intent on giving her child this favourable start in life. She actually breastfed Leo for eleven months. It is possible that the long illness did not just have a somatic but also depressive component. After six months, the mother then took medication, which led to a quick improvement. As her health improved and she was able to get up again, Leo became more aggressive and difficult, whereas in the early months he had often lain for many hours with her under a blanket. His serious problems did not begin until his first birthday. Asked what else they could say about Leo apart from these extremely trying problems, the parents could also report many positive things. Like his parents, Leo loved books and could busy himself with them for a long time on his own, looking at picture books and asking interesting questions. Their life had, however, been subject to constraints as a result of Leo's difficult behaviour, since they could not take him to a restaurant or a coffee house where he would throw himself on the floor, acting up so much that he compelled everyone's attention. The parents thought that Leo would destroy their relationship.

From the first session on, Leo developed a strong positive transference to me as analyst so that the parents decided to let him begin analysis even though he was only two and a half years old. I will describe the development of this child analysis in several detailed excerpts from therapy sessions and the conversations with the parents which took place twice a semester.

## Course of therapy—beginning of analysis

At the beginning of analysis Leo only has a few words at his disposal, which no one except his parents can understand. He is still not toilet trained and oscillates between wild temper tantrums and passive behaviour. Initially Leo appears very unhappy, but from the first session on he makes creative use of the playing material and expresses his problems. He asks fearfully whether his father who had brought him will leave, but then accepts the explanation that Leo will play with me here and then his father will pick him up. When Leo does something he sees as forbidden, he apprehensively asks for his father. He brings me all the toys out of his drawer, tapes himself to me, and in this way shows that he would like to stick to me and come again. He confirms this interpretation with an unequivocal "yes". He takes out wooden figures and wooden animals, puts them in my hand and says I should hold the "bald animals". With this I think he expresses his hope that I will also keep him there along with all his "evil" thoughts. He takes my interpretations very seriously, looking deep in my eyes, checking to see if he can depend on me, impressed to be understood by me. At the end of the session it is difficult to get him to leave.

Leo is capable of expressing his oral wishes and the fears that are closely related to early forms of Oedipal wishes and envy of other imagined babies and of the father. In one session he forms a crocodile that devours babies made of Play-Doh. When I describe this, he says that it is now a crocodile who devoured the king. At home he now wants to constantly have a teething ring in his mouth. In therapy sessions he cuts an eraser in half, sticks one part in his mouth and chews on it, referring to it as "Lulli" (pacifier) or "chewing gum". He throws his pencils and pieces of Play-Doh on the ground, as if unintentionally, looking at me expectantly to see how I react. When I ask whether he thinks that the small part depicts him and he is afraid of also being dumped by me since he messed up everything here he said with a strong emphasis "Yes" and then puts glue all over his chair and the table—as a symbol of gluing himself here, wanting to connect him and me. He shows his anal wishes, his desire to possess and control everything, by marking everything with water (as a substitute for his bodily excretions) as if it should smell of him. He tries to put a fence around all of the animals, which he had put on the table. He then gives me the "bad horse" to hold. He splits everything into good and bad, fearing the intensity of his aggressive impulses and passing them on to me to keep for him. Leo wants to find out whether I was a strong person, not as sick and vulnerable as his fragile mother at the beginning of his life, whether I could survive and understand his aggressions and oral attacks. He gazes at me, moved, when I do not scold him or hit him or close the drawer but instead watch him and try to understand him. Leo had probably noticed how sensitive his mother's health condition had been and had behaved so that he would not harm her.

Interpretation

Leo is a highly intelligent child whose development is inhibited since he had severe inner conflicts. He is afraid of being bad. His jealousy and his difficulties in letting go are expressed in the way he symbolically connects himself to me with tape. Since in his first year of life he was convinced in his magical thinking of being responsible for her mother's illness, he has to keep testing—symbolically and in real terms—whether I can tolerate his being dirty and bad, whether I am a weak person whom he makes sick. His way of accepting my interpretations shows that he feels understood. The simple and robust furnishings of the therapy room allow Leo to express his aggressions. As an analyst I try not to influence the child but to understand the material appearing in play and to interpret it and to reduce his anxiety this way.

Projection of aggression onto the analyst

In another session, Leo projected his aggressions onto me. I was supposed to be the dangerous crocodile, which was first to devour the king, then twice Punch, and finally the crocodile baby. He then became afraid of his aggressions since he was still not able to distinguish between fantasy and reality. In the next session he bit into the cover of the box and wanted me to do the same thing. His wish for us to be both equal without my difference is shown in various ways. He found it difficult to leave after the session and it was not easy for him to accept the separation, racing repeatedly back into the therapy room.

At the same time he wanted to be big, and climbed up onto the table to be bigger than me. When I interpreted this he climbed even higher, up onto the windowsill, and beamed at me. He tried to gain total control over me, to boss me around, for instance, to send me over to his cars. When I told him that he wanted to boss me around he asked fearfully: "Where cars?" When he found them in the drawer where he had left them the previous day he was relieved. He took four cars, climbed up on the table again and made the cars drive along the windowsill into a garage. He took over control but suddenly became apprehensive again and said: "A man is in a car, he wants to go. Everything is packed."

I understood this to express his anxiety that a man (my husband) could come and take me away. I first repeated his words to be sure that I had understood him correctly. His linguistic development had quickly improved. Leo looked out of the window, saw snow, and commented on it. Then he took his blue pencil and drew a large "L" on the table. Now he was the boss again, big Leo. I noticed that he was now the big shot and he wanted to leave his traces everywhere so that everyone knew that he had been there. Leo pointed to the wall where he had left his scribbling in the last session. He said "Leo made it! Poopoo!" He became quite excited when I said he wanted everything to smell of him. Leo stuck the eraser in his mouth, called it "Lulla", and sucked on it with great pleasure. He took me completely in his possession, just like the "Lulla".

In the countertransference I had to be particularly careful not to overly succumb to his charm and to be part of the game instead of interpreting.

Later in the session Leo began to stomp on the table with his two feet, and then he took his cars and drove them into my lap. The cars stood for him; he wanted to push himself into every whole of my body. Then he pretended to cut his finger with the scissors. I told him that he was trying to frighten me and that I would stop him from hurting himself. He plays the game that his father was calling to say that he was picking him up and he asked me to put away all the toys.

At this moment, the father was a good figure, protecting Leo, especially from his wishes that had now become concrete, namely to take me into possession, and from fear of being punished for this or of punishing himself by cutting his finger.

When I spoke to the parents, they told me that Leo's linguistic development was proceeding in a surprisingly positive way and that he listened closely when his parents spoke. His difficulty falling asleep constituted a major problem. He would remain awake for a long time and often acted as if he were already asleep but was still wide awake. When playing he sank into a fantasy world into which he would totally retreat. He would also climb around on his mother a great deal, as if he wanted to get into her like an embryo. He wanted to lie with her under a blanket. Leo's behaviour strongly reminded his mother of her long illness after his birth. At the age of eleven months he had "weaned" himself, she added, which had hurt her deeply. He had only drunk once a day from the breast and liked solid food. Then he had begun to bite her breast and after three days she no longer tried to breastfeed him. Mother and Leo seemed to have a problem with weaning—the transition from breastfeeding to solid food. It seemed to be all or nothing, and the mother had felt rejected.

## Description of his Oedipal wishes and fears

Leo expressed his Oedipal wish in different ways: he crawled into his drawer, lay down and acted as if he were asleep, then threw out a red stone he had called "wolf" who had to be "shot". Leo drew Max and Moritz and said that they would be "hit" and killed by Master Lamp because they were bad. It always surprised me that he used complicated words and animal names. I interpreted this to him as symbolizing that he was very worried about being punished for his wishes. He pretended that a hunter with a big gun was coming to shoot the wolf. He drew a big wolf and gave the hunter a big gun.

Leo oscillated between the wish to take me/his mother away from my husband/his father and his fear of being harmed or injured by the father as retaliation. In order to hide his oedipal wish he tries to get me to participate as if it was my wish to be in a love affair with him.

He began jumping, very wildly and with great glee, on the couch and insisted on my also getting up onto the couch. I interpreted this wish. He then begged me so passionately that I let him pull me up onto the couch. With red cheeks, he jumped high like an acrobat, and wanted to take off my shoes, which I did not allow him to do. He tried to play tag with me, was very excited and wanted to excite me as well. Since he was so small I often let him entice me into going along with him. I interpreted this to him that he wanted to do with me on the couch what daddy and mummy do at night. This little "lover boy" repeatedly succeeded in creating an intensive erotic atmosphere, which, in the end, proved frightening to him. When I interpreted this, he calmed down. I went along a bit with the game and then suggested that we sit down and think about what he wanted to tell me with it. When he was apprehensive, he stuck a piece of string in his nose and said in a sad voice, "I am a clown," as if I should not take what he was saying seriously. It was often difficult to accept his energetic way of presenting his desire to be my lover. When I once smiled he said, "Don't laugh!"

His remark made it clear to me that in smiling I was attempting to avoid taking seriously his pain and his gradual recognition of his inability to replace my husband for me, or to replace his father for his mother.

His listening to sounds at night was an important issue. Leo made both cars, which represented mummy and daddy, collide, repeating this with a mixture of fear and pleasure. He tried to get us both under one blanket. Having failed at this, he placed a blanket over my head and wrapped himself in a different blanket. He built a large apartment for us both in which he wanted to first be in the same room as I but then he built two connecting rooms and wanted us both to sleep there. He wanted us both to get up in the middle of the night and to listen to the sounds. "Do you hear it?" he asked.

He might have experienced the sounds his parents made in the bathroom as frightening and exciting and stimulated himself while holding his penis.

The issue of sexual difference also interested him, but at the same time it was taboo. Even though his parents tried to tell him the facts of life he first refused to deal with this subject.

While playing with male and female wooden figures I once addressed his desire to know something about the difference between men and women, but he was first not receptive and said only, "Human." But then he remembered the tram conductor who had cut off his foot—a story that he had performed in the previous session. When I addressed his fear that something of his body, maybe the penis, could be cut off, he spoke about the wolves who ran about outside and warned me not to leave the apartment. He then went to the toilet and urged me to also do the same thing. I addressed his desire to see if I also had such a "little sparrow" (the word his parents used to refer to his penis) as he did. At the end of the session he "locked" the apartment in playing, so that "no one could come in to my place".

The next time I spoke with his parents they were both very relaxed. Leo now liked to be with his daytime babysitter and she was very much taken with him. He would play make-believe games, build caves for the bear family, and play the bear father himself. At home he played even more wildly. Sometimes he threatened to shoot his father with his gun. Sometimes he would then ask: "Why don't you understand me?"

Later he shows in his play that he understands the act of coitus of his parents as an aggression by the father in a sadomasochistic relationship. He interprets what is going on within the framework of an infantile sexual theory based on the child's own pre-oedipal physical experience with the mother and its result desires. He feared that either the mother would harm the father, biting off his penis and keeping it, or that the father would do something bad to the mother. In the further course of the analysis it became clear that he did not want to fall asleep at night because he would listen to the sounds his parents made during sexual intercourse, which frightened and excited him. The Oedipal theme appeared in various versions. First, he saw his parents as a dangerous Oedipal couple; later, he succeeded in expressing his wishes towards me in play. Instead of regressing to magic thinking—claiming that the crocodile would actually bite off his foot—he could then use words in a symbolic way, that is, separated from the object symbolized. In this connection, I will now cite a sequence from the twenty-eighth session:

> After he had always very much enjoyed coming to the therapy sessions, as if he could hardly wait to come, Leo announced one day, "Today I do not want to play." He climbed up on the table and looked around. By this I think he showed me it was dangerous here and that he wanted to get away. When I interpreted this to him, he wanted to play with his dinosaurs that he had made out of Play-Doh. He then got all worked up, spit on the window pane, licked his spit, and jumped up and down like a disturbed

child. He reacted to my words, when I said that just the thought of the dinosaurs made him all excited, by quieting down, taking out his drawing pad and his crayons, and beginning to draw. I asked what he was making and he answered "A snake." Then he painted, and remarked that he was drawing a hunter whose leg was bandaged. He made dots and small lines on the bandage of the hunter and pointed to his leg to show me how the bandage was fixed. "The crocodile bit off his leg," he said. I was not certain who the crocodile and who the hunter were, whether I was the hunter and whether this explained why did not want to play that day. I said, "You think that the crocodile is biting not only the hunter but also you." He quickly sat down on the windowsill and hid his legs under the table.

He had understood my words not as a description of his fantasy but in concrete terms, as a fact.

I said: "When I say that you think that the crocodile could also bite you it is real for you and you hide your feet." He said: "Don't move away the table!" He did not pay attention to my interpretation and said he was furious because I had taken away his gun. I inquired again since I wasn't sure I had understood him correctly. He quickly climbed down from the table, grabbed a large yellow wooden block and hammered on the locked door: "I am destroying it!" I noted how furious he was that there was an area from which he was excluded. Leo calmed down and said: "I have killed all the wasps, there were so many of them." The wasps stand for his projected fragmented aggressive thoughts. While I interpreted that he was furious because the room is for me and my husband, he made such a racket that I added that he was doing this in order not to hear what I was saying. He immediately stopped hammering and said: "The man will come right away; you can lie down and sleep until he comes." But then he lay down on the couch and acted as if he was sleeping. It was clear that he has the picture of a couple—that is, me and my husband, for whom I was supposed to wait. When I said how jealous he was, when he had to leave at the end of the session and thought that my husband would then come to me, he said: "All wasps are now gone." He ran to me and nestled his head in my lap. I said to him: "You're showing me how important it is for you that I understand you. Then you get really close to me. You would so much like to know what I and my husband or your mummy and your daddy do at night that you stay awake until they go to bed to be able to listen to them."

In a later session Leo said to me on greeting me that he was a "stingray" that would bite me. At the beginning of the session he immediately brought up his excitement and his curiosity about what goes on at night.

He ran right into the therapy room, wildly jumped about on the couch, lay down fevered, covered himself, and said, "Stingray is tired." He stood up and jumped again, asked me to come over and jump with him, and drew me to the couch.

My feelings were contradictory: on the one hand he was very inviting and insistent in the way that he beseeched me, and it was seductive to take him seriously as a little lover, but on the other, it was clear that he was acting out.

I told him that he wants me to jump up and down with him, to do such wild things as he thinks his mummy and daddy do at night. We jumped again, and then he said: "Now the hunter is coming with his gun." I interpreted that to be his fear that the hunter/my husband would come and punish him. Leo said: "Then I will run into the woods and hide. He wants to shoot me. Then he will not find me and is sad." After jumping he hid behind me. I said: "You're afraid that the hunter/my husband is really coming and won't want you to take me away from him; that's why you are hiding." He started jumping again and said: "Now ants are coming." He seemed to be comparing his penis with that of the "hunter" (his father/my husband) and feels that he is as small as an ant. Then he corrected himself and said that they were bringing the stingray something to eat. He sat down, pushing his head into my stomach, and said: "The man is coming." I interpreted that to be his envy of my husband. He wanted to be the person who was boring into me. He thought that my husband/his father stuck his penis in me/(in his mother) and he was doing something very real here by using his head like a penis and boring it into my stomach. I made it clear to him that this thought made him so excited and made it impossible for him to fall asleep. Leo went over to the intercom, which he used as a phone, and said "Hello", before tossing the receiver to the ground. I understood his anger and his desire to get rid of the man.

After this, Leo wanted to play with Play-Doh. He took the animals he and I had made the previous day out of the drawer, and sat down at the table. He took the giraffe, handed me the scorpion so gently as if it actually could sting, and said: "They are fighting now." He took the giraffe and bit off a piece of my scorpion. I spoke with him about his fear, about what would happen if his daddy and mummy had sex, his fear that something dangerous happened. Leo listened attentively, then took his elephant, whose trunk fell off, tried to attach this again, unsuccessfully, and then tossed the trunk to the floor. The bear lost a paw and when I asked which body part it had lost, he emphasized that it was the paw. I thought how important it was that it was the paw and not his willy. I spoke about his fear, that he was anxious that his mother could take away a piece of his father's body or that his father would hurt the mother. Then he said that the animals wanted to go home now, that I should accompany all the animals to his house (in his drawer) with my scorpion.

Another time he made an entire crocodile family out of Play-Doh and emphasized that they were really a family and laid the parent crocodiles in a bed—just as he experienced his family as dangerous and castrating when his parents fought or had sex and did not know the difference between his parents' love or passion and fighting.

The symbolic representation of his parents' sexual union—fantasized via the animals as being something dangerous—helped Leo to express his anxieties. In play, he attributed a dangerous role to me which corresponded to his wishes and anxieties. It was important for me as the analyst to take as little initiative as possible in the role playing but to ask the child again and again what the analyst should do as a hunter or as a crocodile. Only in this way can we learn about the child's fantasies.

When I met with Leo's parents, they explained to me how he reacted with anxiety when they had an argument and how he watched closely when they made up again. They tried to make it clear to him that they had fought but that they now got along again. In playing he could demonstrate to me the anxiety he felt over his parents' sexual union which was perceived as an aggressive act. Working through his anxiety enabled him to diminish it and his problems falling asleep. He also showed his castration fear in "doctor games" that continued over several sessions. He wanted me to play the doctor and to cut him open, after which he quickly announced, "I am a girl." This was closely connected to this fantasy of an aggressively united, violent parental couple and his desires for anal control.

## Separation problems

Leo's problems with toilet training were related to his difficulty in separating and releasing himself, as well as with a strongly phallic cathexis of his bodily excretions. When he became angry with me in a therapy session, he would defecate in his pants at the beginning of analysis so that everything stank. Here are two sequences relating to this from one session:

> Leo drew a long mark with a brown pencil and asked me what it was. Since he drew these signs over several pages, I remarked that it seemed important to him to make many pages "full". He looked for a white page and smeared it. Beaming, he said, "That's a big poop!" He sat on top of his drawing and rolled back and forth.

In a different session when his mother brought him, he was distraught and cried. She explained that Leo was crying because he did not want to let go of her hand when she rang the bell. The mother took his jacket off and left. I asked him why he was crying. He said, "Mommy let go hand." He stopped crying, came in and said, "Am afraid." Then he went to the couch and said, "I am a crab that is tied down. You must cut me free." He showed me how tethered down he felt, he could not free himself. When I acted as if I were untying a ribbon, he said that it would not work that way, I would really have to get some scissors and cut it. "You show me how you were not able to let go of mommy's hand and how difficult it is for you at the end of the session to leave and to also let go of your poop."

Following this session Leo soon became toilet trained. He expressed his desire to go to the toilet as adults do. In a session marked by his strong Oedipal wishes, I took off his nappy and accepted his wish to remain without one. It would have been inappropriate to make a wild "lover" look small and to give him a nappy. He then stayed that way and things went surprisingly well, as his parents reported.

In the first year Leo expressed his desire to remain connected to me and to not become separated with such vehemence that his father's difficulties in getting him out of the room made me act out along with him: at the end of the session, I suggested pushing him out of the room on the small table that he had often used as a train. He accepted willingly, rode with me to the threshold, and then ran to his father. Only when I understood that I was masking Leo's difficulty in creating a transitional space between me and his father could I interpret his anxiety and enable him to accept the parting and discuss his fear of seeing me unchanged the next day. He wanted to control his objects, to remain connected, and feared losing control when he let go.

The end of the analysis, announced on relatively short notice, caused Leo to experience turbulent feelings that once more brought up the theme of weaning. He would cry bitterly at home when his parents informed him of the end of analysis and in the following sessions he was furious with me that I would let him go.

With the wild struggle of two dinosaurs Leo showed me how he was afraid that his bad part would destroy the good part in him and how much he needed my help in integrating the two parts.

Discussion of the end of analysis required working through his weaning, which had been difficult. Leo seemed to need more analysis, and to feel abandoned and left alone in dealing with all his problems, but his parents insisted on terminating it because he had developed so well in all areas. In one of the last sessions Leo brought me a newspaper clipping about a little brown bear that had lost its mother—probably a sign of his anxiety that he would be completely lost without my analytic understanding. He showed me he knew that I knew how much he would still like to come and his trepidation at having to deal with all his inner turbulences on his own.

In a final meeting with the parents after one and a half years of analysis, the parents said that Leo was now very co-operative in the playgroup and at home. He could express himself in a much differentiated way, as well as making many quite nice drawings. He had begun to undress himself and his toilet training had proceeded very quickly. The parents could now take him along to a coffee house where he could express precisely what he wanted and could eat on his own. Other coffee house guests were impressed by him and admired the parents of this independent child. Leo liked going to his all-day babysitter, his language skills were above average, he developed fantasy games, and was very popular with other children.

The early therapeutic intervention enabled Leo to process his confusion over separation and letting go. His development towards a mature solution of his Oedipal conflict had thus been furthered. The sessions with Leo show how complex these issues are and how the different levels of separating from his mother, the rivalry with his father, and his body perception, were all closely interrelated. In the interpretation the analyst tried to address these issues as much as possible in the context of transference (that is, the feelings transferred to the analyst) and countertransference (the feelings that emerge in the analyst). The way in which the child responded to these interpretations, whether it agreed, continued the interpretation in playing, or changed the subject because it felt understood, was closely observed. It is a difficult balancing act to maintain the parents' cooperation without wanting to become a better mother or a better father oneself, and to discuss the parents' jealousy that another person could become so important for their child. The therapeutic work with parents is therefore just as important as the work with the child.

### 5.4.3    Oedipus conflict in the young boy

I have already described in detail that the first love object for a boy is his mother. We assume that he experiences her not only as satisfying but as threatening, since she appears to possess everything he needs. As a baby, he fantasizes his mother to be omnipotent and feels himself to be powerless and needy. We assume that her absence awakens his rage, desire for revenge, and mortal fear, which he projects onto the mother as "raw" perceptions (beta elements). If the mother succeeds in taking in these projected "raw" perceptions, mentally digesting them and "returning" them to her son, he will then gradually develop the image of a whole person and also experience himself as a person with good and bad qualities.

This phase, in which the young boy wishes to have babies as his mother does and envies her for having them ("fecundity envy"), was called the "feminine phase" by Melanie Klein: "At the bottom is a frustrated desire for a special organ. The tendencies to steal and destroy are concerned with the organs of conception, pregnancy and parturition, which the boy assumes to exist in the mother, and further with the vagina and breasts, the fountain of milk" (Klein, 1928: 190). As in the castration-complex of girls, so in the femininity-complex of the male, there is at bottom the frustrated desire for a special organ. The tendencies to steal and destroy are concerned with the organs of conception, pregnancy, and parturition, which the boy assumes to exist in the womb, and further with the vagina and the breasts, the fountain of milk, which are coveted as organs of receptivity and bounty from the time when the libidinal position is purely oral (Klein, 1928: 170). The boy increasingly notices that his mother is not omnipotent, but has a relationship to her husband, the boy's father, that she is loved and desired by him. His own loving relationship to his father helps the boy to separate himself from his mother, fantasized by him as "omnipotent", and to turn towards his father. A relationship between three people comes into being, called a "triangular relationship" by Freud (1924: 176). Compared with his father, the boy is small. His nascent interest in the physical differences between man and woman causes him to see his father as much bigger and wiser than he is—the comparison with penis size as "pars pro toto" symbolizes the difference between adult and child abilities and difference in potency.

The boy would also like to serve his father as a sexual partner, a phenomenon called the "negative Oedipus complex" by Freud (1924: 174), later expressed in homosexuality. The boy wishes to replace his mother and be passively loved by his father in subjugation to him (Freud, 1924).

Freud attributes great importance to the boy's discovery that his mother has no penis. The boy fears that this important part of the body has been taken away from the mother. He sees his father as a rival for the mother's affections, hates him, and wishes to push him aside. At the same time, he loves his father and longs for his attentions. These explosive feelings and fears of being inadequate to his mother, and especially of being punished through castration by his mother or father for his incestuous and forbidden wishes, are termed the "castration fear" (Freud, 1924: 175). Only when the boy has accepted the separate quality of his parents' sexual relationship and his painful exclusion from it can he begin to form a new libidinous constellation. Instead of desiring his mother as a woman, he identifies with his father and tries to model himself on him, in the hope of later becoming like the father and starting his own family.

Since Oedipal conflicts are based in unconscious wishes, postulated by Freud as universal, we have no direct recollection of these wishes. In boys' games, however, elements of these configurations can be observed. Here are two scenes from a psychoanalytic observation of young children.

## Observation of Ben[4]

Ben is a two-and-a-half year-old boy from London. His father is a professional soldier; the mother is a housewife and mother. The scene is described by an observer taking part in a course on "Young Child Observation" held at the Tavistock Clinic, and was filmed by the BBC for *Talking Cure* (a series about the psychoanalytic method the clinic uses in its work with patients; the title making reference to Freud's description of the method of psychoanalytic treatment).

Ben's mother is sitting on a bench at the playground and is holding her friend's six-month-old baby on her lap. Ben is standing next to his mother, staring at the baby, and then runs away. He picks up something, comes back to his mother, places his head on the baby and says like a baby, "Ah, ah." Then he looks tensely at the baby to see how it will react. It smiles and turns to Ben. The mother watches this interaction closely.

Ben's friend Jack goes with Ben to a distant corner of the playground. Ben takes a cloth doll out of a doll pram, stares for a long time at the doll, and then tosses it with great momentum up in the air, letting it fall to the ground. He sits down next to the doll with a serious look on his face and hits it several times very hard on the behind. Full of anger he grabs its hair, turns it, and lets it lie. Ben takes a second doll out of another doll pram, tosses it onto the ground, and hits its behind. Ben places the first doll back in the pram, pushes the pram around, and then tries to toss the doll high up on the wall, which does not succeed at first. His friend Jack has been attracted by Ben's activities; they look at each other like accomplices. Then Jack picks the doll up off the ground and tries to throw it on the wall. The doll falls back down on the ground. Jack picks it up and throws it with a serious, sullen face and after several attempts succeeds in getting it on the wall. Both boys look with great gratification at the lonely doll high up on the wall. Then Jack walks over to the observer who was the only witness of this punishable act, pulls her on the hand and tries to get her to get the doll down from the wall. With a mixture of pride and satisfaction, but also a sense of guilt, Jack looks up at the doll up high.

## Interpretation

Ben and Jack are both at an age when they are interested in the question of whether their parents will have another baby. They keenly

---

[4] Video of the BBC series *Talking Cure* (III), *Damien and Ben*, London 1994.

observe everything that has to do with babies and with the intimacy of their parents' bodies. Their jealousy of other babies can be very pronounced. When Ben sees the unfamiliar baby on his mother's lap, he feels torn. He moves closer and then runs away, showing how ambivalent his feelings are. First he imitates the baby by placing his head on the baby and imitating its sounds. It would be an illusion to believe that a three-year-old is really grown up. It is still in part a baby. Children at that age still like to play baby and parent. One child can assume the baby role, while the other tentatively takes on the role of the mother or the father. But soon jealousy prevails in the game and Ben expresses his wish that the baby—symbolized by the doll—disappear. In the game he is the big and strong man who yells "Hurrah!" and gets rid of the hated rival, throwing it high up in the air and hitting it. The game has a magical quality, giving him a sense of omnipotence. At the end, his guilt feelings win over; he wants an observer to now bring the doll back down again. In the mother–father–child game, the child can also reflect and express its anxiety that there might possibly be more children.

## Observation of Ben (continuation)

The next scene talks place in a large playhouse in which the children can stand or lie down. The observer is standing outside of it and can look down into the playhouse.

Two small girls lie on a mat in a playhouse. Jack walks towards it and lies down very close to a girl. The girls say: "We are babies." Ben takes a toy screwdriver and acts as if he is screwing a screw into their navels. Both look at him smiling. One of the two girls opens her propped legs full of excitement. All three are quite worked up. The observer smiles while watching. Jack has taken a toy bottle that he sticks in his mouth and sucks on. He looks offended at Ben who does not include him in the game. Both girls maintain eye contact with Ben. The girl wearing pink has her legs spread and puts her hand on the inside of her thigh. Ben gives both of the girls a toy car—he tosses it amicably towards their stomachs. The girl wearing pink has put one leg over the other and laughs. Ben has no third car for Jack who sits up disappointedly, gets up, and goes away. Ben runs about and yells at Jack: "Lay down! Lay down right away!" Ben has meanwhile put a teething ring in his mouth, turning it back and forth while sucking it.

Interpretation

In this scene Ben plays the father and husband of the two girls. They say they are babies, but this has more the function of covering over their wish to assume the position of the mother. He is the one who serves both girls, giving them both a present, which they gladly accept with gratified motions. They play what daddy and mummy do together at night, with Jack excluded. The game is very exciting—they all have flushed cheeks and beaming eyes. The healing function of the game also becomes evident in this scene, when Ben is able to project part of his ambivalent feelings on Jack. In the game Jack is the one who is excluded, who feels at a disadvantage—just as Ben perhaps imagines being pushed out of his prince role when the new baby was born. His rivalry with his father is played out in the game with his friend, who is then actually offended. In the previous scene, both formed a team against new babies. Jack's importance for the game can be seen in the fact that Ben runs right after him and does not want him to go away. Ben screams that Jack should stay there in order to play the excluded part.

## 5.4.4   Oedipal conflict in a young girl

The understanding of the Oedipal conflict in a girl is controversial. Freud emphasized that the mother represents the first love object with the same intensity as for the boy. In his "Three Essays on the Theory of Sexuality" Freud (1905a) and in "Female Sexuality" (Freud, 1931: 227) argues that the little girl turns to the mother as the primary loved object as does the "little man". Freud's assumption that the girl knows nothing about her internal sexual organs and her vagina, since there is always only discussion of the clitoris, was very contradictory. Ernest Jones (1935: 264) postulated a "primary femininity". Melanie Klein speaks of the girl's fantasy of attacking the mother's body and the baby that is allegedly inside of it, which points to a concept of female sexual organs. To justify the girl's turning away from the mother and turning to the father as a love object, Freud cites the girl's frustration over the deficiency of her and her mother's sexual endowment, namely the fact that she does not have a penis like her father (Freud, 1931: 228). The girl envies the father for his penis and develops "penis envy". Disappointed, she turns away from the mother and to the father. The desire to have a baby from her father stands symbolically for her wish to have a penis. By contrast, analysts such as Horney, Mitscherlich, and Birksted-Breen have assumed that the girl has an inborn knowledge about its female sexual parts and thus of its value as a girl, that is, a "primary femininity". The wish for a child is seen as primary and not as the result of frustration over not having a penis. In the observation of little girls playing, Erik Erikson (1964) discovered a symbolization of the body's inner space, which he understood as indicating a latent knowledge of the genital inner space. He found gender-specific differences regarding the game's structure that corresponded to the morphology of gender difference. Boys chose playing modes of fighting with phallic objects such as spears, swords, and fishing poles, whereas for girls inner spaces assumed more meaning. They built a house, used cozy corners for playing and cuddling. Bernstein (1990) claimed that girls' anxieties regarding their genitals are less specific than those of boys, and that mental representation of female sexual organs is less clearly delineated since female genital organs are open and provide entry.

In a new pregnancy of the mother, girls are often able to identify with her and to play as if they were pregnant. This play has a salutary effect in providing a way to deal with their emotions.

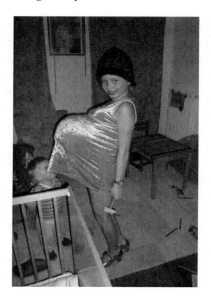

Freud's (1924: 178) often cited statement that "anatomy is destiny"—a variation on a well-known saying of Napoleon—is actually related to a central idea of psychoanalysis, namely that the ego is always physical, that is, always shaped by a female and a male body. The acquisition of gender identity remains contradictory. In psychological terms, we are not born as men or women. Rather, masculinity or femininity is only established in the course of the first eighteen months, irrespective of biological endowment. Freud (1905a: 218) asserted that the seeming clarity of femininity and masculinity "volatizes" or "pales", meaning that a pure femininity or a pure masculinity is not to be found. Birksted-Breen (2005: 148) writes: "It is the very duality and opposition—femininity constructed around lack and dissatisfaction, and a femininity related to the specific female bodily experiences—which to my mind constitutes the female unconscious." The girl must deal with these two perspectives of "positive and negative femininity". Positive femininity refers to the mental representation of her internal organs and a possible motherhood, whereas negative femininity refers to the lack of a penis and the unconscious significance of the phallus as a symbol of power and potency. While the phallic defence in men against the vulnerability and helplessness of their female aspects is manifested in "macho" behaviour, in women the defence of their male aspects consists in presenting themselves as "featherbrained". For both sexes, the healthy cathexis of the penis consists in the ability to establish connections and structures. The psychic possession of a "good inner penis" is as important for both sexes as a good form of bi-sexuality to ensure good mental functioning.

In the girl a homosexual selection of the mother as a love object also exists, which does not require that the libidinous cathexis from infancy be relinquished. Even if the priority is placed on a parent of a different sex, that is, the woman experiences heterosexual sexuality, friendships and deep bonds with persons of the same sex often remain intact for many years.

A mature form of coming to terms with the Oedipal conflict consists in giving up incestuous wishes and recognizing the difference between the relationship between parents and that between parent and child. The parental couple is capable of reflecting on their child and entering into a different type of love relationship with it. How important this cognitive and emotional achievement is can be seen in the effect it has on thinking. In the father–mother– child game played by children, erotic excitement can be seen in their flushed cheeks. Being able to jump around together in the parents' bed, to scuffle in the crib, allows children to do in fantasy what mummy and daddy do at night to make babies.

The child that relinquishes its incestuous wish accepts the reality of its parents' sexual relationship, enabling a mature superego to evolve in the girl and boy. Freud maintained that such a child has introjected the authority of the father into the ego, there forming the nucleus of the superego which "takes over the serenity of the father (and) perpetuates his prohibition against incest" (Freud, 1924: 175). Melanie Klein described the transformation of the early sadistically cruel superego into a moral superego. Instead of self-punishment the child can show empathy for others, feel guilt for its own actions, and make amends for injustice. By being better able to integrate the good and bad aspects of a person and of itself, the bad, persecutory aspects are mitigated, that is, the aggression is lessened by the libido (Klein, 1952: 151). The child can assimilate a calming external world and anchor images of unharmed parents. "That means that the image of his [sic] parents that he initially perceived in a distorted way as idealized and terrifying figures gradually became adjusted to reality" (Klein, 1952: 127). How difficult the development of a mature superego is can be seen in the fact that many people are much stricter and more unrelenting with themselves than with others and have trouble accepting their own unconscious motives.

I would like to argue that the Oedipal configuration is a conflict pattern that remains important throughout a person's entire life. In conflicts it thus always makes sense to ask what the conflict centres on. Does the conflict involve rivalry, jealousy of a third person, whose favour, affection, or love actually shapes the conflict? Even when a baby is born, parents must deal with the fact that their relationship has been expanded into a relationship of three. Early feelings of exclusion are experienced again in particular by fathers, when the baby and the mother enter into an especially close relationship as a "nursing couple". But even the "baby in the mother" can be reactivated on a deep level, with the mother desiring exclusive affection from both the husband and from the baby. In child-rearing, issues of jealousy, disadvantage, and exclusion play an important role not just for the children but also for both parents.

In closing I would like to address two important themes, namely the issue of sexual abuse as a form of perversion and the effects that the resolution of the Oedipal conflict has on thinking.

## 5.5    Sexual abuse—a perversion

Sexuality in early childhood differs considerably from pubertal or adult sexuality and it is thus imperative that adults provide special protection. Acceptance of sexuality in infancy requires special respect for children in dealing with them. Freud wrote how easy it was to seduce children or to force them to perform sexual acts that are a massive transgression:

> It is an instructive fact that under the influence of seduction children become polymorph perverse, and can be led into all possible kinds of sexual irregulations. This shows that an aptitude for them is innately resent in their disposition. There is consequently little resistance towards carrying them out, since mental dams against sexual excesses—shame, disgust and morality have either not yet been constructed at all or are only in the course of construction, according to the age of the child.
>
> (Freud, 1905a: 191)

These violations of boundaries not only injure bodily integrity, but also have a negative impact on the development of personality, since they cause deep emotional and mental confusion. To make things worse, the perpetrators are often loved and respected persons in the family, that is, the same person that the child loves seduces it to perform acts that are simultaneously frightening and exciting. The abused child feels both humiliated and powerful since it was able to elicit strong reactions in the perpetrator. Particularly in the sensitive phase of early childhood when the child is faced with sexual wishes and fantasies related to the parent of the opposite sex, or even of the same sex—and thus feels guilty—sexual transgressions have a particularly damaging effect. The Oedipal conflict primarily has to do with the unconscious wish to transgress the boundaries of generations. The experience of real boundaries between the generations—evident in parental sexuality from which the child is excluded—is painful, but it helps the child to find its own place, to find its bearings in the world, in its family. When an adult actually performs sexual acts with a child, generational boundaries collapse and there is a serious confusion of reality and fantasy, a deep confusion about one's own role and one's own feelings. Forced fellatio frightens and excites a small child. It will then try to repeat this overwhelming and threatening experience in playing by, for instance, stuffing large pieces of cheese or bread into its mouth so that it feels it must vomit. In this way it tries to come to terms with this experience. A sexually abused girl attracted attention in kindergarten and at home because she wanted to bare the genitals of adult men in an aggressive and overly excited way. Her father, however, was able to set clear boundaries and make it unmistakably clear to her that these were his private body parts. She tried it again several more times until the violated boundaries were stabilized again. The child desperately needs adults that are able to maintain these generation boundaries and can help the child deal with the pain, the jealousy, and the frustration.

The sexual abuse of children and infants is a perversion which is, in essence, destructive because sexuality is used as a means to achieve something (Stoller, 1994). Caper (1999: 78) writes about perversion as follows: "We can define it in a psychoanalytic way, purely in terms of the unconscious forces and fantasies behind it: is the activity sexual or destructive in the unconscious?" With homosexual and heterosexual love, it depends on the quality of the relationship, whether it is loving or destructive and thus perverse. Experiencing adult sexuality at an early age is always destructive because it violates the boundaries of generations.[5] An adult man abuses a child instead of protecting it. In therapy, an abused child compared this violent sexual situation with the image of "a flower that was opened too early" (Sinason, 1988).

Is it possible to detect signs of a possible sexual abuse in a child's behaviour? Girls and boys develop different strategies of bearing and surviving an abusive situation. The particular resistance forms employed depend on an individual's life situation, the type of abuse, and the age of the child (Wanke and Triphammer, 1992: 32). Up to the age of five to six, magical thinking still plays a central role, so that children have a hard time distinguishing fantasy from reality. In this period accepting the reality principle develops, but at the same time a more or less pronounced belief in the power of fantasy remains. In addition, the idea of parental sexuality is still strongly linked

---

[5] The exploration of the child's body by another child of the same age can be part of a game based on curiosity when both are acting consensually. If an older child (or several children) put another child under pressure or threaten it by means of force, then this is sexual abuse, since humiliation and exposure predominates. However, it does not have such serious consequences since the generational boundary is not violated.

with aggressive oral and anal tendencies. Much depends on how consolidated the inner world of a child is, and whether it has a good enough relationship with another person to confide in him or her. Even if sexually abused children show different somatic and psychic reactions, attentive, loving adults are necessary to recognize these changes. Children become disturbed; they withdraw or become more aggressive. In playing they may try to stabilize the violated boundaries. A two-year-old girl, for instance, who was abused several times but had a good, stable relationship with her parents, only used red building blocks for building, with great perseverance. It was striking that she strongly opposed any suggestion to use blocks of a different colour, and she cried in despair and went to great pains to separate the various colours. All of the symptoms named are not specific signs of sexual abuse. More important is the desperate nature of play and persistence in play. Adults can only remain open to this possibility, and let their suspicions be substantiated or dispelled by heightened attention and precise observation of the child. Another girl drew one and the same motive over a period of months. It was an idyllic garden with butterflies, flowers, a high tree, and a secure house. She had kept the traumatic experiences locked up inside of her and tried, as a sort of reparation, to find security in a very supportive family. In many instances, after discovering that abuse has taken place, a mother or father can notice a change in the child. In his book *Tatort Kinderseele* (*Crime Scene: Soul of a child*) (1998) Max Friedrich lists changes that often occur.

Possible changes following sexual abuse:

- Sleep disorders.
- Learning disorders such as lack of concentration, poor school performance, lapses, problems of perception, and sudden refusal to learn.
- Eating disorders, such as bulimia, anorexia, or obesity, which usually assume a pronounced form in puberty.
- Disturbances in hygiene manifested in extreme washing compulsion but also in neglect of appearance.
- Sudden changes in behaviour such as increased activity or motivation, self-aggressive behaviour to give outer expression to internal pain, aggression directed at others, or other inexplicable behaviour that is unusual for the child.

- Fear of various things and situations such as taking showers or bathing.
- Diffuse, inexplicable anxiety; trouble falling asleep; separation anxieties.
- Withdrawal and isolation; avoidance of joint activities.
- Flight into a fantasy world to escape from a painful reality.
- Compulsive behaviour, that is, constant repetitions in thinking, speaking, or action that gives the child a minimum level of security.
- Rapidly changing moods ranging from exaggerated cheerfulness, over irritability, to depression.
- Conspicuous sexualized behaviour characterized by excessive use of bawdy language, dirty jokes, hidden and explicit sexual utterances, and behaviour such as public exposure of genitals.
- Illnesses and psychosomatic ailments such as skin eczema, headaches, asthma, chronic sore throat and colds, stomach, intestinal and bladder ailments, diarrhoea, constipation, and constant nausea (all indicating that physical suffering enables the child to bear psychical pain).
- Sexually transmitted diseases, genital fungal infections, and injuries in genital area (bite wounds, haematomas, and so forth) are a relatively sure symptom in small children.
- Running away.

(cf. Friedrich, 1998: 91f)

This long enumeration of possible behavioural changes that can be indicative of sexual abuse shows that there are not specific symptoms. The same symptoms can appear in various inner conflicts, that is, no reverse conclusion is possible. To make things more complicated, small children are still unable to express themselves in a more differentiated way and tend to reveal abuse more through play or in a drawing. A two-year-old girl demonstrated to a young therapist the forced penetration of a penis during play by sitting on top of her and repeatedly pressing a large, cylindrical wooden block in her mouth. When asked whether the girl was showing what her mother and father did at night, the girl said no and named the babysitter and her boyfriend. It was then possible to press charges against the babysitter. When sexual abuse is suspected the social workers called upon must remain open in their own reflection, since an accusation can be real or it can also be a child's fantasy. Accusations have often proven to be inaccurate and have ruined the life of the person against whom charges are pressed ("false-memory syndrome", Loftus and Ketcham, 1994: 65).

At the same time educators should also be sensitized to the fact that the estimated number of unreported cases is very high for sexual abuse and that children often go through a martyrdom lasting months or even years which can have an extremely detrimental effect on their capacity to think and experience. The many offerings of child pornography on the Internet, in which even sexual acts with babies and infants are shown, are indicative of this wide dissemination. It is estimated that in addition to the 600 cases of sexual abuse in which charges are pressed in Austria, a further 25,000 cases remain undiscovered each year. There are more individuals who know about sexual abuse but wish they did not, or remain silent.

> My friends raped a girl,
> a student at the Catholic convent school.
> They took her into the woods
> for a Sunday walk,
> stuck a potato in her mouth.
> They tickled her,
> promised her five schillings
> and a bicycle,
> shoved a pine cone between her legs,
> set her underwear on fire,
> and put out the flame with urine.
> I hid myself nearby
> and kept quiet,
> watching everything.
> One week later
> during the children's mass
> I gave the convent school girl a poem.
> I had copied it from my brother's textbook:
> Many a man curls up and dies
> who flees from evil men;
> He sees not the single loving heart
> watching in silence over him.
> She did not answer me.

> I could have told her so much,
> I could have told her everything
> I had read about Love.
> Only for one question
> I had no answer:
> Why I hadn't helped her.
>
> (Peter Turrini, 1996: 181)

The perpetrators are primarily to be found in the victim's family, and generally have only secondary contact with the victim through their profession or their position of trust and authority. Only rarely do strangers kidnap or abduct a child. Usually there is a complex network of relationships behind an instance of sexual abuse, which makes it possible to ignore the act itself or over a longer period of time. Even though in most cases small girls are the victims and men the perpetrators, it is important to examine the relationship the perpetrator has with the woman he is living with. Often the perpetrators are stepfathers or new life companions who approach a woman living with small girls, or the woman herself who no longer has an interest in sexual contact tolerates or initiates the abuse in order to bind the man to her. Both the perpetrators and accomplices were often victims themselves as children. It is continually surprising how many persons from the neighbourhood have reason to be suspicious without intervening or reporting their suspicions to a social worker. The well-known journalist Gitta Sereny studied the life story of Mary Bell, who as an eleven-year-old killed two boys aged three and four and was sentenced to life in prison. She tells her life story in *Cries Unheard* (Sereny, 1988). Mary was born out of wedlock to a young woman who had been hidden in a convent in Ireland during her pregnancy. While giving birth to the child her mother said, "Take this thing away," referring to her daughter. She spent the first years of her life with a mother who did not love her, before then being put in the care of various institutions. When her mother took Mary back she was working as a prostitute. The frequent sexual abuse of Mary did not remain unknown to her environment, but no one did anything about it. Her contempt for cheerful children growing up in a happy family was so explosive that she lured away and strangled the two small children without any conscious motive. It simply came over her. Afterwards, she said in an interview, they looked as peaceful as angels.

An encounter with small children often triggers strong emotions in adults. The child's helplessness and vulnerability can activate anxiety or the wish to protect the child. The child can also elicit a sense of joy with its vitality and potential for development— and consciously or unconsciously stimulate envy and hate when compared to one's own unhappy childhood. The comparison with one's own early childhood is only very rarely completely accessible to an adult's consciousness, since this evokes primitive ambivalent feelings. Adults who force children or infants to perform sexual acts stage a situation in which children are supposed to experience what they themselves once had to suffer. The more contact they have with their painful feelings as a child and remember their rage, their hate, their excitation, their helplessness and humiliation, the better they are able to break through the vicious circle. If, however, they have repressed their own past experiences and feelings or have played down these painful incidents, there is the danger that they will act them out in reverse roles. Here we are dealing with highly complex emotional phenomena that are linked to a sense of being overwhelmed and a state of helplessness, excitation, omnipotence, rage, and shame. I would like to illustrate the special quality of this highly charged involvement by means of a case study taken from literature and two cases from therapeutic work.

### 5.5.1    Cases of sexual abuse

In her novel *The God of Small Things* Arundhati Roy (1997) provides a compelling description of the main character's sexual abuse by a stranger. In a flashback she tells of Estha, the ten-year-old twin brother who does not speak:

> Estha had gone to the cinema with his parents. Since he was singing loudly he was sent into the foyer. The man selling lemonade noticed him, intimidated him and offered him a free lemonade.

Estha went behind the Refreshments Counter for his Free Cold Drink. He saw the three high stools arranged in a row for the Orangedrink Lemondrink Man to sleep on. The wood shiny from his sitting.

"Now if you'll kindly hold this for me," the Orangedrink Lemondrink Man said, handing Estha his penis through his soft white muslin dhoti, "I'll get you your drink. Orange? Lemon?"

Estha held it because he had to.

"Orange? Lemon?" the Man said. "Lemonorange?"

"Lemon, please," Estha said politely.

He got a cold bottle and a straw. So he held a bottle in one hand and a penis in the other. Hard, hot, veiny. Not a moonbeam.

The Orangedrink Lemondrink Man's hand closed over Estha's. His thumbnail was long like a woman's. He moved Estha's hand up and down. First slowly. Then fastly.

The lemondrink was cold and sweet. The penis hot and hard. The piano keys were watching.

"So your grandmother runs a factory?" the Orangedrink Lemondrink Man said. "What kind of factory?"

"Many products," Estha said, not looking, with the straw in his mouth. (....)

"Good," the Orangedrink Lemondrink Man said. "Excellent". His hand closed tighter over Estha's. Tight and sweaty. And faster still. (....)

Then the gristly-bristly face contorted and Estha's hand was wet and hot and sticky. It had egg white on it. White egg white. Quarter-boiled.

The lemondrink was cold and sweet. The penis was soft and shriveled like an empty leather change-purse. With his discolored rag, the man wiped Estha's other hand.

"Now finish your drink," he said, and affectionately squished a cheek of Estha's bottom.

(Roy, 1997: 103–104)

Roy describes sexual abuse from the boy's perspective—everything seems so natural but at the same time so confusing and threatening. The adult acts as if it were all very ordinary; Estha seems apprehensive, curious, confused, and perhaps even excited. He does not dare contradict the man. How damaging this experience was for him becomes clear afterwards. He tries not to touch anything with his sullied hand and goes back into the cinema. Then he feels nauseous and goes to the toilet with his mother but he is not able to vomit. When she wants to buy him lemonade from the same man,

THE PSYCHOSEXUAL DEVELOPMENT OF A CHILD    231

he strongly refuses, and when she wants to leave him with the man he reacts completely unusually and protests strongly. As so often in reality, this abuse remains undiscovered; no one understands why Estha is so changed and remains so in the following weeks. He himself feels guilty as he thinks he has done something wrong and his mother will therefore love him less.

## Case study of Mira

The sexual abuse by a caregiver in a children's group was uncovered in the process of her analysis of Mira, a seven-year-old girl. She was brought to the therapist because of serious sleeping disorders, nausea attacks, and her anxieties about going to school. Only later did her parents report that at the age of three and a half she was allegedly sexually stimulated during a period of half a year by a caregiver while her nappies were being changed. Mira had completely changed since then, but she kept very close ties to the caregiver. He denied the allegations but was removed from the play group.

Mira is a twin; her sister is good-looking, is well liked by others, and learns easily. Mira is less attractive, has no friends, and is rather clumsy in her movements.

In the first two sessions Mira oscillates between what seems to be a not very genuine wooing and a cruel mocking of me. She wants to show me how stupid people are. When she presents her anxiety of ghosts in playing, she tries to quickly turn it into a joke. I should be the one who is handicapped and silly. She shows how much she suffers from competition with the twin sister she cannot live up to. If she could, she would prefer to start life over—but without a twin sister. She feels rejected. The parents were not expecting the pregnancy and did not count on twins. In playing she always deals with death and cemeteries. She is very suspicious and initially does not believe that I do not tell her parents what she discusses with me in the session. She conveys her unfaltering conviction that she is unwanted and unloved by everybody. She actually succeeded in evoking a feeling of oppression in me. She mocked me and at the same time sought close body contact. Here is a scene to illustrate this.

Mira is playing with wooden building blocks and constructs a village. Three houses stand in one place, and at some distance there is another part of the village with gates, animals, and wooden figures.

When she removes the wooden figures, she calls them in turn mama and papa, the grandparents, herself, and the twin sister. She takes each one and puts it away. I ask her what has happened to the figures. "They are all dead," she replies in a cold voice. She buries them in a cemetery, takes the wooden figure that represents her and puts it in the part of the village with the three houses. I interpret this to her as showing me that she thinks that everything in her is dead and as a statement about how she is sometimes furious with her parents and her twin sister. She then positions the wild animals and builds a fence around these three houses. I understand that she wants to control her aggressive and jealous emotions. I ask her what the three houses symbolize. She looks at me, leans against me with all her weight, and says: "Then I'll be here with you." She expresses her hope that she can say more about her feelings and control them in the three weekly sessions. In some sessions she treats me with disdain and tries to provoke me as if she wanted to get me to send her away, to label her a hopeless case. Then she would have turned me into an incapable analyst and she would have "won". Mira is sceptical as to whether her parents really want her to feel better. As soon as Mira begins to become more self-confident, the parents terminate the analysis.

Interpretation

Mira felt unloved and unwanted, that she was a burden, and that her parents would have preferred to have just had her wonderful sister. Her hate and jealousy of her twin sister have triggered murderous thoughts in her. Her inner world is full of "dead" objects, that is, images of her mother, her father, and her sister whom she has killed in her fantasy. The "special treatment" by the kindergarten teacher probably elicited contradictory feelings. She was the "selected" one, the one who got special treatment. However, the boundaries separating generations were violated and she was left in a state of confusion. The attempted discussion of what had happened by her parents seems to have been a further trauma. Even though she could make good use of therapy, she is burdened by her parents' rejection of it. She reports how deprecatingly her parents would speak of me, shows me how they mimicked me. The parents feel guilty that they cannot love this unattractive daughter as much as her sister and that they did not notice the sexual abuse for so long. When they decide to break off the therapy they say that "they do not want to make the same mistake again", that is, they draw a parallel between the sexual abuse in kindergarten and the processing of the trauma in analysis.

## Case study: abuse in the family

The seventeen-year-old girl I call Olga is the younger of two daughters who were sexually abused several times by their father over a period of a year. The father was convicted and put to jail. Olga availed herself of "victim support", which enabled her to seek therapy. She is an excellent student in all her main subjects but in music she is on the verge of failing. The teachers state that she is restless and agitated. She is "chaotic" and often daydreams. The mother had increasing disciplinary problems with her and was worried that she "might not put her foot down" to get respect from her daughter. A young analyst who worked with Olga allowed me to use the following material.

In the first two therapy sessions Olga showed both sides of her problem. In the first session she was cheerful and active. In describing her sister she spoke vividly about her sister and her husband and that she had just had a baby and that they had moved to Italy. She did not mention her father and mother.

Later she described her two cats. She went to great pains to draw the cat's head, but when she went to start drawing the body she suddenly stopped. The analyst linked this with her experiences, that she didn't want to know about everything happening to her body and that she wanted to focus only on her mind and on learning. This interpretation also preoccupied her in the next session. She showed her desperation and sheer hopelessness and said that she did not need any help. Then she drew an eagle trying to catch a mouse, with the mouse twice as big as a rat. In the second drawing the mouse had disappeared into a mouse hole and she wrote "happy end" over it. In the corner she drew a high mountain and a nest with eagle chicks which were being fed by one of the parents with a dead mouse.

## Interpretation

Recovering from sexual abuse can be a long process, especially when the abuse was suffered over a longer period of time. After the abuse

234     THE EARLY YEARS OF LIFE

is discovered it is important to prevent any further meeting between the victim and the abuser. Our understanding of the importance of abuse can differ distinctly from the victim's understanding. The victim can be corrupted and find the abuse fascinating, can be afraid of the abuser, or may love him. The first step could be withdrawal. The abuse, however, can also affect the victim's entire personality. Grandiosity can be used as a defence against feelings of impotence and helplessness. In Olga's case, five years went by between the traumatic experiences and the beginning of therapy. I think that Olga had protected herself by the idea of being able to control the situation of abuse herself. Her drawing of the cat with a beautifully detailed head but without a body showed Olga's concealed problem. Not mentioning her father and mother when talking about her family also allows one to conclude that there were large unconscious or conscious conflicts with them. Olga had often told the story about the abuse to the police, the social worker, to her mother, and so on, and had put together a protective, formalizing narrative. The analytic form of free association or of free play and drawing had got by her defence system. She was frightened by the picture she had drawn as well as by the interpretation. Accurate interpretation had probably been given too early and had threatened Olga's fragile inner defence system. Olga did not want to remember her story of abuse nor the feelings that it had triggered. She had asked her mother to tell the therapist she had often drawn cats with bodies at home. Through the interpretation, her defence was apparently lifted and the tremendous despair lying behind it revealed. Now the therapist had become a threatening figure, an eagle, and Olga had become a threatened big mouse. In the further work with Olga it was important to make the different aspects of the abuse visible in her drawings and to discuss them.

In work with traumatized children sexual abuse constitutes a traumatic experience. It is important to assimilate the feelings projected onto the therapist and to contain them emotionally for the child, as Anne Alvarez (1992: 155) describes in her text "Child Sexual Abuse". It would be excessive to want to recall the "total" situation. It can be important to process the individual steps at the child's own pace.

Is there a way to prevent sexual abuse or is it possible to break the vicious circle that turns victims into abusers or accomplices of abusers?

## 5.5.2    *Prevention of sexual abuse*

One approach to preventing sexual abuse, perceived in the last decade, is therapeutic work with potential perpetrators, that is, with
individuals who feel the urge to have sexual relations with children.
This inner compulsion is a severe psychological disturbance which
cannot be changed without therapeutic support.

In her "Prevention of Sexual Abuse from Early Childhood with
a Focus on the Practical Implementation in Kindergartens and Primary Schools" Ingrid Kurz (2005) cited various forms of prevention.
She draws a distinction between:

- primary prevention that aims at a child's self-determined approach
  to its own body;
- secondary prevention that provides for a training of detection
  of possible symptoms in a child that has experienced sexual
  abuse; and
- tertiary prevention that focuses on preventing secondary damage
  during interrogating of victims and "secondary denial".

The extent to which a child succeeds in resisting pressure exerted by
adults to engage in sexual acts, to seek help or to confide in another
person, depends largely on how good its relationship is with its
parents, whether or not it feels accepted and trusted. The two case
studies I have discussed dealt with girls who had felt unloved or
unwanted, with or without reason. Such unloved, neglected, or
deprived children are more susceptible to seduction.

More than a hundred years ago Freud pointed to the significance
of sexual education. In his text "The Sexual Enlightenment of Children (An Open Letter to Dr. M. Fürst)", Freud responded to the
inquiry of Dr. Fürst in Hamburg:

> I am expected, therefore, to answer questions on the following
> points: whether children ought to be given any enlightenment
> at all about the facts of sexual life, at what age this ought to
> happen and in what manner it should be carried out. Let me
> admit to you at once that I find a discussion of the second and
> third points perfectly reasonable, but that to my mind it is quite
> incomprehensible how there should be a difference of opinion
> on the first point.

> (Freud, 1907: 131)

Freud emphasizes that the child's intellectual interest in the mysteries of sexual life, its desire for sexual knowledge, is already expressed in the early years. He perceived secrecy and the stork myths as detrimental to a child's development and its trust in its parents. Today there is consensus that it makes sense to answer clearly and honestly any questions a child might ask. Typically, the child will first address the physical difference between boys and girls and only later ask where babies come from. Even if the child is often sceptical about the adult's explanations because it harbours oral or anal sexual fantasies (Freud, 1908), it can later return to these issues.

## 5.6    The resolution of the Oedipus conflict and its effect on thinking/the internal world

Father Reading to his Children.

The resolution of the Oedipus conflict represents a new dimension in the process of psychical maturation. Rather as the decimal system created a new mathematical reference system and made it possible to solve new tasks, so the insight into the Oedipus conflict revealed a new dimension of thinking. It shows that in addition to the relationship of the couple it is possible to also internalize a recognizable conception of a three-person relationship—a triangular relationship. We should remember that at the beginning of the Oedipal phase, the child has the wish to constitute a love pair with the parent of the opposite sex so as to be able to make a baby. The parent of the same sex is experienced as a rival that must be done away with, but at the same time this person is someone that the small child loves tenderly. These contradictory emotions are linked to turbulence and guilt feelings. At the same time the child also fears the punitive revenge of the "kings" that have been dethroned in its fantasies. I have already addressed the different developments taking place in the boy and the girl. It is just as important to point out the varying constellations in the "negative Oedipal conflict", that is, when the parent of the same sex is desired, since in this case, too, we are dealing with a triadic constellation.

The child's new view of itself and the active individuals—father, mother, and child—results in a balance within the triad. The end of the mature development is marked by the renunciation of the incestuous Oedipal desire, an acceptance of being excluded from the parents' sexual relationship, and the awareness of the different quality of the parents' sexual connection in the love of their child. The child experiences parents' who consider it and at the same time relate to each other—also opening a "triangular space" (Britton, 1989: 86). The parents' model, the way they think of their child, is internalized by the child so that a basis is created for self-reflection and the ability to learn from experience. Britton (1998: 87) writes:

> The capacity to envisage a benign parental relationship influences the development of a space outside of the self, capable of being observed and thought about, which provides the basis for a belief in a secure and stable world (Britton, 1989: 87).

The frightening fantasy of a combined aggressive Oedipal couple (paranoid-schizoid position) has been superseded, and the child can now understand the parents' sexual relation as benign and loving, accepting that it is excluded (depressive position). Normal thinking is promoted since the child can experience the father and the mother as separate individuals who are able to have a sexual relationship and then part again—a model of connecting and separating without any catastrophe. If the child can acknowledge the parents as separate, their sexual union is no longer experienced as being directed against the child and the child can introject a benign oedipal couple. Instead, the parents' positive relationship as a couple represents a stable basis for the family and thus also for the child. When this developmental stage leading to normal thinking is not possible due to internal conflicts, the child remains caught up in its fears. Melanie Klein (1932), in her analysis of Rita, describes how this child was convinced that the parents' sexual union only took place to torment and punish her. Her inability to internalize her parents as a real Oedipal couple resulted in her incapacity to envisage being observed. The parents' intercourse as a threatening act was supplemented by the fantasy of a destroyed couple in a destroyed, threatening world. The next step, to normal rivalry and relinquishment, is then not possible.

Feldman describes an important result of the viewpoint of the Oedipal configuration on the development of a child's internal world:

> If the patient negotiated the Oedipus complex in a relatively healthy way, he [sic] has an internal model of an intercourse that is on balance, a creative activity. This model seems to be directly connected with the development of the patient's capacity to allow thoughts and ideas to interact in a kind of healthy intercourse. On the other hand the fantasy that any connection forms a bizarre or predominately destructive couple seems to result in a damaged, perverse or severely inhibited forms of thinking.

> (Feldman, 1998: 106)

This analogy of a kind of creative intercourse of thoughts to bring forth something new with the act of sexual intercourse may strike some people as farfetched, but it does underscore the fundamental significance of the recognition of the parents' sexual relationship for the development of thinking. This close connection between normal, creative thinking and the acceptance of the parents' sexual relation proves helpful in recognizing early disturbances. Mature thinking enables a person to develop a space outside of the self, an outside perspective. This person is then able to think about different opinions and arguments and to bear the pain of different viewpoints instead of taking them to be attacks against him or herself. Bion (1992: 25) also emphasizes the ability to bear not-knowing without resorting to hasty solutions: "Only through renunciation of both premature knowledge and the belief in knowledge that has been secured once and for all is growth and development possible." If this mature thinking is not possible it is not possible for an individual to tolerate other opinions; it will want to hear its opinion be confirmed by others or will experience other views as being directed against it, as deconstructive, as attack, or at best as misunderstanding, that is, it is also unable to learn from experience, to modify its own opinion, to think something new.

On the basis of an example taken from a psychoanalytic observation in kindergarten, I would like to show how development is able to take place in a creative and imaginative way towards a mature resolution of the Oedipal conflict. This scene stems from an observation group in the university study programme "Psychoanalytic Observation Studies" at the Alpen Adria University in Klagenfurt. In it, a child with its immediate environment was observed at a kindergarten throughout half a year by Bachmann (2004).

## 5.6.1    Observation of Benni playing

Benni is a little boy just shy of three years old. Four weeks ago his mother had a little sister. His Austrian father, who lives in Africa, had been with the family at the birth but had to return to his place of work. In recent weeks Benni had been sick and had gotten a new nanny who took him to kindergarten.

I enter the group room, wave briefly to welcome everyone and look around me. My gaze drifts through the group of children; I see Benni sitting at a table with two little girls.

Benni is engrossed in his book. I sit down on the chair behind him and notice that he is looking at a book about animals. His fingers touch or trace the individual illustrations. Sometimes he whispers a few words such as "wau-wau" or "miau-miau". He leafs through about half of the book, lifts it up, and asks the kindergarten teacher's assistant Anni where the lions are. Anni answers that he would have to continue leafing through the book. When he gets to the page with the exotic animals, he points at the lions and shouts to Anni: "Daddy is there with the lions in Africa!" Anni nods and says, "Yes, Benni, you already told me!" Benni squints and growls, lifts his arms, makes fists, and yells loudly, "I am also the lion, I am in Africa!" The two little girls giggle. When Benni moves towards them with his growling face they look for protection. Anni calms them by saying that Benni is just playing the lion but Benni then yells: "No, no, I AM the lion, I must go back to Africa!" He goes over to Anni, growls, makes fists with his hands, and yells: "Right away!" Anni strokes his back and says: "Dear lion, it's nice here too, isn't it?" Benni makes an even more horrifying growl and yells back: "But I want to Africa!"

Susi, the kindergarten teacher, looks over at Benni and Anni and then stands up, saying: "Dear, dear Benni-lion, we all really like you so much if you want to go to Africa we'll all be very sad. Just stay here and tell us about your Africa!" Benni holds his hands still bent stiff like claws, with his head hanging slightly to side and his gaze quite pensive. Then he cuddles up next to Susi who is sitting next to him on a stool. After a few moments of reflection he says: "Well, OK, because otherwise you'll cry, right, if I go away!"

Susi gently turns Benni towards her, looks at him with big eyes, and says: "Yes, Benni, then I will cry and the kids too!" Lisa, one of the little girls, also comes up to Benni and takes his hand. (I have the impression that she is just about to cry.) Lisa says: "Benni, dear Benni, stay here!" Benni's lips begin to form a smile. He takes her by the hand and says: "Will you cry then, Lisa? Will you cry when I go way, way away to Africa, far, far away?" The corners of Lisa's mouth begin to tremble and she actually begins to cry. Even the other little girl who is standing next to Anna begins to cry. Susi takes Lisa on her lap and consoles her by saying that Benni will not go away, at least not for the moment. Anni also reassures little Katja. Benni tenderly touches Lisa's hair and says: "Lisa, I am here, I can be the lion here, here "in kindergarten" and you're my lion baby, Lisi!" Lisa turns around forcefully, wipes her face with her hand, and whispers, "Good, Benni, not gone!"

In the meantime Benni has gotten down on all fours and crawls growling in front of Lisa's and Susi's legs. Lisa seems to have gotten over her anguish and imitates Benni. Katja also lets go of Anni's arm and joins the "action". The children growl, giggle, and crawl in alternation around the table. The "lion group" has moved towards the entrance to the cozy corner. The children lumber on all fours up the few steps, while giggling and squealing. Once they have reached the top Benni sits up and says, "Now we have to build a cave before it gets dark."

He takes several cushions and stacks them in a circle. Lisa and Katja help him. (The children's building activities seem harmonious …) When their work appears finished the children crawl in the middle of the circle, after Benni has asked them to do so. Since things seem very cramped, Benni pulls Lisa onto his lap. Lisa lets him do this without showing any resistance and rests her head on Benni's shoulder. Benni's face is flushed; he orders Katja to sit on Lisa's lap. This doesn't work; Lisa and Katja roll off to the side and laugh. Benni throws himself to the side as well, holding two cushions and squealing with pleasure. A cheerful "ruckus" ensues. The children roll around with the cushions. The whole thing becomes a sort of "pillow fight". The children's laughter and squeals become even louder. Anni, who is sitting at the table with the drawing children, shouts energetically, "Benni, not so loud, don't be so wild, you're going to hurt each other!" Benni answers, almost singing, "But we're lions, lions are so wild!" The two girls join in: "Lions are so wild, are so wild!" The children laugh and begin to crawl around on all fours.

The kindergarten teacher Susi comes and sits down next to me at the beginning of the staircase, explains to the children that they are smart little lions and should be careful. Otherwise they might fall down the mountain (she points at the steps leading downward) and could hurt themselves. Benni straightens himself up, his body completely upright. He interrupts her monologue by stating that he was not a small lion but instead a large one, actually the father of the two "lion girls"! He adds that he had allowed them to be so wild and loud because he was the father after all and lions, as he again emphasizes, are simply like that. (His voice keeps getting louder and his body is as taut as an arch.)

I notice how Susi, the kindergarten teacher, has tried to refrain from laughing while Benni was showing the right "lion behaviour". He takes a deep breath and then says that being a bit wild was part of being a lion, but that he should also be careful and watch out for the small ones. Benni continues to squat, begins to growl and asks whether Susi would like to be the mother. Lisa and Katja shout: "Yes, yes mother lion!" Benni kneels in front of Susi and hammers on the ground with his fists. "Children, quiet, Mami lion needs silence!" He crawls on all fours and gets a cushion to hand to Susi. Susi plays the mother lion a couple of times; she lays her head on the cushion and comments how tired she is from hunting. Then she suggests to Benni that Lisa or Katja could now play mama lion. Benni shakes his head wildly and says: "No, that doesn't work, they are so small, they are only children!" Then he walks on his toes (as if he wanted to show how tall he really is). The kindergarten teacher explains to Benni that there are also small mummies. Benni does not accept this. He says: "No, but not such small ones, they do not exist, not in Vienna, and not in Africa, no way!" Susi has to laugh loudly. Benni looks at her flabbergasted; he pushes his lip forward (appears hurt), stomps on the ground with his foot, and says that he now has to leave.

(Bachmann, 2004: 3)

## Interpretation

In his play, Benni reveals his identification with his father, symbolizing this through the lion father. He is powerful and strong, and at the end he is even able to win the kindergarten teacher as his "lion spouse". He is very determined and argues that the girls are too small, that no such small lion mothers exist. It is often difficult to remain serious for adults when Oedipal wishes become so visible. Benni is, however, completely offended when the kindergarten teacher laughs at him and he withdraws, with his self-pride wounded.

At the beginning of the playing session Benni shows his sadness about his father who was in Africa. He is animated to feel like a lion by the illustration of the lion in the book. However, he is very jealous of his little sister and feels lonely because of the absence of his beloved father. He does not show his feelings but he manages to act while playing so that both girls feel the pain of parting. They cry for him in proxy and ask Benni not to leave (it is possible that Benni begged his father not to return to Africa and to leave him alone). Anni, the kindergarten teacher's assistant, shows no interest in Benni's story about his father in Africa. This then prompts Benni to actually become the strong lion, he "is" the lion—as a symbolic equation. Benni receives confirmation of the fact that he is really a dangerous lion both through the girls' fear and their sadness when he threatens to leave. The kindergarten teacher is able to contain Benni's fear and to put his feelings in words. She moves very close to Benni and asks him to stay since they all

THE PSYCHOSEXUAL DEVELOPMENT OF A CHILD 243

like him there. Benni cuddles up to her and thus shows that he feels understood by her. Now he has become a sweet lion father.

By reassuring Benni that everyone likes him and that he should stay, the kindergarten teacher has added a new dimension to the playing session. The two little girls who were so upset about Benni's threat to leave are now transformed into his lion children. The lions' playful scuffle is so exciting that it resembles a childish, erotic game that all of them enjoy. They withdraw into the cozy corner and build their camp there.

In his description of the lion, Benni also articulates his father's threatening aspect, who drives away anyone who wants to take away Benni's lion mother and fights with anyone who wants to rob him of his masculinity (castration fear).

Benni has succeeded in being the game's active player. Although he has not been left behind alone by his father with his mother and the new baby, it is he who threatens to leave the girls and to start a new lion family. He is no longer the jealous, ousted prince but a lion father with two lion girls. Ultimately, he also gets an adult lion mother. The erotic tension, however, seems to have been so great that the kindergarten teacher laughs out loud and thus hurts Benni. Of course, he, too, knows in the back of his mind that he is not the lion father, but he would like to believe it. The pleasurable aspect of the game facilitates an internal development in Benni and the two girls—a development that has an effect both on the emotional realm and on thinking.

## The liberating effect of children's play

The play of children opens up a path to a child's internal world. Through play, creativity is given just as much space as destructivity, which can also be expressed in a playful way. In play the child establishes a connection between its wishes, feelings, and fears and external reality. The child experiments like a "scientist" with the outside world; it begins to express itself symbolically and can learn from experience. Fantasy is a crucial part of its inner reality. Inhibited play is thus always indicative of a serious disturbance, since the child is unable to establish contact with other persons and objects. In child analysis, the observation of children playing and their way of entering into contact with the therapist offers access to their inner world. "Playing is an important means of exploring the relationship between internal reality and external reality," as Caper (1999: 85) writes. The seriousness with which children play points to their fundamentally scientific, exploratory attitude: "When I do this what will happen?" Children are excellent observers and spend a great deal of time closely studying how, for instance, their own parents act towards their children. Some parents are worried about their child because it is not active and "only watches". A child, however, is active in its watching, it assimilates, examines, compares, assesses, and acquaints itself with the social world and the world of objects. In Benni's play described above, there are "healing forces" at work, as Zulliger (1970: 24) has said, since play gives the child a possibility to express its pain at being abandoned, to even trigger these feelings in other children, and to compensate for them in a conciliatory fashion through the affectionate romping of the lion family. For a short time even his Oedipal wish to become the kindergarten teacher's husband and to transform her into a lion mummy is fulfilled, but at the same time he is keenly aware of the fact that this is only a game.

I would like to close with a quote taken from Heraclitis (Patrick, 2006: 75):

*We come closest to ourselves when we attain the gravity of the child at play.*

# CHAPTER SIX

# Epilogue

In my attempt to describe the psychoanalytic understanding of the early years of life based on the ideas of Freud, Klein, and Bion, I have tried to make complex theories accessible by linking them to the parent–infant interaction found in everyday family situations. Freud took the work on the symptom as his starting point for psychoanalysis, the symptom being for him the most alien thing to the ego to be found in the psyche. The symptom stems from repression, serving as a proxy before the ego. Freud even went so far as to describe the repressed element as the "inner foreign country" and reality as its "outer foreign country" (Freud, 1915: 165). Psychoanalytic developmental theory seeks to understand the emergence of the deep layers of the personality and various psychic mechanisms influenced by the overcoming of primitive anxieties, and dealing with more mature forms of thinking and feeling.

Proceeding from theoretical concepts, I have cited not only examples of pathological development but also scenes observed in so-called "normal" families. These families are also juxtaposed with children whose development is problematic and who could be helped in an analytic treatment. My approach is intended to make it easier for the reader to understand the interlocking of unconscious and conscious processes without the risk of labelling these phenomena, noted in oneself or in one's children, as pathological. Freud's assertion that pathological disturbances only differ incrementally from normal development, that is, that there is a bridge connecting normal and pathological modes of behaviour, is encouraging, since it makes crises and mental or emotional disturbances appear treatable, but at the same time is also disquieting, since anybody considered as "normal" could also at some point develop pathological symptoms.

Several subjects are addressed in detail with the goal of analyzing individual processes of development, while other issues could only be briefly discussed. The author's intention was to connect complex metapsychological theoretical constructions with illustrations taken from everyday life. Here I was also aware of the danger of simplification, since concessions with regard to detail and subtleties had to be made for the sake of exposition. Still, the author hopes she has made clear the impressive diversity of the development process and the interplay of external and internal factors. The reader should be encouraged to read Freud, Klein, and Bion in order to gain a deeper understanding of these concepts in the original texts.

What makes psychoanalytic development theory so special is its focus on the development of the child's inner world. It becomes clear that the interplay of the outside world and inner motives, affects, the life and death drive, and fantasy, shape the inner world. We are always dealing with two children—one the real outer child and the other the reader's "inner child" and the "inner infant". When we speak of early primitive fears and archaic forms of thinking and feeling, manifested in a defencive splitting into good and bad, the persecutory anxieties and fantasies of omnipotence, we are also alluding to the deep "psychotic core" of each individual. This entails an understanding of an individual's many-layered psyche.

In Melanie Klein's theory of development, focus is not on the understanding of a stage-like development consisting in consecutive phases. Instead, she speaks of "positions" or phases marking the typical experiential modes of the baby and the infant—positions that remain relevant throughout our entire life in different manifestations (Klein, 1928: 189). Wilfried Bion (1962b), in particular, referred to this dynamic understanding in a way that was helpful for understanding the analytic process. The understanding of the radical alternation of moods and states of the infant as well of the primitive mechanisms of splitting and concrete thinking is useful in the analytic process since it makes clinical material more accessible. In the Kleinian technique of understanding the analytic process as a "total situation", focus is on the effect that the patient wishes to produce either consciously or unconsciously on the analyst (Joseph, 1985). Instead of the content of what is narrated serving as a basis for orientation, the process of interaction between the patient and the analyst is the central focus. The analyst seeks to reconstruct the patient's emotional story in the here and now of transference and countertransference. Instead of offering wide-ranging interpretations the analyst tries to describe precisely how the patient sees the analyst, him or herself, and what is taking place between them, at a given moment, and to trace each change in the patient's behaviour as carefully as possible.

In this process, observation of the analyst's countertransference reactions is paramount. Detailed description of the interaction between mother and baby in Infant Observation as provided in this book can help refine attention on details of interaction and their emotional significance. Just as the patient as a baby and infant establishes relationships to its most important caregivers, modifying and internalizing them in their fantasy, they will unconsciously try to let the analyst experience their feelings—mainly those stemming from the phase of pre-linguistic development. An understanding of the experiential modes of the first years of life can enable therapists, social workers, and educators to better detect early anxieties, hopes, and wishes in others and themselves. Examples from observations of children at play help the reader gain access to "children's language" as manifested in images and playing activities.

Explanations of the roles assumed by mother and father in the first years of a child's life show that the parents' personalities exercise an influence in either promoting or hampering a child's development. It is crucial that the parents provide their children with adequate care—which, of course, means that there is no ideal family scenario free of ambivalences, conflicts, or problems.

The impression could sometimes be made that the psychoanalytic theories presented here constitute "definitive" knowledge. Kleinian theory is, however, not a finished construction. A number of questions are still being pursued and are often the subject of heated debate, which means that we are dealing with an open system that is being further developed through new insights and clinical material.

The author hopes that the views and positions presented here have awaken the reader's interest in individual development and will help promote a better understanding of human development. This form of exposition should not only serve to convey the complexity of the developmental process and the intricacy of the emergence of the inner world but also help the reader reflect on the special quality of the emotional and mental development of each child.

# BIBLIOGRAPHY

Alvarez, A. (1992). "Child Sexual Abuse", in A. Alvarez (ed.) *Live Company: Psychoanalytic Psychotherapy with Autistic, Borderline, Deprived and Abused Children*, London: Routledge. pp. 151–162.

Alvarez, A. (1992; 2001). *Live Company: Psychoanalytic Psychotherapy with Autistic, Borderline, Deprived and Abused Children*, London/New York: Tavistock/Routledge.

Alvarez, A. and Ried, S. (eds.) (1999). *Autism and Personality: Findings from the Tavistock Autism Workshop*, London/New York: Routledge.

Anderssen-Plaut, G. (1997). "Ungehaltene Eltern—ungehaltene Kinder: Psychische Auswirkungen kultureller Differenzen", *Kinderanalyse* 3: 227–246.

Asserate, A.-W. (2005). *Manieren*. München, dtv.

Atwood, M. (1997). "Making Poison", in M. Atwood (ed.) *Murder in the Dark*, London: Virago. pp. 5–8.

Bachmann, M.T. (2004). Die Verarbeitung kindlicher Angst—Benni der starke, traurige Löwe. Jahresarbeit des Universitätslehrganges "Persönlichkeitsentwicklung und Lernen" am IFF (unveröff. Arbeit).

Badinter, E. (1980). Die Mutterliebe. Geschichte eines Gefühls *vom 17.* Jahrhundert bis heute. München, Zürich, dtv. (Original in French: *L'amour en plus* [1980] Paris: Flammarion.)

Bahrick, L.R. and Watson, J.S. (1985). "Detection of intermodal proprioceptive-visual contingency as a potential basis of self-perception in infancy", *Developmental Psychology* 21: 963–973.

Bahrik, A. and Watson, J.S. (1995). "Self-orientation in early infancy: the general role of contingency and the specific case of research to the mouth", in P. Rochar (ed.) *The Self in Infancy: Theory and Research*, Amsterdam: Elsevier. pp. 375–393.

Barnett, L. (1985). *Sunday's Child: The development of individuality*. The Short version; 0–2 years. Video.

Barnett, L. (2005). *Monday's Child: A Baby is Born in Nepal*. Video.

Barnett, L. (2006). "Creating and using video for teaching child development", *Int. Journal of Infant Observation and its Applications* 9(2): 179–189.

Basilides, S. (2006). Neuorientierung: Wie Muttersein das Leben verändert. Abschlussarbeit zur Erlangung des "Master in Psychoanalytic Observational Studies" an der Universität Klagenfurt, Wien.

Bates, E. *et al.*, (1979). "Cognition and communication from 9–13 months: Correlational Findings" in E. Bates (ed.) *The Emergence of Symbols: Cognition and Communication in Infancy*. New York: Academic Press. pp. 25–34.

Bauer, J. (2005). *Warum ich fühle, was du fühlst: intuitive Kommunikation und das Geheimnis der Spiegelneurone*. Hamburg: Hoffmann und Campe.

Berk, L.E. (2004). *Development through the Lifespan*. Allyn & Bacon.

Berk, L.E. (2005). Entwicklungspsychologie, 3. Auflage. München, Boston, Pearson Education (engl.: Development through the Lifespan, 2004).

Bernhofer, R. (1998). "Spielräume der Wahrnehmung: Die Eltern-Kind-Interaktion als Schlüssel zum Verständnis und zur Behandlung der Wahrnehmungsstörungen", *Zeitschrift für Individualpsychologie* 23: 13–22.

Bernstein, D. (1990). "Female genital anxieties, conflicts and zypical mastery modes", *International Journal of Psychoanalysis* 71: 151–165.

Bettelheim, B. (1977). *Kinder brauchen Märchen*, Stuttgart: DVA. (English: The Use of Enchantment).

Bible (2001). English Standard Edition.

Bick, E. (1964). "Notes on Infant Observation in Psychoanalytic Training", *Int. Jour. of Psych. Ana.* 45: 558–566.

Bick, E. (1968). "The Experience of the Skin in Early Object Relations", *Int. Jour. of Psych. Ana.* 49: 484–489.

Bick, E. (1986). "Further considerations of the function of the skin in early object relations", *Brother* 2: 292–299.

Bion, W.R. (1959). "Attackes on Linking", *Int. Journal of Psycho-Analysis*, 40(5–6): 308–315. (Reprinted: Bion, W.W. [1967] *Second thoughts*, London: Karnac. Reprinted: 1990. pp. 93–109.)

Bion, W. (1962a). *Learning from Experience*. London: Heinemann Medical Books.
Bion, W. (1962b). "A theory of thinking", *Int. Journ. of Psycho-Anal.* 43: 306–310. (Reprinted in: Spillius, E.B. (ed.) (1988) *Melanie Klein Today, Vol. 1, Mainly Theory*, London/New York: Routledge. pp. 178–186.)
Bion, W.R. (1963). *The Elements of Psycho-Analysis*. London: Heinemann Medical Books.
Bion, W.R. (1985). *All My Sins Remembered: Another Part of My Life, The Other Side of a Genius. Family Letters*. London/New York: Karnac.
Bion, W.R. (2005). *The Tavistock Seminars Wilfried R. Bion*. London/ New York: Karnac.
Birksted-Breen, D. (2005). "The feminine", in S. Budd and R. Rusbridger (eds.) *Introducing Psychoanalysis: Essential Themes and Topica*, London/ New York: Routledge. pp. 142–152.
Brenman, E. (2006). *Recovery of the Lost Good Object*. London/New York: Routledge.
Britton, R. (1989). "The missing link: parental sexuality in the Oedipus complex", in R. Britton, M. Feldman, and E. O'Shaughnessy (eds.) *The Oedipus Complex Today*, London: Karnac Books. pp. 83–102.
Brosig, B. and Gieler, U. (Hrsg.) (2004). *Die Haut als psychische Hülle*, Gießen: Psychosozial Verlag.
Budd, S. and Rusbridger, R. (eds.) *Introducing Psychoanalysis: Essential themes and topics*, London, New York: Routledge.
Caper, R. (1988; 2000). *Immaterial Facts: Freud's Discovery of Psychic Reality and Klein's Development of His Work*, Northvale (New Jersey) London: Jason Aronson.
Caper, R. (1999). "Psychopatholgy and primitive mental states", in R. Caper (ed.) *A Mind of One's Own: A Kleinian View of Self and Object*, London/New York: Karnac. pp. 70–83.
Caper, R. (1999). *A Mind of One's Own: A Kleinian View of Self and Object*, London/New York: Karnac.
Caper, R. (2000). *Seelische Wirklichkeit: Von Freud zu Melanie Klein*, Stuttgart: Klett-Cotta.
Cavell, M. (1997). *Freud und die analytische Philosophie des Geistes: Überlegungen zu einer psychoanalytischen Semantik*, Stuttgart: Klett-Cotta. (English: *The Psychoanalytic Mind: From Freud to Philosophy*.)
Chugani, H., Behen, M., Muzik, O., Juhasz, C. and Nagy, F. (2001). "Local brain functional activity following early deprivation: a study of post-institutionalised Romanian orphans", *Neuroimage 14*: 1,290–1,301.
Cox, M., Paley, J. and Harter, K. (2001). "Interparental conflict and parent–child relationship", in J.H. Grych and F.D. Fincham (eds.) *Interparental conflict and child development: Theory, research, and applications*, New York: Cambridge University Press. pp. 249–272.

Damasio, A. (1994). *Descartes' Error*. London: Pan Macmillan.

Damasio, A. (1995). *Descartes Irrtum*. München: List.

Damasio, A.R. (1999). *The Feeling of What Happens: Body and the making of consciousness*, New York: Harcourt Brace & Company.

Damasio, A. (2004). *Ich fühle, also bin ich: Die Entschlüsselung des Bewusstseins*, München: List.

Datler, W. (1997). "Vom Erklären frühester "Verhaltensauffälligkeiten" zur Suche nach ihrer Bedeutung", in W. Jantzen (Hrsg.) *Geschlechterverhältnisse in der Behindertenpädagogik. Subjekt/Objekt-Verhältnisse in Wissenschaft und Praxis*, Luzern: Edition SZH der Schweizerischen Zentralstelle für Heilpädagogik. pp. 110–119.

Datler, W. (2004). "Die Abhängigkeit des behinderten Säuglings von stimulierender Feinfühligkeit", in B. Ahrbeck and B. Rauh (Hrsg.) *Behinderung zwischen Autonomie und Angewiesensein*, Stuttgart: Kohlhammer. pp. 45–69.

Davidson, R. and Fox, N. (1992). "Asymmetrical brain activity discriminates between positive v. negative affective stimuli in human infants", *Science 218*: 1,235–1,237.

Davis, T., Howell, R.T. and Gardner, A. (2001). *Human Genetics*, New York: Oxford University Press.

Daws, D. (1993). *Through the Night: Helping parents and sleepless infants.* London: Free Association Books.

deMause, L. (1977). *Hört ihr die Kinder weinen: Eine psychogenetische Geschichte der Kindheit*, Frankfurt: Suhrkamp.

Diem-Wille, G. (1993). *Babybeobachtung von Elias*, unveröff. Manuskript.

Diem-Wille, G. (1996). *Karrierefrauen und Karrieremänner: Eine psychoanalytisch orientierte Untersuchung ihrer Lebensgeschichte und Familiendynamik*, Opladen: Westdeutscher Verlag.

Diem-Wille, G. (1997). "Observed families revisited—two years on: a follow-up study", in S. Reid (ed.) *Developments in Infant Observation: The Tavistock Model*, London: Routledge. pp. 182–206.

Diem-Wille, G. (1999). "Niemand hat mir je etwas davon gesagt ..." Die Falldarstellung einer Eltern-Kleinkind Therapie aus der Tavistock Clinic, in *Jahrbuch für Psychoanalytische Pädagogik 10: Themenschwerpunkt: Die frühe Kindheit*. Gießen, Psychosozial Verlag, 101–115.

Diem-Wille, G. (2003, 2009). *Das Kleinkind und seine Eltern: Perspektiven psychoanalytischer Babybeobachtung*, Stuttgart: Kohlhammer.

Diem-Wille, G. (2004). Psychoanalytische Aspekte der Schwangerschaft als Umgestaltungder inneren Welt der werdenden Eltern, in *Psychotherapie Forum*, Vol. 12, 3. Wien/New York: Springer. pp. 130–139.

Die Welt in Geschichten. Leser leben besser: Für diese einfache Botschaft wirbt die Stiftung Lesen. *Die Zeit*, Wochenzeitung für Politik, Wirtschaft und Kultur, Hamburg, 2006, 10.

Dornes, M. (1993). *Der kompetente Säugling: Die präverbale Entwicklung des Menschen*, Frankfurt: Fischer.

Dornes, M. (2001a). Die frühe Kindheit: Entwicklungspsychologie der ersten Lebensjahre, Frankfurt, Fischer, 5. Auflage.

Dornes, M. (2001b). Die emotionale Welt des Kindes, Frankfurt, Fischer, 2. Auflage.

Dornes, M. (2005). "Infantile Sexualität und Säuglingsforschung", in I. Quindeau and V. Sigusch (Hrsg.) *Freud und das Sexuelle*, Frankfurt: Campus Verlag. pp. 112–134.

Elias, N. (1939). *Über den Prozeß der Zivilisation*. Suhrkamp: Basel. (English: *The Civilizing Process: Sociogenetic and Psychogenetic Investigations*.)

Emanuel, L. and Bradley, E. (eds.) (2008). *What can the matter be?: Therapeutic interventions with parents, infants and young children*. London.

Erikson, E. (1964). *Womanhood and inner space: Identity, youth and crisis*, New York: Norton.

Feldman, M. (1989). "The Oedipus Complex: Manifestations in the Inner World and the Therapeutic Situation", in R. Britton, M. Feldman and E. O'Schaughnessy (eds.). *The Oedipus Complex Today*, London: Karnac. pp. 103–128.

Fiegl, J. (2004). *Unerfüllter Kinderwunsch: Das Wechselspiel von Körper und Seele*, Düsseldorf, Zürich: Walter.

Flaubert, G. (1857; 1979). *Madame Bovary: Sitten der Provinz*. Zürich: Diogenes. (English: *Madame Bovary: Provincial Manners*.)

Fonagy, P. (1996). "Die Bedeutung der Entwicklung metakognitiver Kontrolle der mentalen Repräsentanzen für die Betreuung und das Wachstum des Kindes", *Psyche 52*: 349–368.

Fonagy, P. and Target, M. (2002). Neubewertung der Entwicklung der Affektregulation, in *Psyche, Sonderheft: Entwicklungsforschung, Bindungstheorie, Lebenszyklus*. Stuttgart, Klett-Cotta, 839–862.

Fraiberg, P. (1969). "Libidinal Object Constancy and Mental Representation", *Psychoanal St. Child 24*: 9–47.

Fraiberg, S. (1980a). *Die magischen Jahre in der Persönlichkeitsentwicklung des Vorschulkindes. Psychoanalytische Erziehungsberatung*, 4. Aufl. Reinbek: Rowohlt.

Fraiberg, S. (1980b). "Ghosts in the nursery", in S. Fraiberg (ed.) *Clinical Studies in Infant Mental Health: The First Year of Life*, London: Tavistock Publiations.

Fraser, F.C. and Nora, J.J. (1986). *Genetics of man*, Philadelphia: Lea & Febiger.

Freud, A. (1965). "Wege und Irrwege in der Kinderentwicklung" in A. Freud (Hrsg.). *Die Schriften der Anna Freud, Bd. VIII*. Frankfurt: Fischer.

Freud, A. (1969). *Das Ich und die Abwehrmechanismen*, in A. Freud. (Hrsg.) *Die Schriften der Anna Freud. Bd. I.*, München: Kindler. (English: *The Ego and the Mechanisms of Defence.*)

Freud, A. (1980). "Das Ich und die Abwehrmechanismen", in A. Freud. (Hrsg.) *Die Schriften der Anna Freud. Bd. I.*, München: Kindler. pp. 193–356.

Freud, S. (1895). *Über die Berechtigung von der Neurasthenie einen bestimmten Symptomkomplexals "Angstneurose" abzutrennen.* Studiensausgabe, Bd. VI, Frankfurt: Fischer. (English: *On the grounds for detaching a particular syndrome for neurasthenia under the description "anxiety neurosis".*)

Freud, S. (1900). *Die Traumdeutung.* Studienausgabe, Bd. III. Frankfurt: Fischer. (English: *The Interpretation of Dreams.*)

Freud, S. (1904). *Psychopathologie des Alltagslebens.* Frankfurt: Fischer.

Freud, S. (1905). *Drei Abhandlungen zur Sexualtheorie.* Studienausgabe, Bd. III. Frankfurt: Fischer. (English: *Three Essays on the Theory of Sexuality.*)

Freud, S. (1905a). *Bruchstücke einer Hysterie-Analyse.* Studienausgabe, Bd. VI. Frankfurt: Fischer. (Englilsh: *Fragment of an analysis of a case of hysteria.*)

Freud, S. (1907). *Zur sexuellen Aufklärung der Kinder.* Studienausgabe, Bd. V. Frankfurt: Fischer.

Freud, S. (1908). *Charakter und Analerotik.* Studienausgabe, Bd. VII. Frankfurt: Fischer. (English: *Character and Anal Eroticism.*)

Freud, S. (1909). *Analyse einer Phobie eines vierjährigen Knaben, "Der kleine Hans".* Studienausgabe, Bd. VIII. Frankfurt: Fischer. (English: *Analysis of a phobia in a five-year-old boy.*)

Freud, S. (1910). *Über "wilde" Psychoanalyse, Studienausgabe, Ergänzungsband,* Frankfurt: Fischer.

Freud, S. (1911). *Über einen autobiographisch beschriebenen Fall von Paranoia.* Studienausgabe, Bd. VII. Frankfurt: Fischer. (English: *Psychoanalytic notes on the auto-biographical account of a case of paranoia.*)

Freud, S. (1912/13). *Totem und Tabu: Einige Übereinstimmungen im Seelenleben derWildenund der Neurotiker.* Studienausgabe, Bd. IX. Frankfurt: Fischer. (English: *Totem and Taboo: Resemblances between the psychic lives of savages and neurotics.*)

Freud, S. (1914). On Narcissism, *The Standard Edition of the Complete Psychological Works of Sigmund Freud, Volume XIV (1914–1916): On the History of the Psycho-Analytic Movement, Papers on Metapsychology and Other Works,* 67–102.

Freud, S. (1915a). Trieb und Triebschicksale, G.S.V, 443 (English: *Instincts and their Vicissitudes*). *The Standard Edition of the Complete Psychological Works of Sigmund Freud, Volume XIV (1914–1916): On the History of the Psycho-Analytic Movement, Papers on Metapsychology and Other Works,* 109–140.

Freud, S. (1915b). *Das Unbewußte*. Studienausgabe, Bd. III. Frankfurt: Fischer. (English: *The Unconscious*.)

Freud, S. (1915c). Mitteilung eines der psychoanalytischen Theorie widersprechenden Falles von Paranoia, G.S. V, 288. (English: A Case of Paranoia Running Counter to the Psycho-Analytic Theory of the Disease), *The Standard Edition of the Complete Psychological Works of Sigmund Freud, Volume XIV (1914–1916): On the History of the Psycho-Analytic Movement, Papers on Metapsychology and Other Works*, 261–272.)

Freud, S. (1917). *Über Triebumsetzung, insbesondere der Analerotik*. Studienausgabe, Bd. VII. Frankfurt: Fischer. (English: *On the Transformations of Instinct as Exemplified in Anal Eroticism*.)

Freud, S. (1917). *Vorlesungen zur Einführung in die Psychoanalyse*, G.S. VII. (English: Introductory Lectures on Psycho-Analysis), *The Standard Edition of the Complete Psychological Works of Sigmund Freud, Volume XVI (1916–1917): Introductory Lectures on Psycho Analysis (Part III)*, 241–463.

Freud, S. (1918). *Aus der Geschichte einer infantilen Neurose, "Der Wolfsmann"*. Studienausgabe, Bd. VIII. Frankfurt: Fischer. (English: *From the History of an Infantile Neurosis*.)

Freud, S. (1920). *Jenseits des Lustprinzips,*. (English: *Beyond the Pleasure Prinziple*, S.E., XVIII, 1–64.).

Freud, S. (1923). *Das Ich und das Es*. Studienausgabe. Bd. III. Frankfurt: Fischer. (English: *The Ego and the Id*.)

Freud, S. (1924). *Der Untergang des Ödipuskomplexes*. Studienausgabe, Bd. V. Frankfurt: Fischer. (English: *The Dissolution of the Oedipus Complex*.)

Freud, S. (1925). *Notiz über den "Wunderblock"*. Studienausgabe, Bd. III. Frankfurt: Fischer. (English: A Note Upon the "Mystic Writing-Pad".)

Freud, S. (1926). *Hemmung, Symptom und Angst*. Studienausgabe, Bd. VI. Frankfurt: Fischer. (English: *Inhibitions, Symptoms and Anxiety*.)

Freud, S. (1931). "Über die weibliche Sexualität". (English: "Female Sexuality"). *The Standard Edition of the Complete Psychological Works of Sigmund Freud, Volume XXI (1927–1931): The Future of an Illusion, Civilization and its Discontents, and Other Works*, 221–244.

Freud, S. (1933). *Über die weibliche Sexualität*. Studienausgabe, Bd. V. Frankfurt: Fischer. (English: *Female Sexuality*.)

Freud, S. (1937). Analysis terminable and interminable, *S.E, 23*: 209–253.

Friedrich, M. (1998). *Tatort Kinderseele: Sexueller Missbrauch und die Folgen*. Wien: Ueberreuter.

Frith, U. (1989). *Autism: Explaining the Enigma*. Oxford: Blackwell.

Gabbard, G.O. (1994). "Mind and Brain in Psychiatric Treatment", *Bulletin of the Menninger Clinic 58*: 427–446.

Gaddini, E. (1998). "Das Ich ist vor allem ein Körperliches", in G. Jappe and B. Strehow (Hrsg.) *Beiträge zur Psychoanalyse der ersten Strukturen,* Tübingen: edition diskord.

Gaschke, S. (2006). Sybil Gräfin Schönfeldt im Gespräch. Die Zeit Wochenzeitung für Politik, Wirtschaft und Kultur, Hamburg 10.

Gehlen, A. (1971). *Der Mensch: Seine Natur und seine Stellung in der Welt.* Frankfurt, Athenum, (English: *Man, His Nature and Place in the World.*)

Gergely, G. (1995). "The role of parental mirroring of affects in early psychic structuringation", Vortrag vor der 5, IPA Conference on Psychoanalytic Research, London.

Gergely, G. and Watson, J. (1996). "The social-biofeedback model of parental affect-mirroring", *Int. Journ. of Psycho-Analys. 77:* 1,181–1,212.

Gerhardt, S. (2004). *Why Love Matters: How Affection Shape a Baby's Brain.* London/New York: Routledge.

Gibbons, A. (1998). "Which of our Genes Makes us Human?" *Science 281:* 1,432–1,434.

Goldbrunner, H. (1989). *Arbeit mit Problemfamilien: Systemische Perspektiven für Familientherapie.* Mainz: Grünewald.

Gori, R. (1977). "Zwischen Schrei und Sprache: Der Sprechakt", in D. Anzieu *et al.,* (Hrsg) *Psychoanalyse und Sprache: Vom Körper zum Sprechen,* Paderborn: Jugferman. pp. 91–130.

Gould, J.L. and Keeton, W.T. (1997). *Biological science.* New York: Norton.

Green, A. (1993). "The Dead Mother", in A. Green (ed.) *On Private Madness,* Conneticut: Int. University Press.

Green, A. (1994). "Psychoanalyse und gewohntes Denken", in J. Sandler (Hrsg.) *Dimensionen der Psychoanalyse: Die Freud Memorial Lectures: Beiträge zu einem interdisziplinären Dialog.* Stuttgart: Klett-Cotta.

Greenson, R. (1954). "About the Sound "Mm …" ", *The Psychoanalytic Quarterly 23:* 234–239.

Grinberg, L., Sor, D. and Bianchedi, E. (eds.) (1993). *New Introduction to the Work of Bion.* Revised Edition. Northvale, New Jersey/London: Jason Aronson.

Haag, G. (2001). "In the footsteps of Francis Tustin: further reflections on the contribution of the body-ego", *Int Journal of Infant Observation June:* 7–22.

Habermas, J. (1963). *Theorie und Praxis: Sozialphilosophische Studien.* Frankfurt: Suhrkamp.

Habermas, J. (1968). *Erkenntnis und Interesse.* Frankfurt: Suhrkamp. (English: *Knowledge and Human Interests.*)

Haddon, M. (2003). *The Curious Incident of the Dog in the Night-Time*. London: Doubleday.

Halliday, J.L.,Watson, L.F., Lumley, J., Danks, D.M. and Sheffield, L. (1995). "New estimates of Down syndrome risks of chorionic villus sampling, amniocentesis, and live birth in women of advanced maternal age from a uniquely defined population", *Prenatal Diagnosis 15*: 455–465.

Heintel, P. and Broer, K. (2005). *Hirnforschung als dialektische Sozialwissenschaft*, Wien: Lit Verlag.

Hermann, U. (1902; 1992). *Das Jahrhundert des Kindes*. Weinham/Basel: Beltz, Verlag.

Hines, S. and Bennette, F. (1996). "Effectiveness of early intervention for children with Down syndrome", *Mental Retardation and Developmental Disabilities Research Reviews 2*: 96–101.

Hinselwood, R.D. (1991). *A Dictionary of Kleinian Thought*. London: Free Association Books.

Hobson, P. (1993). *Autism and the Development of Mind*. Hove: Laurence Erlbaum.

Horn, J.M. (1983). "The Texas Adoption Project: Adopted children and their intellectual resemblance to biological and adoptive parents", *Child Development 54*: 268–275.

Huston, A.C. (1984). *Do adopted children resemble their biological parents more than theiradoptive parents? No. A note on the study of behavioral genetics*. University of Kansas, unpublished manuscipt.

Isaacs, S. (1948). "The nature and function of phantasy", *Int. J. Psycho-Anal. 29*: 73–97.

Jacobson, E. (1964). *Das Selbst und die Welt der Objekte*, Frankfurt: Suhrkamp.

Jahoda, M., Zeissel, H. and Lazersfeld, P. (1960). *Die Arbeitslosen von Marienthal*. Wien: Springer.

Jahoda, M., Zeissel, H. and Lazersfeld, P. (1972). *Marienthal: The Sociography of an Unemployed Community*, London: Tavistock Publications.

Jones, E. (1935). "Early female sexuality", *International Journal of Psychoanalysis 16*: 313–336.

Joseph, B. (1985). "Transference: the total situation", in B. Joseph (ed.) *Psychic Equilibrium and Psychic Change*, London/New York: Routledge. pp. 156–167.

Joseph, B. (1993). *Psychic Equilibrium and Psychic Change*. London/New York: Routledge.

Joseph, B. (2003). *Vortrag gehalten bei der Wiener Psychoanalytischen Vereinigung*, unveröff manuskript. (English: *Thinking about the* playroom, the setting: the essential similarities in child and adult psychoanalysis.)

Joseph, B. (2005). "The paranoid-schizoid position", in S. Budd and R. Rusbridger (eds.) *Introducing Psychoanalysis: Essential Themes and Topics*. London/New York: Routledge. pp. 39–46.

Kanner, L. (1943). "Autistic Disturbances of Affective Control", *Nervous Child* 2: 217–250.

Kant, E. (1956). *Kritik der reinen Vernunft, Theorie—Werkausgabe*. Wiesbaden: Insel.

Kinsey, A.C. (1945). *Das sexuelle Verhalten des Mannes*. Frankfurt: S. Fischer Literatur.

Kinsey, A.C. (1948). *Sexual Behavior in the Human Male*, Philadelphia Pa: W.B. Saunders.

Kinsey, A.C. (1953). *Das sexuelle Verhalten der Frau*. Frankfurt: S. Fischer.

Klein, M. (1924). "Die Zwangsneurose eines sechsjährigen Mädchens", in von Ruth Cycon (Hrsg.) *Melanie Klein: Gesammelte Schriften, Bd. II. Die Psychoanalyse des Kindes*, Stuttgart: Frommann-Holzboog. pp. 56–82.

Klein, M. (1926). "The psychological principles of early analysis", *Int. J. Psyho-Anal. 8*: 25–37.

Klein, M. (1928). "Early stages of the Oedipus conflict", *Int. J. Psych-Anal. 9*: 169–180.

Klein, M. (1930). "The Importance of Symbol-Formation in the Development of the Ego", *Int. J. Psycho-Anal. 11*: 24–39.

Klein, M. (1932). *The International Psycho-Analytical Library*. London: The Hogarth Press.

Klein, M. (1933). "The early development of conscience in the child", in L. Sandor (ed.) *Psych-Analysis Today*. New York: Covici-Friede. pp. 149–162.

Klein, M. (1934). "On criminality", *Brit. J. Med. Psycol. 14*: 312–315.

Klein, M. (1935). "A Contribution to the Psychogenesis of Manic-Depressive States", *International Journal of Psychoanalysis 16*: 145–174.

Klein, M. (1940). "Mourning and its relationship to manic-depressive states", *Int.J. Psycho-Anal. 21*: 125–153.

Klein, M. (1945). "The Oedipus complex in the light of early anxieties", *Int. J. Psycho-Anal. 26*: 11–33.

Klein, M. (1946). "Notes on Some Schizoid Mechanisms", *Int. J. Psyho-Anal. 27*: 99–110.

Klein, M. (1952). "Some theoretical conclusions regarding the emotional life of the infant", in *Dev Psa*, 198–236, WMK III, 61–93.

Klein, M. (1957). *Envy and Gratitude: A Study of Unconscious Sources*, London: Tavistock.

Klein, M. (1975). "The Psycho-Analytic Play Technique: Its history and significance", in M. Masud and R. Khan (eds.) *Envy and Gratitude and Other Works 1946–1963*, London: The Hogarth Press.

Krejci, E. (1992). "Vorwort", in W. Bion (Hrsg.) *Elemente der Psychoanalyse*, Frankfurt: Suhrkamp. pp. 7–25.

Krejci, E. (1999). *Psychogenese im ersten Lebensjahr: Perspektiven kleinianischer Psychoanalyse, Bd. 6*, Tübingen: Edition discord.

Kümmel, P. (2006). Beckett—Der Seher. Wir haben ihn überlebt, aber wir werden ihn nicht überwinden. Zum 100. Geburtstag des Schriftstellers Samuel Beckett. Die Zeit, Wochenzeitung für Politik, Wirtschaft und Kultur, Hamburg, Nr. 16, 49–50.

Kurz, I. (2005). *Prävention von sexuellen Missbrauch ab dem frühen Kindesalter mit dem Schwerpunkt der praktischen Umsetzung in Kindergarten und Volkschule*, Diplomarbeit, Universität Wien, Wien.

Laufer, M.E. (2005). "Gender identity and reality", in S. Budd and R. Rusbridger (eds.) *Introducing Psychoanalysis: Essential Themes and Topica*, London/New York: Routledge. pp. 129–141.

Lazar, R.A., Lehmann, N. and Häußlinger, G. (1986). "Die psychoanalytische Beobachtung von Babys innerhalb der Familie" in J. Stork (Hrsg.) *Zur Psychologie und Psychopathologiedes Säuglings—neue Ergebnisse in der psychoanalytischen Reflexion*. Stuttgart: Frommann-Holzboog.

Lazar, R.A. (1999). " "Mrs Klein" und "WRB": Die Kleinianischen Wurzeln des "Bionschen Denkens" ", *Kinderanalyse 3*: 189–222.

Lecours, S. and Bouchard, M.-A. (1977). "Dimensions of Mentalisation: Outlining levels of psychic transformation", *International Journal of Psychoanalysis 78*, 855–875.

Le Guiun, U.K. (1998). *A Book about the Way and the Power of the Way*, Boston & London: Shambala.

Leslie, A.M. (1987). "Pretence and Representation: The Origins of Theory of Mind", *Psychological Review 94*.

Liebletsberger, K. (2005). *"Ich lerne vom Verhalten meiner Betreuerin". Über Chancen und Möglichkeiten von Multiproblemfamilien im Rahmen einer psychoanalytisch-pädagogisch orientierten Familienintensivbetreuung*, Diplomarbeit, Universität Wien, Wien.

Loftus, F. and Ketcham, K. (1994). *Die therapeutische Erinnerung: Vom Mythos der Verdrängung bei Anklagen wegen sexuellen Mißbrauchs*, Hamburg: Klein.

Lüders, K. (2002). "Bions Container-Contained-Model", in R. Kennel and G. Reerink (Hrsg.) *Klein–Bion: Eine Einführung*. Tübingen: edition diskord.

Mahler, M. (1979). *Symbiose und Individuation. Band I. Psychose im Frühen Kindesalter*, Stuttgart: Klett-Cotta.

Malatesta, C.Z. and Izard, C.E. (1984). "The ontogenesis of human social signals: from biological imperative to symbol utilization" in N.A. Fox and R.J. Davison (eds.) *The Psychobiology of Affective Development*, Hillsdale: Erlbaum. pp. 161–206.

McDougall, J. (1989). *Theaters of the Body*, New York: Norton.

Meyer, S. (2006). *"Auch wenn es eine negative Antwort ist, ich will es wissen"*: *Autismus: Wahrnehmungsstörung oder Beziehungsstörung*, Diplomarbeit, Universität Wien, Wien.

Miller, L., Rustin, M., Rustin, M. and Shuttleworth, J. (eds.) (1989). *Closely Observed Infants*, London: Duckworth.

Mitscherlich, A. (1954). "50 Jahre später: Einige Empfehlungen an den Leser", in S. Freud (1904). *Psychopathologie des Alltagslebens*, Frankfurt: Fischer. pp. 7–10.

Montessori, M. (1936; 1982). *The Secret of Childhood*, New Jersey: Ballantine Books.

Moore, K.L. (1982). *The developing human: Clinically oriented embryology*, 3. Aufl. Philadelphia: Sanders.

Moore, E.G.J. (1986). "Family socialization and the IQ test performance of traditionally and transracially adopted black children", *Developmental Psychology* 22: 317–326.

Morris, C. (1938). "Foundations of the theory of signs", in *International Encyclopedia of Unified Science*, Chicago: University Chicago Press.

Mussen, P., Conger, J., Kagan, J. and Huston, A. (1990). *Lehrbuch der Kinderpsychologie, Bd. 1 und 2*. Stuttgart: Klett-Cotta.

Nietzsche, F. (1886). *Jenseits von Gut und Böse: Vorspiel einer Philosophie der Zukunft*, Wien o.J.: Nietzsches Werke. (English: *Beyond Good and Evil: Prelude to a Philosophy of the Future.*)

Neitzsche, F. (2005). *Thus Spoke Zarathustra: A book for everyone and nobody*, trans. G. Parkes, Oxford: Oxford University Press.

Nietzschke, B. (1988). "Die Bedeutung der Sexualität im Werk Sigmund Freuds", in B. Nietzschke (Hrsg.) *Sexualität und Männlichkeit. Zwischen Symbiosewunsch und Gewalt*, Reinbek: Rohwolt. pp. 282–346.

Nietzschke, B. (2005). *Die Bedeutung der Sexualität im Werk Sigmund Freuds*. Available at: http://home.subnet.at/werkblatt/nietzschke/text/sexualität.htn, S1–60.

Norman, J. (2001). "The psychoanalyst and the baby: a new look at work with infants", *International Journal of Psychoanalysis* 82: 83–100.

O'Shaughnessy, E. (1988). "W.R. Bion's theory of thinking and new techniques in child analysis", in E.B. Spillius (ed.) *Melanie Klein Today: Developments in theory and practice. Vol. 2, Mainly Practice*, London/ New York: Routledge. pp. 177–190.

Papousek, H. and Papousek, M. (1987). "Intuitive parenting: a dialectic counterpart to the infant's integrative competence" in J.D. Osofsky (Hrsg.) *Handbook of Infant Development*, New York: Wiley. pp. 669–720.

Parker, B. (1972). *A Mingled Yarn: Chronicle of a Troubled Family*. Yale: Yale University Press.

Parker, B. (1974). *Meine Sprache bin ich: Modell einer Psychotherapie*. Frankfurt: Suhrkamp.

Parker, B. (1975). "Chronik einer gestörten Familie" in A.v. Mitscherlich (Hrsg.) *Literatur der Psychoanalyse*. Frankfurt: Suhrkamp.

Patrick, G.T.W. (ed.) (2006). *The Fragments of the Work of Heraclitus of Ephesus on Nature and Hercliti Ephesii Reliquiae*, Kessinger Publishing, LLC.

Pelikan, J. (2004). "Der Gebrauch von Sprache als Übergangsphänomen", *Kinderanalyse 12(2)*: 136–166.

Piaget, J. (1969). *Nachahmung, Spiel und Traum*, Stuttgart: Klett.

Piaget, J. (1999). *Das Weltbild des Kindes. 6. Aufl.* München: dtv.

Piaget, J. (2001). *The Psychology of Intelligence*, London: Routledge.

Pick, I.B. (1985). "Working through in the counter-transference" in E.B. Spillius (ed.) *Melanie Klein Today*, Vol. 2. pp. 35–47.

Pick, I.B. (1992). "The Emergence of Early Object Relations in the Psychoanalytic Setting", *New Lib. of Psycho-Anal. 14*: 24–33.

Pines, D. (1993). *A Woman's Unconscious Use of Her Body: A psychoanalytical Perspective*, London: Virago Press.

Piontelli, A. (2002). *Twins: From Fetus to Child*, London/New York: Routledge.

Portmann, A. (1951). *Biologische Fragmente zu einer Lehre vom Menschen*, Basel: Schwabe.

Pozzi, M.E. (2003). *Psychic Hooks and Bolts: Psychoanalytic Work with Children Under Five and Their Families*, London: Karnac.

Raphael-Leff, J. (1993). *Pregnancy: The Inside Story*, London: Sheldon Press.

Rauchfleich, U. (1996). *Menschen in psychosozialer Not. Beratung, Betreuung, Psychotherapie*, Göttingen. Vandenhoeck & Ruprecht.

Rees, L. (2005). *Auschwitz: The Nazis and the "Final Solution"*, London: BBC Books.

Reid, S. (1997). *Development in Infant Observation: The Tavistock Model*, London: Routledge.

Reid, S. (1999). "The assessment of the child with autism: a family perspective" in A. Alvarez and S. Ried (eds.) *Autism and Personality: Findings from the Tavistock Autism Workshop*, London/New York: Routledge. pp. 13–32.

Rizzolatti, G., Fogassi, L. and Gallese, V. (2006). "Mirrors in the Mind", *Scientific American 295(5)*: 30–37.

Rogers, S. and Pennington, B. (1991). "A theoretical approach to the deficits in infantile autism", *Development and Psychopathology* 3: 137–162.

Rolls, E. (1999). *The Brain and Emotions*, Oxford: University Press.

Roth, P. (2005). "The depressive position", in S. Budd and R. Rusbridger (eds) *Introducing Psychoanalysis*, London/New York: Routledge. pp. 47–58.

Rousseau, J.J. (1762). *Emile ou, de l'éducation*, trans. Allan Bloom, New York: Basic Books.

Roy, A. (1997). *Der Gott der kleinen Dinge* (English: *The God of Small Things*), München: Karl Blessing.

Rymer, R. (1994). *Genie: A Scientific Tragedy*, London: Penguin.

Sacks, O. (1985). *The Man Who Mistook His Wife for a Hat*, London: Picador.

Salzberger-Wittenberg, I. (1970; 1999). *Psycho-Analytic Insight and Relationships: A Kleinian Approach*, London/New York: Routledge.

Sandler, J. (1960). "The background of safety", *International Journal of Psychoanalysis 41*: 352–356.

Scarr, S. and Kidd, K.K. (1983). "Developmental behavior genetics" in M. Haith and J. Campos (eds.) *Handbook of Child Psychology, Bd. 2, Infancy and developmental psychobiology*. New York: Wiley. pp. 345–435.

Scarr, S. and Weinberg, R.A. (1976). "IQ test performance of black children adopted by white Families", *American Psychologist 31*: 726–739.

Schatzman, M. (1973). *Soul Murder: Persecution in the family*, New York: Random House.

Schatzman, M. (1974). *Die Angst vor dem Vater: Langzeitwirkung einer Erziehungsmethode; eine Analyse am Fall Schreber*, Reinbek: Rowohlt.

Schiff, M., Duyme, M., Dumaret, A. and Tomkiewicz, S. (1978). "Intellectual status of working-class children adopted early into middle-class families", *Science 200*: 1,503–1,504.

Schiff, M., Duyme, M., Dumaret, A. and Tomkiewicz, S. (1982). "How much could we boost scholastic achievement and IQ scores: A direct answer from a French adoption study", *Cognition 12*: 165–196.

Schore, A. (1994). *Affect Regulations and the Origin of the Self*, Hillsdale, New York: Lawrence Erlbaum Associates Inc.

Schore, A.N. (1997). "A Century After Freud's Project: Is A Rapprochement Between Psychoanalysis And Neurobiology At Hand?", *J Amer. Psychoanal. Assn 45*: 807–840.

Schore, A. (2003). *Affect Dysregulation and Disorder of the Self*, New York: Norton.

Schreber, D.G.M. (1879). *Ärztliche Zimmergymnastik*, Leipzig: Heyne.

Schreber, D.G.M. (1891). *Das Buch der Erziehung an Leib und Seele, 3. Aufl*, Leipzig: Heyne.

Schreber, P. (1903). *Denkwürdigkeiten eines Nervenkranken*, Leipzig: Oswald Mutze.

Schwartz, J.M., Stoessel, P.W., Baxter, L.R. Jr., Martin, K.M. and Phelps, M.E. (1996). "Systematic cerebral glucose metabolic rate change after successful behavior modification treatment of obsessive-compulsive disorder", *Archive of General Psychiatry 53*: 109–113.

Segal, H. (1957). "Notes on Symbol formation", in H. Segal (ed.) *Delusion and Artistic Creativity and other Psychoanalytic Essays*, London: Free Ass. Press. pp. 49–65.

Segal, H. (1991). "Symbolism", in H. Segal (ed.) *Dream, Phantasy and Art*, London/New York: Routledge. pp. 31–48.

Sereny, G. (1998). *Cries Unheard: The Story of Mary Bell*, London: Pan Mamillan.

Sinason, V.E. (1988). "Smiling, swallowing, sickening and stupefying: the effect of abuse on the child", *Psychoanalytic Psychotherapy 3(2)*: 34–39.

Spillius, E.B. (1988). "Introduction to part Three: on thinking", in: *Melanie Klein Today. Developments in theory and practice, Vol. I.*, London, New York: Routledge. pp. 153–159.

Spillius, E.B. (1993). "Varieties of Envious Experience", *Int. Journ. of Psycho-Analy. 74*: 1,274–1,280.

Spillius, E.B. (1994). "Developments in Kleinian Thought: Overview and Personal View", in *Psychoanalytic Inquiry*, Contemporary Kleinian Psychoanalysis, New Jersey, 324–365.

Spillius, E.B. (2002). "Unterschiedliche Formen des Neiderlebens" in C. Frank and H. Weiß (Hrsg.) *Kleinianische Theorie in klinischer Praxis*, Stuttgart: Klett-Cotta. pp. 147–181.

Spitz, R. (1945). *Hospitalism: The Psychoanalytic Study of the Child. I.*, New York: International University Press.

Steiner, J. (1993). *Psychic Retreats*, London: Routledge.

Stern, D. (1977). *The First Relationship: Infant and Mother*, Cambridge, Massachusetts: Harvard University Press.

Stern, D. (1985). *The Interpersonal World of the Infant: A view from psychoanalysis and developmental psychology*, Basic Books.

Stern, D. (1995). *The Motherhood Constellation. A unified view of patient–infant psychotherapy*, London: Karnac Books.

Stierlin, H. (1980). *Eltern und Kinder: Das Drama von Trennung und Versöhnung im Jugendalter*, Frankfurt: Suhrkamp.

Stierlin, H. (1989). *Delegation und Familie: Beiträge zum Heidelberger familiendynamischen Konzept,* Frankfurt: Suhrkamp.

Stoller, R. (1968). *Sex and Gender: The Development of Masculinity and Femininity,* New York: Jason Aroson.

Stoller, R. (1994). *Perversion: The Erotic Form of Hatred,* New York: Brunner-Mazel.

*Talking Cure* (1994). Ben and Damien, BBC-Video Tape.

*Talking Cure: Mind and Method of the Tavistock Clinic* (1999). Edited by David Taylof, London: Duckworth.

Target, M. and Fonargy, P. (1966). "Playing with reality II: The development of psychic reality from a theoretical perspective", *Int. Journ. of Psycho-Analy.* 77: 459–479.

Thorner, H.A. (1981). "Notes on the Desire for Knowledge", *International Journal of Psychoanalysis* 62: 73–80.

Throughton, J. (1994). *Tortoise's Dream: An African Folk Tale,* London: Picture Puffins.

Titze, M. (1995). *Die heilende Kraft des Lachens: Mit therapeutischem Humor frühere Beschämungen heilen,* München: Kösel.

Trevarthen, C., Aitken, K., Papoudi, D. and Robarts, J. (1996). *Children with Autism: Diagnosis and Interventions to Meet Their Needs.* London, Bristol PA: Jessica Kingley.

Turrini, P. (1980). *Ein paar Schritte zurück.* Gedichte. München: AutorenEdition.

Turrini, P. (1996). *Shooting rats, other plays and poems,* Ariadne Press.

Tyson, P. and Tyson, R. (1990; 2001). *Psychoanalytic Theories of Development: An integration,* Yale: Yale University Press.

Wanke, P. and Triphammer, M. (1992). *Sexueller Missbrauch von Kindern,* Wien: Jugend and Volk.

Watson, J.S. (1994). "Detection of the self: The perfect algorithm", in S. Parker, R. Mitchell and M. Boccia (eds) *Self-Awareness in Animals and Humans: Developmental Perspectives,* Cambridge: Cambridge UP. pp. 131–149.

Watson, J.S. (1995). "Self-orientation in early infancy: The general role of contingency and the specific case of reaching to the mouth", in P. Rochat (ed.) *The Self in Infancy: Theory and Research,* Amsterdam: Elsevier. pp. 375–393.

Watt, D. (2001). *Emotion and consciousness: implications of affective neuroscience for extended reticular thalamic activating system theories of consciousness.* www.phil.vt.edu/ASSC/watt/default

Weininger, O. (1903). *Geschlecht und Charakter,* Wien.

Wiener, H. (1989). "The dynamics of the organism: implications of recent biological thought for psychosomatic theory and research", *Psychosomatic Medicine 51:* 608–635.

Williams, G. (2003). *Innenwelten und Fremdkörper*, Stuttgart: Klett Cotta.

Winnicott, D.W. (1947). "Hate in the Counter transference", *International Journal of Psychoanalysis 100*: 1–325.

Winnicott, D.W. (1947). "Hate in the Counter transference", *International Journal of Psychoanalysis*: 69–74, 1949.

Winnicott, D.W. (1951.) "Transitional Objects and Transitional Phenomena", *International Journal of Psychoanalysis 34*, 1953, reprinted in *Collected Papers: Through Paediatrics to Psycho-Analysis*. London: Tavistock Publication, 1958.

Winnicott, D.W. (1956). "Primary Maternal Preoccupation", in D.W. Winnicott (ed.) *Through Paediatrics to Psycho-Analysis*, London: The Hogarth Press and the Institute of Psycho-Analysis. pp. 300–305.

Winnicott, D.W. (1960). "Ego Distortion in Terms of True and False Self", in *The Maturational Processes and the Facilitating Environment: Studies in the Theory of Emotional Development*. London: Hogarth Press, 1965.

Winnicott, D.W. (1963). "The Development of the Capacity for Concern", in D.W. Winnicott (ed.) *The Maturational Processes*, London: The Hogarth Press and the Institute of Psycho-Analysis. pp. 73–79.

Zulliger, H. (1970). *Heilende Kräfte im kindlichen Spiel*, Stuttgart: Fischer.

Zwettler-Otte, S. (2006). *Die Melodie des Abschieds: Eine psychoanalytische Studie zur Trennungsangst*, Stuttgart: Kohlhammer.

# INDEX